MW00425165

Anne Boleyn in London

Anne Boleyn in London

Lissa Chapman

First published in Great Britain in 2017 by
Pen & Sword History
an imprint of
Pen & Sword Books Ltd
47 Church Street
Barnsley
South Yorkshire
S70 2AS

ISBN 978 1 47384 361 5

Typeset in Ehrhardt by
Mac Style Ltd, Bridlington, East Yorkshire
Printed and bound in the UK by CPI Group (UK) Ltd,
Croydon, CRO 4YY

Pen & Sword Books Ltd incorporates the imprints of Pen & Sword
Archaeology, Atlas, Aviation, Battleground, Discovery, Family
History, History, Maritime, Military, Naval, Politics, Railways,
Select, Transport, True Crime, and Fiction, Frontline Books, Leo
Cooper, Praetorian Press, Seaforth Publishing and Wharncliffe.

For a complete list of Pen & Sword titles please contact
PEN & SWORD BOOKS LIMITED
47 Church Street, Barnsley, South Yorkshire, S70 2AS, England
E-mail: enquiries@pen-and-sword.co.uk
Website: www.pen-and-sword.co.uk

Contents

Chapter 1

A Walk Through London: 1522

The London Anne Boleyn returned to as a young woman would be virtually unrecognisable to a visitor from the twenty-first century. Not even the River Thames looked the same – it was wider in those days before the Embankment, shallower and crossed by only one bridge. The Tower of London was there, in a neighbourhood of warehouses, the moat full of water and the area within the walls full of unfamiliar buildings, with Tower Hill a more obvious landmark than it is today. The Tower would probably do, however, to help the time traveller to find her way. And it would soon be obvious that Tudor London was tiny in comparison to what it has become. Estimates vary as to how many people lived there in the 1520s – perhaps 70,000.[1] There were, as yet, no census returns: even parish registers were not to be required until the 1530s. There was some development to the south of the river at Southwark, to the east in Stepney and Bethnal Green, and to the north in Clerkenwell. Kensington and Islington, however, were still rural villages. Hackney, a 3-mile walk away and a favoured country retreat, was famous for its market gardens, excellent turnips and healthy air. There was a farm at Tottenham Court, and marshes around the Tyburn and Westbourne streams, by then getting silted up and fetid because so much water was being diverted to London for its civilians to drink. Knightsbridge was best avoided, as it was a hotspot for footpads, and at Mayfair there were only a few cottages to mark a place that came alive on its market days. London would have seemed not only small, but probably provincial to someone who was used to Paris, which at that time was the largest city in the world, with a population of perhaps 300,000.

The river was not only wider and shallower, but smellier, as it served as the capital's main sewer. It was also busy to the point of congestion, as it was the main transport route. Rich Londoners had their own barges; the rest made do with calling a waterman – the Tudor version of a black cab. The bridge was about 30 metres from the present-day London Bridge – the north end of it is marked by a plaque near the church of St Magnus the Martyr. It had been rebuilt after the murder of Thomas a Becket, and by the 1520s it was crowded with up to 200 shops, private houses and warehouses, which virtually joined together overhead, leaving a space only about 12 feet wide for people, carts and animals to find their way through. The roof of the gatehouse at the southern end of the bridge featured spikes topped with the tarred and boiled heads of traitors – a macabre welcome to visitors. Rivers long culverted in the present day still flowed, trickled or meandered their way into the Thames. The bridge also made the navigation of the river highly dangerous, as the buttress supports took up five sixths of the width of the river, leaving the water to rush ferociously through the gaps. At some stages of the tide the levels of the water would be up to 6 feet higher on one side than on the other. Prudent travellers would disembark to leave the boatman to find his way through, and get back on board once he had done so.

Once in the city, the street layout was very similar to that of the twenty-first century. However, the streets themselves, cobbled at best, were more often surfaced simply with trodden earth, muddy, icy or dusty according to weather and season. Gravel would be put down in preparation for important events. The streets were mostly narrow and dark, as the wooden-framed houses had upper storeys that projected over the lower ones, meaning that there was little space between the top floors. There were also dozens of house signs over pedestrians' head – these, resembling modern pub signs, were used to identify locations in the days before street numbering. An address might be, for example 'At the sign of the Lock, near St Mary's Church in Bow Lane'. No sensible citizen would venture out unaccompanied at night – people of high status would have their own servants to go with them. Shops had wooden shutters that were raised so that goods could be displayed in opening hours; most shopkeepers lived on the premises, giving over the front room to trade, the back premises as a kitchen or as a workshop, and the rooms above to domestic life. At ground-floor level, windows were placed high up and, at the front of the house, usually kept shuttered. Doors had stout locks and bolts and, very often, a security grille so the people inside could inspect their potential visitor before committing themselves by opening the door. No one expected city streets to be safe.

Inside, even the houses of the prosperous were dark and sparsely furnished. The darkness was because windows were small. Glass was expensive, thick and did not let all the light through. Inside the rooms, most finishes were wooden – but it was only the Victorians who decided the past was brown. The Tudors liked bright colours, and so the panelling that lined many walls was generally painted, and the tapestries fashionable among those who could afford them were usually in bright colours, as were the painted cloths of the less affluent. Floors on the ground level of poorer houses were still often of rammed earth, covered with rushes. The better off had floorboards. Those few who could afford carpets usually used them as table coverings – Cardinal Wolsey had just negotiated the import of sixty Damascene carpets via Venice, and seems to have been the first person in England to use them to walk on. For most, furniture was sturdy, simple and largely made of oak. The main room of a middle-class house might contain a table, a couple of benches, perhaps a chair or two for the master and mistress of the house, a few jointed stools and a cupboard for the household's silver or best pewter. A bedroom would contain little more than beds (few people slept alone) and clothes chests. Only the main rooms would have a fireplace, fuelled with wood or the more expensive sea coal.

Some privileged households had piped water. This was available in limited areas from private water companies, including one enterprise that pumped water from a chalybeate spring in Hackney, to Aldgate. But most people had to make do with pumps, wells, and the conduits that were set up in many London streets including Cheapside and Fleet Street. It is easy to understand why few people drank water which was known to be a source of illness, but which was needed for washing. Although bathrooms only existed in Royal palaces, the same was not true of baths, which were generally slipper shaped, wooden and lined with sheets before use. They had to be filled by hand with water, drawn and then heated over the fire. The dirty water was then removed and disposed of – having a bath was onerous and time consuming. This does not mean, however, that Londoners did not make great efforts to keep clean, but usually washed themselves from a hand basin (there are many recipes for homemade soap and scented washes). The same applied to washing clothes, in particular the linen shirts and smocks that men and women almost universally wore next to the skin. Those who could afford to, would change these very frequently.

Clothes were extremely expensive and expected to last a lifetime, and good ones were often left in wills. Tudor Londoners expected to be able to work out the social status of anyone they met, just by looking them up and down. It did not always work like that, but for another century efforts would be made to enforce the sumptuary laws that sought to dictate in great detail who could wear what. The regulations applied to both men and women, and covered everything from kinds and qualities of fabric, to colours and jewellery to furs.[2] The legislation included threats of confiscation and fines for anyone who disobeyed. At the top of the social scale, purple silk was reserved to the King and his immediate family; Earls could wear cloth of gold and sable, while lords and knights had to content themselves with imported wool, and the colours crimson and blue. Serving men were not allowed to have long gowns using more than 3 yards of fabric, while servants, shepherds and labourers might not pay more than two shillings for the cloth for their outer clothes. The fact that these laws were reissued so often suggests that they were broken with great frequency, and it is notable that those of high status could wear virtually anything they pleased. Churchmen were supposed to dress simply and modestly, and, if they rode, they were to do so on a mule in emulation of Christ. Cardinal Wolsey, the King's chief minister and Archbishop of York, kept the mule, but gave his a harness of red and gold leather. When he rode out, he was preceded by servants carrying two huge silver crosses and calling out 'Make way for my lord's Grace'. He was generally dressed in red, as befitted a Cardinal, but favoured silk and velvet, with ermine linings for winter – he lived in a grander style than the King.

References to imported wool suggest that one of the motivations for the lawmakers was to support the wool industry, by far England's most lucrative trade. Wool cloth could be anything from exquisitely fine 'nun's veiling', through to smooth but durable broadcloth and on to coarse, plain frieze cloth. Scarlet was a quality of cloth as well as a colour, but it appears that red was very popular for both men and women. This was long before the clothes of most male Londoners became virtually monochrome. The limiting factor as to colour was that of the dyes that were available and at what price. The brightest reds were made with cochineal, and were very expensive. A true black, too, was expensive to produce and was, therefore, usually seen on people of high status. The cheapest dyes were those that could be produced from plant sources such as woad, for blue, and weld, for yellow. Cheapest of all was to leave wool in its natural colour. Most, but not all, underclothing was made of linen – cotton, although it was known, was uncommon, and its use was largely confined to upholstery. New clothes were a major undertaking, involving choosing the fabric and fittings with a tailor – in the following decade, Lady Lisle, living in Calais, sent frequent shopping lists to her factor, John Husee, in London. Just one consignment of fabric included £5 4s 11d worth of worsted, buckram, damask, velvet, camlet and satin.[3]

Our time traveller, looking at Tudor Londoners, would immediately notice that everyone, including small children, was wearing a hat of some kind. For men this was generally a round, brimmed cap. Some older men wore a coif underneath. Most London women wore their hair entirely covered, sometimes with several layers of coifs of different shapes. Some women wore a hood over this – in the 1520s this was a gable-shaped hood with long flaps reaching down to the shoulders. Apart from small girls, only brides and queens wore their hair loose in public. Indeed, when the French hood came into fashion, probably popularised at court, although not introduced, by Anne Boleyn, it was considered very daring because the front few inches of the wearer's hair were displayed. No decent person, either, would have shown their arms uncovered, even on the hottest day. A kirtle with its removable sleeves pinned up and turned back to show the wearer's smock, would be considered distinctly risqué. Working from the skin outwards, a woman's clothing consisted of a smock, the only undergarment, usually linen, with a kirtle over it, and possibly a gown worn over that. There were few, if any, corsets worn by Englishwomen until the end of the century – support was provided by a well-fitted kirtle with an interfaced bodice. Men had a linen shirt, with a doublet, upper hose (tight breeches), nether hose (stockings) and a gown as an outer garment. Shoes took the form of soft leather sandals for both sexes – men had boots for riding, but these do not appear to have been worn at other times.

Although London had spilled out of the confines of the city walls, those walls and their gates were still an important feature of 1520's life. The walls were still largely the ones that had been built by the Romans; in the sixteenth century they were still viable as a defence, and were patrolled as such. The gates were the way into London – their names and locations still live on as Ludgate, Billingsgate, Moorgate and the rest. They were locked for the night for curfew by 9pm in summer, dusk in winter; after those times no one was supposed to enter or leave; the rule was that shops and taverns should close up for the night and everyone go home. All through the night until 4am, watchmen patrolled, calling the time and a reassurance that all was well – they were instructed to rouse a neighbourhood in the case of fire or crime. The Great Fire of 1666 was only the last, and most catastrophic, of the fires that broke out quite frequently, threatening London's overwhelmingly timber buildings. Attempts were made to include stone fire walls in new houses, but these were piecemeal and inadequate. Inside, most people seem to have gone to bed early – candles were expensive, and most people could not afford to burn enough to work by. Tudor days were inclined to begin and end early.

For those who had the money, the wharves between the Bridge and the Tower were the place to find almost anything from almost anywhere in the known world. You needed the contacts as well as the funds, as some things were risky to deal in. Fabric and clothing were one thing – a mercer with the right connections could bypass import restrictions and demarcation between guilds; but something really controversial called for more circumspection. Most of the business of the Customs House, south west of All Hallows by the Tower, was concerned with weighing the vast quantities of English wool being exported and collecting the dues on it – a useful source of income for the Crown. Officials could, in theory, search any incoming ship. When Anne Boleyn came to London, it was only five years since Martin Luther had nailed his challenge to a church door. His ideas soon did the sixteenth century equivalent of 'going viral' – pamphlets were printed in each town, distributed and passed on to the next printer. The first copies were only just getting to England, brought in quietly by returning diplomats and traders. The authorities were scarcely aware of them yet, but there were already 'known men' – people of reformist sympathies – in London. Lollards had been in existence for a century, and when a young priest called William Tyndale arrived in London to ask the Bishop to help with his project to translate the whole of the New Testament into English, he was only the latest in a long tradition.

It is impossible to over emphasise the importance of religion to Londoners of Anne Boleyn's generation. All aspects of life were undertaken and perceived in terms of faith, and every Londoner belonged to the same church. Despite the early signs of a tidal movement towards reform, the structures belonging to nearly a millennium of an all-powerful church hierarchy were so ubiquitous that it is highly unlikely that most people would have questioned them. In terms of actual religious practice, not only did almost everyone attend church regularly for Mass, but it was taken for granted that individuals would also pray in private. Wills and inventories show that very many people possessed rosaries, and that it was very common for homes to contain crucifixes and images of saints. One farming book of the time begins with an exhortation to the reader to begin each day by making the sign of the cross and saying several prayers.[4] Neither was there much distinction between religious and secular life. Most organisation was done by the parish, and meetings and decisions happened in and around the church. It was at church where you were most likely to see your neighbours and catch up with news. This was especially necessary at a time when it is likely that less than half of Londoners could read. Even the well to do could often not sign their own names – making the literate parish priest an even more useful and important person. For anyone with property to leave, it was usual to make a will beginning with a prayer and funeral arrangements – often with some money left for masses for the testator's soul.

Perhaps the one element about early Tudor London that is most difficult to imagine is that of the omnipresence of the Church, and of churches. It has been estimated that one quarter of the city was Church property. Of the most impressive buildings in the capital, the Tower of London and the Guildhall were secular – the rest were mostly churches or parts of monasteries and nunneries – there were over 100 churches within the city walls. Names such as Covent Garden, the Minories and Whitefriars and Blackfriars recall the religious houses – Tudor Londoners lived with the reality, and each monastic house owned several acres of land. For example, when Blackfriars came to be dissolved, there was room for an entire exclusive housing development in its precincts. And, near what is now the Bank of England, the Austin Friars had enough land to spare to lease several plots out, so that Thomas Cromwell was able to live in a gated community. The church also held extensive additional property, as wealthy people made bequests for the good of their souls – very often the rent from a house would pay for a chantry chapel with a full-time priest to pray for the souls of several generations of a family.

The St Paul's Cathedral of the 1520s was utterly different from the one the time traveller knows today, although it was on the same site. Old St Paul's was a vast, gothic structure – it consisted of nave, choir, transepts and spire; parts of it were nearly a thousand years old. To Londoners, it was infinitely familiar. Famously, its nave was a walkway and short cut, with traders occupying recognised stalls along its length; they hired and paid rent for these, and goods and services of all kinds were offered. Outside, there were small shops built up against the cathedral walls – the rents were a useful source of extra income for the church. Given the level of population, it seems unlikely that there were enough potential members of the congregation to go round the 100 other churches – but this was hardly the point, not least because services for the local population were far from being the only, and often not the most important, use for a church. They also operated as family chapels, meeting places, shops, places of burial, pubs, storage spaces and courts. The church door was the place to post information, and was also the location for weddings. A number of churches also had connections with livery companies, and might also house a chapel for the use of guild members.

London was also a centre of education, even though it was to be some three centuries before it acquired its own university. There were, however, a great many schools. To the north of St Paul's Cathedral, our time traveller may see the extensive and still new buildings of Dean Colet's school. Colet, an intellectual, son of a Lord Mayor of London and the friend of Erasmus and More as well as a university contemporary of Cardinal Wolsey, died in 1519, leaving his school generously endowed and with a carefully planned governing document ensuring that its future course would be steered by like-minded people – and not by priests. John Colet, although he was Dean of St Paul's, went on record as believing 'there is no heresy more dangerous to the church than the vicious lives of its priests. A reformation is needed, beginning with the bishops, and extended to the priests ...'. His views brought him into conflict with More and the bishops – but Colet was too well connected and too clever for them.[5] All round London, on a smaller scale, there were schools in private houses and in rooms over church porches. Most of these charged modest fees. There were also dame schools, where a woman taught perhaps half a dozen children in her own home. Thomas More reckoned that sixty per cent of English adults could read and write.[6] It should, however, be remembered that at this time reading and writing were taught separately, and many people who were signing their names with an 'x' could read. This may have been especially true of girls, who were less likely to be sent to school, but who were often taught to read at home by their mothers. The sophisticated education given to Royal ladies, and to Thomas More's own three daughters, was unusual but not unprecedented.

The people interested in religious reform were talking about change from within the church. Most Londoners had not yet heard of Martin Luther, and the idea of challenging the authority of the church was unthinkable to almost everyone. Mass every Sunday was a matter of course – and it was in Latin, a holy but incomprehensible rite of which most of the congregation could understand little. There might be a sermon in English, possibly accompanied with an exposition of a Biblical text relating to a particular time of year. This was the way it had always been, and the church held sway over many aspects of life, including not only weddings, christenings and funerals but property transactions, the making of wills and the law. Children were taught to have a general idea of what was said and done during the mass, but most of the responsibility and authority lay with the priest, who turned away from the congregation for much of the service, speaking directly to God. For some, this was ceasing to be enough. Dissatisfaction was not, of course, entirely new, and it was in London that many of the dissatisfied were to be found.

Our time traveller is likely to also notice some of the halls of the livery companies, although, from the street, they could well be mistaken for rich houses, generally entered through a discreet, and well-fortified, street door and often built round a courtyard. It was inside livery halls that some of the most crucial deals were done. A mixture of training college, trade union, dining club and charity, the richest and most influential provided the men who became sheriffs and lord mayors, carving up areas of influence with one another and with the church. It was virtually impossible to make your way in 1520's London without access to one or the other. Among the livery companies themselves, it was important to have friends among one of the ultra-high status 'Great Twelve', headed by the Mercers, Grocers, and Drapers. In those days before the invention of banks, it was also the livery companies that held the city's financial power. Sovereigns went straight to them to seek backing for the more expensive parts of their foreign policy, with mixed results. By the 1520s, city grandees had had more than a decade of paying towards Henry VIII's foreign wars, and were increasingly reluctant to part with yet more money they would never see again. Liverymen were, however, anxious both to stay on good terms with the King, and to gain and keep the enormous buying power of the crown – so they kept paying up.

Near the western boundary of the city, the Fleet was a navigable waterway, flowing into the Thames south of Ludgate, where there was a stone bridge. Wide barges full of food and fuel plied the river up as far as

Holborn – named for the higher reaches of the river – where there was another bridge as the river flowed south from its source in the heights of Hampstead. Just to the west of what is now New Bridge Street, south of St Bride's Church, lay the newly and fashionably built Bridewell Palace. It was constructed round two courtyards, with a grand processional staircase but without a great hall: the latest in elegant royal living. The King could always use the great hall at Blackfriars, just on the other side of the Fleet. The other main waterway in London was the Walbrook – writing towards the end of the century, John Stow had heard that it had once been 'a fair brook of sweet water', but that was long ago. By Tudor times it was little but a sewer, so noxious that many sections were already covered over.[7]

Shopping, especially for food, was an important and time-consuming activity. Up to four fifths of the income of poorer people went on food, and in London there was less possibility of growing your own. There were a number of markets, each one with its own specialism – Billingsgate for fish, Gracechurch Street for dairy products, Cheap for vegetables. There were also many permanent shops. London households could not be self sufficient as larger country homes often were. Vegetables, fruit and meat all had to be bought in, often every day, as it was difficult to keep food fresh. Ale was drunk with almost every meal, as there was no tea, coffee or chocolate, the water was often not safe to drink and milk, often scarce, was mostly for children. Some households made their own ale, or it could be bought from the many alehouses. London kitchens were often not big enough to house a bread oven, so usually bread would be bought too. This was a major item, as it provided the main carbohydrate element in most people's diet: there was as yet no pasta or potatoes and little rice, and if a middle-class housewife wanted a pie for her family, she would be likely to take it to the baker's to be cooked.

In the early sixteenth century the richer you were, the more meat you were likely to eat. This was not, however, just in the form of roast joints, although these were appreciated, but in many complicated spiced dishes, pies and stews. The Tudors ate a bewildering variety of animals and birds, from blackbirds and larks to kids and hares. Venison was reserved for the King and not offered for sale. In a prosperous household there would be good food all the year round, but everyone had, by law, to observe the fast at Lent, every Friday, and some Saturdays too, which meant that not only meat but dairy products were forbidden (except, in the case of Lent, on Sundays). Fish, however, was available in great profusion and variety. Vegetables were certainly eaten when they were available, but many of those familiar today were not yet known – most famously, potatoes and tomatoes. Additionally, a great many of those that were known were very different. Carrots were small, scrawny and purple or white but not orange, while peas and beans were recognisable but much smaller. Cabbages, onions, cauliflowers, cucumbers and turnips would have been familiar – all, of course, only available in their English season. Londoners were fortunate, as there were already many market gardens within reach of the city, and for the prosperous, there was a limited amount of imported citrus fruit. All fruit was popular but regarded as unhealthy if eaten raw, so pies, tarts and preserves were often served. Cheese was generally regarded as coarse stuff, and does not often feature in recipes, but was certainly very welcome among those who could not afford much meat. The basic food of the poor was pottage, which was essentially a grain mixture with cabbage, root vegetables and perhaps some bacon. Richer people had pottage too, but theirs were likely to be enriched with spices and almonds.

There were sumptuary laws relating to food as well as to clothes – people of different degrees were limited as to how many main dishes they could have for dinner.[8] A cardinal was allowed nine, while dukes, marquises, bishops and earls rated seven. At gentry level, the number dropped to three. If you had someone of a higher rank coming to dinner, you could trade up to the number of dishes they were allowed. In prosperous households there were usually two courses, with a pottage at each. On special occasions there might be a dessert course for the guests, offering the sweet things, such as gingerbread and marzipan, of which the Tudors were very fond, although the price and scarcity of sugar made them prohibitively expensive. The better-off would have wine with their dinner, which was served at 10 or 11am, although ale was the basic drink of almost everyone, including children. All this was, however, completely academic to poorer Londoners, who would be limited to bread and ale for breakfast, with a dinner of pottage (likely to contain a mixture of pulses and vegetables, with perhaps a little meat), plus more bread and a supper of the same. And that was the moderately fortunate who did not go hungry. Some years, at the end of winter, after a bad harvest, there was scarcely enough food for even those who could pay.

Inside the city walls, the streets were thronged not only with monks and nuns but those who were employed in the religious houses. The 'religious' themselves were immediately identifiable by the habits prescribed by each order – so visible that neighbourhoods were named after them. The Blackfriars were Dominicans; there were Greyfriars and Whitefriars further to the west, and the Minories was the home of the Minoresses of St Clare, an order of Franciscan nuns, and to the Crutched Friars. The present-day Covent Garden provided orchards for the monks of Westminster Abbey, and north of Smithfield was the house of the Carthusian monks where Thomas More was in the habit of visiting on retreat. South of the river at St Thomas's Hospital, monks and nuns had been caring for the poor, the sick and the homeless for at least four hundred years. The real Dick Whittington had added a ward for unmarried pregnant women so that they could give birth in safety. Near the church of St Bartholomew the Great, monks and nuns were attempting cures.

The monastic orders were not only religious and political players, but the providers of most of London's health care and social services. Bedlam, the hospital of St Mary of Bethlehem, occupied a site near where Liverpool Street station now stands – the monks there began to care for the insane as early as the fourteenth century; by the 1520s it had a secular master, a lucrative post that was to be held in the 1530s by George Boleyn. St Bartholomew's hospital in Smithfield had been founded by Rahere, Henry II's jester, and St Thomas's by the monks of Bermondsey to commemorate Thomas A. Becket. By the time of Henry VIII, it too had a secular master, six brothers and three lay sisters, who had the care of forty sick, poor people. These represented virtually the only safety net for the poor if they fell ill or grew old and feeble, for lepers and for unwanted babies.

The Strand was a ribbon development of ecclesiastical palaces, with just a few grand houses reserved for secular lords and for lawyers. The term 'inn' (still preserved in the Inns of Court) meant great house – the furthest west of the Strand palaces was Durham Place, which was the London home of the Prince Bishops of Durham. Next door, the former Palace of the Savoy now operated as a hospital, set up by Henry VII. To the north of the Strand, there was a lane leading off in the direction of St Giles in the Field, and nearby, a number of what Stow described as 'houses for gentlemen and men of honour'[9] Further west, beyond Charing Cross, the estates of the Abbot of Westminster covered several hundred acres as far as the horse ferry and north to Mayfair. Bloomsbury, Soho, Piccadilly, St Giles and St James all belonged to monastic houses, and much of the present-day South Bank belonged to assorted southern English bishops. South of the river, the Bishop of Winchester owned much of Southwark, which was already notorious as a safe haven for gambling houses and brothels. The bishops made good money from the rents, and the prostitutes became known as the Bishop of Winchester's geese.

Further west, the time traveller finds herself outside another magnificent mansion. This was York Place, the London residence of the Archbishops of York. When Anne Boleyn returned to London, Thomas Wolsey was at the height of his power and magnificence. He had extended his palace considerably, and also bought artwork, jewellery, tapestries, glasses from Venice, silver and silver gilt for his tables and display boards, books, musical instruments and any novelty he might be offered. Wolsey was famous for the wonderful entertainments he held – just a couple of years before Anne Boleyn's arrival in London there had been an evening, described by Wolsey's biographer Cavendish, somewhere between a masquerade, a concert and a supper party, during which the King, his sister Mary and ten companions had arrived in disguise, masked and by water. Several hours of alternating dancing, drinking, theatrical entertainment and eating followed. Eye witnesses said the specially made costumes gleamed in the candlelight as the revellers danced until dawn.

Westminster Abbey, scene of coronations and Royal burials, was under the control of monks – the Abbot of Westminster was one of the great powers in the land. The time traveller might find Parliament in session round and about the Palace of Westminster. This, however, was relatively uncommon – Parliament sat only when the King called it, and there was no suggestion that he should do so as a matter of course at any particular interval – the summons usually came when the King needed extra money. The Lords had a designated space in the Queen's Chamber; the Commons appear to have fitted in as and when they could. The King visited not only to open and proceedings, but stayed to speak to the Lords, making the case for whatever legislation he wanted – generally the passing of a subsidy, the contemporary form of income tax.

If she was looking for the King, our time traveller has probably come to the wrong place. In the early 1520s the court was most often at Greenwich in the winter. In the summer months, those seeking to track the King down might well be in for a long and possibly frustrating journey, as he and a chosen group of courtiers spent months at a time on progress, travelling between palaces, with stop-overs at the country homes of favoured friends. They would spend most of their days hunting, and their evenings eating, drinking and exchanging hunting stories – nothing of significance could happen in court circles for weeks at a time. Wolsey was left behind to get on with the work of running the country while, back in London, other kinds of work – and other lives – went on.

Chapter 2

'Your very humble obedient daughter' 1501–22

nne Boleyn was born into the ruling class – but it is fair to say that she was not born a very important member of that class. The Boleyns were certainly of gentle status, and with noble connections, but the births of their children, especially their daughters, did not make a special impact on the world. So, we are still not sure when Anne was born or where, although it was probably in 1501 at Blickling in Norfolk.

The Boleyn family were originally from Norfolk – there are records of Boleyns living in Salle in the fourteenth century, where they were gentlefolk, although not rich or particularly influential. The family's fortune was made by Geoffrey Boleyn, who left Norfolk in the 1420s, becoming first a hatter and then a mercer – it is likely he was a younger son, as it was usual for an eldest to stay at home to learn how to run his future inheritance, while the younger ones were apprenticed to trades. Geoffrey's was hardly a rags to riches story, as he had not started life in the least ragged, but he certainly made serious money in London Geoffrey Boleyn, in turn, became an Alderman and Lord Mayor of London in 1457-8, having transferred to the more prestigious Mercers' Company. He was also an MP for the City of London, and acquired property. As this was a time long before the nobility found anything distasteful about City wealth, he was able to marry the daughter of a baron, Thomas, Lord Hoo, and to acquire Hever Castle in Kent. Their son, William, appears to have been content with the life of a Norfolk gentleman, but married even higher up the social scale – his bride was Margaret, daughter and co-heiress of the Earl of Ormonde, and it was their son, Thomas, who was to become the father of Anne Boleyn.

Although Geoffrey Boleyn had spent much of his career in London, there is no evidence that the Boleyns had retained many permanent

connections there. In addition to their home at Blickling, the family had a
town house in Norwich, and appear to have spent large sums on updating
Hever. But with that they were content – evidently they had not, and
did not, in the last years of the fifteenth century, aspire to have national
influence. At this time the upper nobility would expect to maintain a
London house – many of the grandest of these lined the Strand; others
were in the premier streets of the city, especially those in the Cheapside
area – as well as their country estates. William Boleyn was highly regarded
in Norfolk. He was knighted in 1483, was a justice of the peace and was
among those called upon as a trouble-shooter by the crown in times of
unrest. He was also a close associate of the Duke of Norfolk, and was
therefore in a position to negotiate a marriage between his 18-year-old
son, Thomas, who had been born in 1477, and Lady Elizabeth Howard,
thus bringing the Boleyns a further step up, in terms of status, in the
world. By this time the Boleyns had considerable wealth – when Geoffrey
died in 1462, he had land in five counties besides Norfolk, and this was
added to by William once he inherited on the death of his elder brother,
Thomas.

It was left to William's son, Thomas, to rediscover whatever London
might have to offer. He had already made an excellent marriage, although
it is true that the Howards' fortunes were in decline at this time. The Duke
of Norfolk's son, the Earl of Surrey, had made the mistake of backing
Richard III at the time of the Battle of Bosworth, with the result that he
had lost virtually all his possessions to the newly made King Henry VII,
and had to spend several expensive years negotiating to buy the Howard
lands back. So the social and economic gap between Thomas Boleyn and
Elizabeth Howard was smaller than it would otherwise have been. Sir
William Boleyn made his son an annuity of £50 a year, and they would
also have had whatever money Elizabeth brought to the marriage. At a
time when a London baker would be happy to take home £5 a year, this
was far from poverty, especially as the young family were able to live first
at Blickling and then, after William's death in 1505, at Hever (William's
younger son, James, lived at Blickling after this date). However, Thomas
Boleyn was to write plaintively of what he regarded as having been the

poverty of his early married years, especially as, he said, his wife had a baby every year.[1] Although only three of their children lived into adulthood, we know they had at least two other sons, Henry and Thomas – there may also have been other babies who died in infancy.

Certainly Thomas Boleyn worked hard, and with some success, to make his way in the wider world. Some historians, especially in the nineteenth century, have written disapprovingly of the enthusiasm with which he greeted the opportunities brought when each of his daughters, in turn, caught the king's eye. However the record of his appointments leaves no doubt that, from the earliest stage of his career, Thomas had the trick of pleasing, and evidently this applied to Henry VII as well as his son. It is likely, too, that this was a man of some genuine ability. As early as 1501, he attended the wedding of Arthur, Prince of Wales and Catherine of Aragon, and in 1503 was one of those who escorted the King's eldest daughter Margaret to Scotland where she was to start her new life as the wife of its King, James. Thomas began his career with a relatively junior appointment as a Yeoman of the Crown, and was then appointed a Squire of the Body, earning a salary of £30 a year and the right of Bouge of Court (that is, to food and fuel as well as accommodation). In 1509 he took part in the funeral procession of Henry VII. In opting for a life at court, Thomas Boleyn was choosing a career in the place where much, though not all, real national power was wielded. It was also the place where much, though not all, real money was made. At this date the City of London, where Thomas's grandfather had made his money and rose to the top of its hierarchy, was still also a place of power and prestige in its own right. It is notable that, after the death of Geoffrey Boleyn, not only does it appear that the family had no London house (Geoffrey's was probably in the Barnard Castle area, as he served that ward as an alderman) and also appear to have lacked any close relatives in the city hierarchy after Sir Geoffrey's time. It might have been expected that Thomas's younger brother, James, would have followed his grandfather's route to riches via a London apprenticeship – it was still common for younger sons of influential families to do this, usually in the higher status trades such as goldsmith, vintner or mercer. In the event James Boleyn held some minor appointments at court, was knighted in 1520 and was a member of the Reformation parliament in 1529, and lived on, perhaps below the political radar, to inherit his brother's property, and, just before he died, to see his great niece, Elizabeth, become Queen. But his career was evidently always hampered by lack of property. It may be, too, that he was content to barter less success for less risk.

It is likely that Thomas and Elizabeth spent much of their time apart during their early married life, with Thomas in attendance on the King, and Elizabeth either pregnant or with their small children, first at Blickling and then, after William's death in 1505, at Hever. It is almost certain that their daughter, Anne, was born at Blickling, as, after her death, one of her former chaplains, Matthew Parker, recalled that they were 'countrymen', meaning that they were both born in the same county, Norfolk. There is, however, still some disagreement about when she was born, although most historians now believe that the year of her birth was 1501. Neither is there a consensus about the number of siblings she had or the order in which they were born. Only three children, Mary, Anne and George, lived to grow up, but two other sons, Thomas and Henry, were born, died young and have memorials at St John the Baptist, Penshurst (where there were family connections) and St Peter's, Hever, respectively. It has recently been suggested[2] that Thomas, who was probably the eldest, may have been born as early as 1497 and have lived into adolescence, dying as late as 1520, with Henry also living into his teens. It does not appear that there is much evidence for this as the suggestion is based largely on the dating of their two, very similar, small memorial crosses, which can be dated stylistically to about 1520. This may simply mean that the family did not mark their sons' graves until 1520, which could well have been several years after they died. There is no direct mention of Thomas or Henry in the historical record, so it is impossible to be sure, but the idea that the Boleyn nursery was home to five, rather than three, children during Anne's formative years is an interesting one. Of the surviving siblings, it is usually now agreed that Mary was the eldest, born in around 1500, followed by Anne in 1501 and George in 1503. Elizabeth may well have given birth to other babies who were either stillborn or short lived.

In those days, long before birth certificates or even parish registers, the births of children, even from influential families, often went unrecorded. Up to a quarter of all babies born did not live to see their fifth birthday.

Hever Castle, where Anne Boleyn spent much of her childhood, still stands, although much altered and extended. The Astor family, who owned the property in the early twentieth century, turned it into a romantic – and much more comfortable – version of what the Edwardians thought a castle should be, although in Anne's time it was more accurately a fortified manor house rather than a defendable stronghold. The charming tower room now said to have been Anne's bedroom, for example, was almost certainly no such thing – Tudor children, even of the upper classes, did not have a room to themselves. The castle is in a low-lying position, and would have been cold and damp in winter, despite the improvements made by Thomas Boleyn, who added a new hallway, front door and stairs. In Anne's time it was also surrounded by woodland. There was a vast kitchen, with its own well, later gutted by the Astors and turned into a reception room. The mediaeval heart of the house was the great hall, with its dais at one end where the family ate, while the rest of the large household had their meals in the main hall. Behind the dais was, and still is, a withdrawing room where the Boleyn family probably ate at least some of their meals in private. A long gallery at the top of the house provided the possibility of exercise in bad weather, and it is likely that there was a garden in the sixteenth century. The vast lake, parterres and waterfalls were all installed, at a similarly vast expense, by the Astors – the surroundings of the castle would probably not be recognisable to the Boleyns. However uncomfortable the Hever of five centuries ago would seem by modern standards, this was a highly privileged place – the fact that Anne Boleyn grew up as a child in a household of this status serves to demonstrate how little the taunts that she was an upstart are justified.

We do not know who taught Anne Boleyn to read and write – this may have been her own mother or, equally likely, the family may have employed a tutor for the children. Anne evidently learned well, and it is likely that she was taught Latin and French, music and dance as well as reading and writing. It was the fashion at that time among aristocratic families to educate daughters as well as sons. If, as seems likely, Thomas Boleyn was seeking to find places at court for his children, he would have taken care to ensure that they were all learned and accomplished so that they would make a good impression on potential employers. The nursery at Hever was presided over by Mrs Mary Orchard, who was to stay with the family for the whole of Anne's life, being one of those appointed to attend her in the Tower. It is likely that there were several other female servants to help look after the children and, in the absence of both parents, the nursery would have been the Boleyn children's world. This was completely usual in Tudor upper-class households – high status women were not expected to take day-to-day responsibility for their children's care.

We do not know how often Anne left Hever during her first twelve years. Thomas Boleyn evidently spent much time at court – and so may Elizabeth, once she had finished bearing children. There is some evidence that visibly pregnant ladies were not expected to appear at court. It is not clear whether she held any court office in her own right, but her status meant that she was likely to have waited on Catherine of Aragon in addition to the important occasions such as the Field of the Cloth of Gold when she appears in the historical record. Meanwhile, Thomas's career blossomed. He was made a Knight of the Bath in Henry VIII's Coronation Jousts in 1509, then a pall bearer at the funeral of the baby Prince Henry who lived for six weeks in 1511. As Thomas was nearly fifteen years older than Henry he was not made a Gentleman of the Privy Chamber (these were the men in closest everyday attendance, and were the nearest Henry had to friends), but he served on the King's Council and was made a Knight of the Body. In May 1512 he was appointed as an ambassador to Margaret of Austria – an appointment that was to have far-reaching effects, both for Thomas and for his daughters. Although the diplomatic mission met with only limited success, Thomas succeeded in winning the confidence of the Regent of the Low Countries who, although still in her early thirties, was universally respected, was addressed as '*tres redoutee dame*', and whose palace at Mechelin, near Antwerp, was a great centre of the high culture of the time. At some point during the negotiations Margaret agreed to receive Thomas's daughter, Anne, as one of her maids of honour – a wonderful opportunity for the young girl to finish her education at Europe's most sophisticated court. There is no evidence as to why Anne was chosen rather than her elder sister, Mary – either the first steps in Mary's Court career were already planned, or it may be that Anne was regarded as being the more promising of the two sisters.

Anne set off from home without either of her parents. She was accompanied to Mechelin, the palace that was Margaret of Austria's main home, by a Flemish nobleman, Claude Bouton. There would almost certainly have been at least two servants in the entourage, and the journey is likely to have taken around a week, depending on the winds and weather they encountered when they arrived at Dover for the crossing – of course, by sailing boat. The rest of the journey is likely to have been either on horseback or, for Anne herself, in a horse litter. The days of comfortable wheeled carriages were still in the future. There is no record of how much time Anne and her family had to prepare for her leaving home – she was not to return to England for nine years. No doubt she was expected to be exemplary in her behaviour and to lose no opportunity for her own and her family's advancement. It was a great deal to expect of a 12-year-old girl – but Thomas Boleyn would almost certainly have said, and believed, that he was ensuring his promising daughter was being offered the best possible start in the world.

At Mechelin, Anne became one of the Regent's eighteen *filles d'honneur*. At twelve or thirteen she was probably the youngest of them – but all were carefully supervised by Margaret, who ensured they were taught languages, music and dancing from the greatest teachers of the day, as well as deportment and the art of how to operate gracefully and safely in the sometimes febrile atmosphere of a court where courtly love was supposed to rule, but with decorum.

Soon after Anne's arrival, Margaret wrote to Thomas Boleyn:

'I have received your letter by the Esquire Bouton, who has presented your daughter to me, who is very welcome, and I am confident of being able to deal with her in a way which will give you satisfaction, so that on your return the two of us will need no intermediary other than she. I find her so bright and pleasant for her young age that I am more beholden to you for sending her to me that you are to me.'[3]

So it is clear that Anne's learning of fluent French was part of the deal, and Margaret duly set her to work with a tutor named Symonnet. Soon Anne was fluent enough in the language to be able to write an independent letter to her father, written from Margaret's summer palace near Brussels. Evidently Thomas had previously written to Anne reminding her of all that was expected of her, as her reply, which unexpectedly survives and is now in the Library of Corpus Christi College, Cambridge, reads in part and in translation:

> 'Sir, I understand from your letter that you desire me to be a woman
> of good reputation when I come to court, and you will tell me that
> the queen will take the trouble to converse with me, and it gives
> me great joy to think of conversing with such a wise and virtuous
> person. This will make me all the keener to persevere in speaking
> French well, and also especially because you have told me to, and
> advised me for my own part to work at it as much as I can.'[4]

As Eric Ives has observed,[5] the spelling is highly idiosyncratic, even for the early sixteenth century, and Anne was still clearly in the early stages of writing in French. However, this one letter is extremely persuasive in dating her birth as 1501 and not 1507 – the handwriting is most certainly not that of a 6-year-old. This letter also indicates just how much Anne was aware that her career path was mapped out by her father – she was to stay with Margaret of Austria, probably for an agreed two or three years, during which she was to acquire all the learning, graces and accomplishments that were on offer in this most sophisticated of environments. It may be that the 'Queen' referred to means Catherine of Aragon, in which case a future career path is being mapped out as well as plans for the next few years (at this stage the move to France was not foreseeable). In being ambitious for his child, and in expecting her to uphold the family honour, Thomas Boleyn was behaving in a way typical of his class and time – advancement was conducted by networks of kinship and obligation, and anyone given an opportunity was expected not only to make the most of it for themselves, but also on behalf of their extended family and friends and of the clients among whom they gave and received favours. So, Anne was being given not only a great opportunity but a set of future responsibilities.

All the evidence points to Anne having been as good as her word and her father's expectations of her time with Margaret. She appears to have absorbed the culture of the place, which owed much to the influences of the high culture of Burgundy and Flanders, and was the focal point in northern Europe for music, painting and architecture. In comparison, London was still a cultural backwater. The palace at Mechelin where Anne spent much of her time during the next two years, was brick built, and offered every comfort then available. The household inventories survive, and tell us that inside, the palace contained the most luxurious textiles, the richest tapestries, the most exquisitely illuminated manuscripts and the most beautiful paintings. It was here that Anne acquired many of her tastes. A music manuscript that belonged to her survives in the Royal College of Music, and contains around thirty pieces, of which over half are by composers associated with Margaret of Austria. We know, too, that Anne became an accomplished musician, and was probably taught by organist Henri Bredemers, who was on the payroll at Mechelin. During this time she may well also have met Henry VIII, who was among the leaders of a renewed war with France. He, and probably also Anne Boleyn, were also present during the peace negotiations that followed at Lille and Tournai, when Anne could well have made herself useful as a translator. The story goes that during these negotiations Margaret and King Henry's friend, Charles Brandon, Duke of Suffolk, entered into a flirtation which came to an abrupt end when he made what she had supposed to be a mock marriage proposal, but which he chose to take seriously, to the point she had to make an official denial of any agreement to marry him. If the gossip of the time has any truth, Brandon may well have been less than keen to re-acquaint a girl who had witnessed what appears to have been an episode that ended in embarrassment for him. She was to be an intermittent thorn in his side for the next twenty years.

It was to be European politics that put an end to Anne's time at Mechelin. A peace with France was successfully negotiated, and its terms included a marriage between Henry VIII's 18-year-old sister, Mary, and the ailing 52-year-old King of France, Louis XII. As Mary had previously been due to marry Margaret of Austria's nephew, Charles V – an agreement only made the previous year – this news can hardly have been welcome to the Regent, who already had her own reasons for disliking France. And she appears, understandably, to have been less than pleased to receive an embarrassed letter from Thomas Boleyn, written from Greenwich in August 1514. Boleyn wrote that the lists were being compiled of ladies to accompany Mary, and French speakers were in demand. So Anne had been specifically requested, and, her father wrote, 'to this request I could not, nor did I know how to refuse'.[6] It is not to be supposed that Thomas had even wanted to refuse – the advantages to Anne and her family were too great. In any case Anne would probably have not stayed in Mechelin more than another year or two – it was the timing and circumstances of her departure that were the difficulty. It seems Thomas Boleyn had done extremely well for his family, as not only Anne but her elder sister, Mary, were included in the list of maids of honour to accompany the new French Queen. Given the intense competition there would certainly have been for these appointments, this was a major coup.

It appears that Margaret may indeed have made difficulties over Anne's departure, as her name does not appear on the list of those who accompanied the new Queen of France on her journey from London, although that of her sister, Mary, is included. Mary and her brother, King Henry had always been close, and it seems that she and he had agreed that, if Mary agreed to this marriage, when the King of France died, she could choose for herself the next time. So the elaborate but hasty preparations went ahead. It is possible that it was decided that it was pointless for Anne to make such a long three-cornered journey, and that, with the agreement of all concerned, she travelled directly to Paris in the autumn of 1514 and met the English party there. However, it is on record that Margaret was indeed personally affronted by the marriage, and this may very well have led her to delay Anne's departure.

It is likely Anne arrived in time to witness the new Queen's coronation, triumphal entrance into Paris, complete with playlets, mechanical wonders, fresh roses and lilies in November, and a second wedding ceremony. Thereafter, King Louis wrote that he was delighted with his bride, and after their wedding night was making appreciative comments about having 'crossed the river three times', but followed this up by dismissing most of his new Queen's English ladies, on the pretext that they were interfering between him and her. Although she was allowed to retain some of her younger maids of honour, including, apparently, both Boleyn girls, Mary was, understandably, both outraged and frightened by this development, which left her with no English confidante in a foreign city – and which, of course, was what Louis had in mind. However, the marriage was not to last long – the French king was, even for the early sixteenth century, a very old fifty-two, and had suffered from leprosy for years. By the time of the Christmas celebrations he was observing the festivities from a couch, and died on 1 January 1515 after only eighty-two days of marriage.

Louis's successor was his cousin, François, who was also the husband of his daughter, Claude (in France women were specifically barred from inheriting the crown). Before François could be confirmed as King, everyone had to be sure that Mary was not pregnant. By tradition a newly widowed Queen of France observed forty days of strict seclusion, during which time she remained, swathed in white veils, in a shuttered and curtained room lit only by candles and supposedly attended only by her ladies. As well as being a formal observance, this served the highly practical purpose of keeping the queen concerned under close observation. It is clear that Mary found this time both trying and frightening, as she was isolated and with few sources of advice. It is likely that the seclusion was less than total, and some historians, including A. F. Pollard, have believed that François tried to seduce her; this is uncertain, but he was certainly keen to control who she might marry next.

It is highly likely that both Mary and Anne Boleyn were in attendance of Mary Tudor at this time – some writers have said that, baulked of the Queen, François instead conducted a brief affair with Mary Boleyn.

However, there is no evidence of this other than one malicious remark that François may, or may not, have made twenty years later. This was reported by Rodolfo Pio, the Papal Nuncio in Paris in early 1536, when salacious gossip about the Boleyns was going down well in Papal circles – he wrote that the French King had 'known' Mary in France *'per una grandissima ribald et infame sopre tutte'* ('for a very great whore, more infamous than all the rest').[7] Pio does not actually state that François claimed to have had an affair with Mary himself – the comment can certainly be interpreted that way, or equally, that François was commenting on Mary's reputation at his court. If it is true that Mary was only at the French court between November 1514 and April 1515, she must have been a fast worker to have become known for promiscuity in what was certainly a fairly permissive environment. However, as most of Mary Tudor's elder ladies had been sent home, the remaining younger ones – and Mary Boleyn was around sixteen at this time – may have had little protection in a foreign land. It is not clear how many of them spoke fluent French; if some of them did not, then that would have increased their isolation. It is not difficult to imagine that the more naïve among them may have looked like easy pickings, either to the notoriously lecherous François himself, or to some of his friends, or both. It is equally easy to imagine that, even at fourteen, Anne Boleyn's time at Mechelin had given her enough sophistication and toughness to avoid becoming a passing entertainment, as well as the fluent French that would have enabled her to turn down unwanted offers with wit. This is complete speculation – but it does fit in with what is known of the sequence of events, and of the characters of the two sisters.

What is on record is that Henry dispatched Charles Brandon to France to make an agreement with the new French King, fetch his sister home, and to collect as much as possible of her dowry and jewels. Henry knew that there had been a previous attachment between Brandon and Mary, and appears to have extracted a promise that he would do nothing about it until back on English soil. However, Brandon was not proof against Mary's determination – they began a secret affair, closely followed by an equally secret marriage, after which they had the problem of reconciling Henry to the distinctly undignified fait accompli. They both maintained that it was Mary who had insisted they marry straight away, and it is likely that this was true – and, put this way, they were more likely to be forgiven. François was happy to support them, as this new marriage had the effect of removing Mary from the international marriage market. Both the Boleyn girls must have known about what was going on – and Anne must also have been a witness to Brandon's previous somewhat asinine behaviour around Margaret of Austria. It is quite possible that she disapproved of, or even disliked, him and that, at fourteen, she failed to keep her feelings to herself. This may well have been the beginning of the dislike that Mary Tudor and, perhaps to a somewhat lesser extent, Brandon himself were to display towards Anne in later years.

When, in April 1515, Mary Tudor and her new husband set off for Calais, England, with the task of mending bridges with Henry, Anne Boleyn did not go with them. Instead, she had performed, or had performed for her, the feat of securing a place in the household of the new Queen of France, Claude, the daughter of Louis and wife of François, who was at this time only 15 years old. The explanation may be that Claude had met and taken a liking to Anne as a contemporary, or Anne may have acted as interpreter in conversations between Claude and Mary Tudor in the preceding months. Anne was to stay in France nearly another seven years, and during this period became as accomplished a courtier as her father. Claude, who was gentle, deeply religious and born lame, was almost constantly pregnant, and spent much of her time away from Paris at the Loire palaces of Blois and Ambois. It may not have been the most lively of households, but we know that Anne used her time well, and continued to hone her musical talents – in future years, even hostile commentators were to admit she was a skilled lutenist and dancer.

Opinions vary as to whether Mary Boleyn went back to England with Mary Tudor, stayed at the French court or, according to one tradition, did not secure a place with Queen Claude, but stayed on in France at the household of a French nobleman near Brie. This theory comes from a story given later in the sixteenth century by William Rastell, Thomas More's first biographer, who claimed that Anne Boleyn was sent to France in disgrace as a teenager. At least one recent writer[8] has speculated that this story was a distortion of a real occurrence, but that the Boleyn daughter who lived for a time in the household of Philippe du Moulin was in fact Mary. It is also possible that she remained in Mary Tudor's household, for which complete accounts do not survive. There is no direct evidence to support any of these possibilities, and Mary disappears from the official record until 1520, when she was certainly back in England for her wedding. Some commentators have assumed that the marriage, to William Carey of the King's Privy Chamber, was a disappointing one for a Boleyn, and that she was being married off to mask an affair with the King. In fact, the Careys were a landed family that could trace their lineage back to the twelfth century and held land in several counties, although William was a younger son of a younger son with no inherited land and his own way to make in the world. He was one of the 'new men' so highly regarded by the King, and had arrived at court under the patronage of the Earl of Devon, who was a remote cousin of the Tudors. Soon after his arrival at court in 1518 he obtained a Privy Chamber appointment as Esquire of the Body, and in the New Year of 1519 was entrusted with a thousand crowns (£250 in the currency of the time – a very substantial sum) of the King's gambling money, and was given 4s 2d for delivering it safely. He is also recorded as playing tennis on the King's tennis court and, later in the year, was included in a list of the relatively few courtiers entitled to extra privileges, including being served breakfast. Carey could also keep four servants and two horses at court. Carey's status was reminiscent of that of Thomas Boleyn at the same age, and it is likely that the Boleyns thought Carey was likely to 'come good' in the same way. The wedding took place in February 1520, and the King was among the guests, making an offering of 6s 8d during the marriage service.

1520 was also the year of the Field of the Cloth of Gold – a famous, stylish, immensely expensive and ultimately abortive piece of diplomacy. Part of the ever-shifting tide of European politics, the peace treaty between England and France this summit meeting was called to ratify, was soon to vanish into the sand. However as a tale of splendour and competitive over-spending, its fame lives on. A temporary township of pavilions and marquees was constructed in Calais, and much of the

English court packed its bags and crossed the Channel to take part. The English contingent included Thomas and Elizabeth Boleyn, their daughter, Mary, and her new husband. It is likely that Anne Boleyn was there in attendance on the Queen of France. And it may be that her brother George, by now 16 years old, was there too, probably attending his father (those who took part officially were allowed to have attendants of their own). If so, this would have been the first occasion on which Anne's birth family had been together for several years – probably since Anne had left for Mechelin. It is likely that Thomas was the only relative apart from Mary whom Anne had seen in the years since; she had almost certainly not seen her mother since leaving England. If it is true that the two eldest Boleyn sons, Henry and Thomas, may have lived on into their early teens, dying not long before this event, then their absence may have rendered the meeting of the survivors more poignant. However, this was a time when the future looked promising for the Boleyn family. Thomas' diplomatic career was going well, and he was now an ever-richer man; Elizabeth was often at Court in attendance on Catherine of Aragon; Mary had made a good marriage and was also at Court as part of her husband's household; and George, too young at sixteen to have any independent appointments as yet, was waiting in the wings, perhaps putting in a year or two at university, to start his own career.

Anne was to stay with Queen Claude until late 1521 and when she was recalled, it was partly because of the once more deteriorating relations between England and France, and partly because there was a plan that she should be married. At twenty, in sixteenth-century terms, it was certainly time for a match to be made for her. The one that was proposed was intended to resolve a long-running conflict. Sir Thomas Boleyn was, through his mother, one of two possible claimants for the Irish Earldom of Ormonde. The King had found in his favour at the time of the death of the last Earl, Thomas Butler, in 1516. Over in Ireland, however, the matter looked rather different. A cousin, Piers Butler, claimed that, as the nearest male relative of the late Earl, the title should go to him – and he had gained the support of a number of Irish lords. Piers' son, James, was being brought up (or being kept hostage, depending on your point of view) in the household of Cardinal Wolsey, and now the suggestion was made that a possible way forward might be for James Butler and Anne Boleyn to marry. This solution was favoured both by the all-powerful Wolsey and by Anne's uncle, the Duke of Norfolk, who, between them, persuaded the King to support their plan. So, Thomas Boleyn had little alternative other than to go along with them, at least in the first instance, and Anne was duly recalled in late 1521.

There is no surviving evidence about exactly when Anne was told she was to return to England, who gave her the news, how she felt about it or how and in whose company she made her return journey – this time, possibly a winter voyage. Anne would, in company with all travellers of her day, have made the return journey by sailing boat, crossing, this time, from Calais to Dover. It may well be that she continued her journey directly to London rather than stopping off at her childhood home of Hever. If so, it is quite possible that this would have been her first sight of the city that was to be her main home for the remaining fifteen years of her life. Her departure from Hever to Mechelin was almost certainly via Dover. However, by this date, Thomas Boleyn had been appointed Treasurer to the Royal Household – a position senior enough that he was entitled to good accommodation wherever the court was, plus food and the right to keep several servants and horses. He would in any case have been able to find a bed for his newly returned daughter – but it is highly likely that Anne went straight into an appointment as Maid of Honour to the Queen.

Chapter 3

Queen in Waiting: 1522–33

T he first direct sighting we have of Anne back in England is extremely high profile, and precisely datable – on 1 March 1522, she took part in a very notable event. Life at Henry VIII's court was punctuated by entertainments of all kinds – jousts, processions, celebrations, the high points of the church year, weddings, christenings, and even funerals, all had their form of ceremonial. In all of these events, performance in the form of music, poetry and dance would have their place. For the most part these events would take place under the King's roof, but sometimes the court would visit the home of a significant courtier. One such gathering took place at York Place, the London home of Cardinal Wolsey, on Shrove Tuesday 1522. This was the day of Carnival – the day before the start of Lent, the forty-day run-up to Easter, during which no one was allowed to eat meat or dairy products except on Sundays, and everyone was supposed to observe a period of penitence and contemplation. Possibly just as important, yet another European treaty, this time with the Emperor Charles V, was about to be signed, and his ambassadors were in London and needed to be entertained and impressed.

That day's entertainments had a unifying theme – that of the cruelty of unrequited love. The day included tournaments, during which the participating knights almost certainly made great play with shields bearing mottos such as bleeding hearts, women's hands and the like. There would also have been much eating, drinking and the giving of prizes. The high point of the festivities was reserved for the evening, with the staging of a pageant entitled *The Assault on the Chateau Vert*. This was a performance piece including music, dance and spectacle, and the cast included both courtiers and the Master and Children of the Chapel Royal. The piece appears to have been written for the occasion by the Master, William

Cornish, who also directed the show. The whole was, we are told, in the style of the pageants held at the court of Burgundy, and featured a mobile wooden castle, which could be wheeled on and off stage, but was big enough to accommodate eight ladies climbing on it. It is clear that the story, simple as it was, contained contemporary messages in the way of a modern pantomime. The scenario was that the Green Castle was defended by women and attacked by men. Eight ladies of the court, including Anne and her sister, Mary, were cast in roles indicative of what were regarded as female attributes, including beauty, nobility and kindness. Each wore white satin, with the names of their characters picked out in yellow satin, and their head dresses were cauls of Venetian gold topped with Milan bonnets. The complementary male characters bore the names of so-called male virtues including Nobleness, Youth, Loyalty, Pleasure and Liberty. The storyline was simple – the men stormed the castle, the women, aided by boys of the Chapel Royal in drag, portraying 'female' vices such as back biting, resisted by throwing missiles such as rose water bombs. The men prevailed and the women were led out to dance. The action was probably accompanied by appropriate background music.

We know that performances such as this were designed to function on several different levels. Some are obvious – they provided an evening's pastime; they marked a significant day of the year or a celebration; they would impress any foreign visitor invited to attend; they displayed the taste and spending power of whoever commissioned them; and they served as a showcase for the beauty (in either sex) and possibly the talent of those currently in favour. It seems, too, that, as we will see in a later chapter, for those in the know, there may sometimes have been an extra storyline. In this instance the entertainment was not a fully-developed play – but some of the casting may well have been telling. The glamorous Mary Tudor, now Duchess of Suffolk but still known as the French Queen, was cast as Beauty, and her remote but still royally descended cousin, the Countess of Devon, as Honour. Constancy was played by Jane Parker, who was one day to marry George Boleyn, and the newly returned Anne Boleyn was Perseverance. Other ladies played Bounty, Mercy and Pity, while Mary Boleyn was Kindness. So far, so apparently innocuous

– unless one considers that it is likely that Mary had recently begun an affair with the King.

Like most of the King's extra–marital adventures, this one was conducted with some discretion – to the point where some historians have doubted that it happened. However, the existence of the relationship is proved beyond reasonable doubt by several factors. Firstly, during the negotiations for the divorce from Catherine of Aragon, the King was to commit the tactical error of asking the Pope for a conditional dispensation to remarry a wife (Anne Boleyn) who was within the 'forbidden bounds' because Henry had slept with a close relative of his intended bride. And secondly, when several years later, the King was accused to his face of having slept with Anne Boleyn's mother and sister, he was so taken aback that he was only able to stammer 'never with the mother' (it was left to Thomas Cromwell to chip in 'not with the sister, either').[1] There is also other persuasive circumstantial evidence, starting with the fact that, beginning in 1522, Mary Boleyn's husband, William Carey, begun to receive a series of uncommonly generous grants, the first of which was the keepership of the estate of Beaulieu in Essex[2] – the just reward of looking the other way? If so he was not the first and would not be the last. It must be remembered that, at this time, a Royal affair was generally regarded, within the court at least, as an opportunity for advancement – no one, with the possible exception of the Queen, would disapprove – and in this context, Mary's casting can seem like a moderately gentle insider joke.

However, Mary was to gain remarkably little from her affair. Some historians have claimed that this began as early as 1519, and that Mary's marriage was a sham, entered into purely to cover up for the King's interest in her. There is no evidence either for this or for the accompanying idea that Mary did not have sex with her husband until the King was done with her, and that she had been able to avoid becoming pregnant during their relationship. This theory credits Mary with a reliable method of contraception that was unknown to other women of her time, and asserts that as soon as she was 'handed over' to her husband, sometime in 1524, she became pregnant by him, and gave birth to a son and daughter in the next few years. In fact persuasive evidence has now come to light to indicate that Mary's daughter, Catherine, was her eldest child, born as early as April 1524. Some commentators have concluded that the King cannot have believed this was his daughter on the grounds that he made to attempt to acknowledge her publicly. It is likely that he had at least one and possibly two other 'unofficial' daughters, and it was only in the case of Elizabeth Blount's son, Henry Fitzroy, that he publicly accepted the paternity of any illegitimate child. Daughters he could take or leave, however, looking at the grants made to Mary Boleyn and her husband, there is some evidence that the King was trying to make sure that both Mary and her daughter would be at least modestly provided for. It is also true that a portrait of Catherine Carey, painted when she was in her thirties, does give her a strong facial resemblance to pictures of Henry VIII.

There is no direct evidence of how the people most closely concerned felt about the affair, let alone how it appeared to the sister of the King's latest mistress. However, looking at what we know of how the Boleyns treated Mary in later years, they may well have been considerably less than impressed, perhaps not so much with the fact that she was sleeping with the King, but by how little she got out of the relationship. There is nothing to indicate that Thomas Boleyn either forced or manoeuvred his elder daughter into the King's bed, given the pragmatic view that the court in general appears to have taken over such affairs. However he may well have been disappointed by the modesty of the benefits acquired more than disapproving of the relationship itself. It is true that a number of grants were made to the couple in the early 1520s,[3] but these hardly added up to the level of spoils acquired by Royal mistresses in, for example, France. When William Carey died of the sweating sickness in 1528, and Mary was left with little income, it was to take a direct request from the King before Thomas Boleyn stepped in to help. And when, six years later, Mary made a secret second marriage to William Stafford, a relatively poor man several years her junior, and was banished from court as a result, she was too much afraid to approach her parents, sister or brother directly, instead asking Thomas Cromwell to intercede for her. So it seems more than possible that Anne Boleyn, who must have known all about her sister's affair, regarded it as an object lesson in how not to conduct a relationship with the King.

But at this time Anne had problems of her own. Negotiations for the suggested marriage with James Butler soon stalled. But Anne, if we are to believe a number of later accounts, was soon one of the most sought-after ladies at court. She was never a beauty, although everyone admired her lustrous dark hair and her black eyes, but she was elegant, sophisticated, highly intelligent and charming. She was also an accomplished musician who played the lute and the organ, a good dancer and, after her years abroad, an excellent linguist. The stories of warts, goitres and sixth fingers largely originate from hostile Catholic sources, some of them from half a century after her death. However, George Wyatt, grandson of Sir Thomas Wyatt, who in the 1590s gathered material for a biography of Anne, was to write:

'There was found, indeed, on the side of her nail, upon one of her fingers, some little show of a nail, which yet was so small, by the report of those that have seen her, as the work master seemed to leave it an occasion of greater grace to her hand, which, with the tip of one of her other fingers might be, and was usually by her hidden without any blemish to it'[4]

Clearly George Wyatt, writing at the end of the century, was relying on hearsay, but he was able to call on the evidence of people in his own circle of family and friends who had known Anne Boleyn, and who were not hostile witnesses. It should be noted that no one who had actually seen Anne, ever mentioned a sixth nail or any other malformation of her hand. It is impossible to be sure – but it does seem feasible that Wyatt's informers were correct and Anne did have a sixth nail which she was so clever at concealing that few people ever noticed it.

Whatever the truth about her appearance, it is evident that Anne took quickly to life at the English court. It would have been surprising if she had not, as court life was all she had known since she was 12 years old. But she was now entering her twenties, and for a Tudor lady, it was high time she made a good marriage. For Tudor ladies, the usual way to go about this was for her parents to arrange a match. The kinder ones might take their daughter's views on the matter into account. We do not know whether Anne's parents were giving any consideration to an alternative match for her, or whether they still believed the Butler marriage was a viable possibility – whatever was being discussed, Anne did not wait for them to act, but became secretly engaged to a very eligible bachelor indeed. This was Henry Percy, heir of the Earl of Northumberland.

Percy was a member of the household of Cardinal Wolsey, and would certainly have met Anne during the Cardinal's frequent visits to court. Another member of that household, George Cavendish, was to write a biography of his master, so we have an eye witness – but not necessarily unbiased – version of what happened next. Cavendish tells us that, during his visits to court, Percy 'fell to dalliance among the Queen's maidens, being at the last more conversant with Mistress Anne Boleyn than any other, so that there grew such a secret love between them that at length they were ensured together intending to marry.' Cavendish then asserts that the King, already interested in Anne on his own account, ordered the Cardinal to put a stop to the relationship, which he did by tearing Percy off a strip for getting entangled with 'a foolish girl yonder in the court', when he was intended by his father and the King for a much better match. He also claimed the King had other plans for Anne. Apparently Percy, reduced to tears, begged the Cardinal to intercede for him in the matter, saying that he was now morally if not legally committed to the marriage, but the Cardinal refused to help, instead sending for Percy's father. In this version of events, father and Cardinal got together with lawyers to find a way out of the betrothal, got Anne banished from court and hastily married Percy off to the daughter of the Earl of Shrewsbury, after which Anne nourished an implacable hatred of the Cardinal.

There is still argument over how much of this story is true. The crucial question is the date of Percy's marriage to Mary Talbot – and it is clear that the negotiations for this took years. What is less certain is when the marriage took place. If Eric Ives was correct in supposing it was in the new year of 1524,[5] then that is far too early for the King to have been involved – he was almost certainly in the midst of his affair with Anne's sister at that time, and there is no other evidence of his interest in Anne beginning until 1526. In that alternative case, it is more likely to have been Wolsey himself, still looking to bring about Anne's marriage to James Butler, who was the main objector, and threatened Royal wrath to frighten Percy. However, David Starkey believes that the date of the marriage was almost certainly August 1526',[6] that the King was indeed already interested in Anne, and that Cavendish is correct that Wolsey was acting under orders. Whatever the truth of this aspect of the story, it seems likely that the commitment between Anne and Percy was just as serious as Cavendish claimed. Certainly Percy does not emerge from the story as a very heroic figure, caving in over his commitment to Anne, and then marrying the woman of his father's and Wolsey's choice. His is a rather sad story – the marriage was a disaster, his health gave way, and when he was appointed to act as one of the judges at Anne's trial in 1536, he collapsed after adding his voice to the chorus of 'guilty' verdicts. He died only a few months later.

If it is true, as some have claimed, that Anne was banished from court for a period as a result of this, then there is no contemporary record of it, and we do not know when she returned. The next evidence we have about her concerns another possible love affair, but this, if it existed, was a very different relationship – not an engagement to marry with the heir to an earldom but an entanglement with a married poet. Thomas Wyatt was, like the Boleyns, a professional courtier. His childhood home, Allington Castle, was in Kent, only some 20 miles from Hever, and it is highly likely the two families knew each other. However, Anne and Thomas may never have met as children, especially as he was a couple of years younger than she. According to his grandson, George, they met on her return from France: '...after much more with her witty and graceful speech, his ear also had him chained unto her, so as finally his heart seemed to say, I could gladly yield to be tied forever with the knot of her love, as somewhere in his verses hath been thought his meaning was to express.'

So far, so romantic. But this is another relationship that has been hotly argued over since it had, or had not, taken place. Both Anne and

Wyatt, as courtiers, were well versed in the rules of courtly love. And
if, as seems fairly clear, both were towards the centre of a cultured and
witty elite circle, it would have been surprising if they were not on, at
the least, terms of elegant flirtation. What we do not know is how much
genuine feeling was involved on either side. As Anne was undoubtedly
well aware, Wyatt was miserably and inextricably married – and as she
was now in her mid-twenties, marriage must surely been uppermost in
her mind. This does not, of course, mean that she was not happy either
to enjoy a flirtation or to add an accomplished and handsome courtier
to her circle of admirers – and it may be that genuine feeling played a
part. Some later writers have claimed that this was a full-scale affair and,
of course, this is possible – but, on Anne's part, this would have meant
the serious risk of ruining her reputation, without the possibility of the
relationship becoming permanent. Wyatt was one of those arrested at the
time of Anne's fall, and the poetry he wrote then strongly suggests an
intensity of feeling of which a 'serious' relationship of some kind would
make sense. And there is the story that, when Wyatt realised that the King
really meant to marry Anne, he took the extraordinarily risky course of
confessing to a sexual relationship with her:

> 'I beseech your grace to be well advised what you do, for she is not
> meet to be coupled with your grace, her conversation hath been so
> loose and base, which thing I know not so much by hearsay as by my
> own experience as one that have had my carnal pleasure with her.'

Like so many other stories told to Anne's detriment, this one came from a
later Catholic writer, Nicholas Harpsfield, who said he had heard it from
the merchant, Antonio Bonvisi, who in turn had heard it from an unnamed
person who was supposedly 'likely to know the truth thereof'. Bonvisi, a
lifelong friend of Thomas More, spoke to Harpsfield twenty years after
the event. It may well be that the story is a spiteful invention – but, as at
least one recent writer has pointed out,[7] this is a story of an unexpected
and audacious act on Wyatt's part. Harpsfield's account continues that the
King, although very much taken aback, then refused to believe the tale.

There is no real evidence that this encounter ever took place, although the existence of the story does demonstrate that Bonvisi, who was at least in a position to know the insider gossip of the time, thought it a likely enough tale to pass on. This observation should, however, be set in the context of a time when no accusation was too bad to throw at Anne, and of a teller who would have been only too pleased to discredit her further.

Another story may date from the early days of the King's interest in Anne, and is told by George Wyatt, who claims that Thomas Wyatt had helped himself to a jewel on a ribbon that Anne used to carry around with her. At this time the King had acquired, by unknown means, a ring of Anne's, which he took to wearing on his little finger. Both men were aware of, and resentful of, the other's interest in her – and there ensued a scene after a game of bowls which they both claimed to have won. The real conflict, however, was about Anne. The King, staring meaningfully at the ring on his finger, said 'Wyatt, I tell thee it is mine,' to which Wyatt replied by asking to be allowed to measure out the ground, upon which he took Anne's jewel on its ribbon from around his own neck, and used it for the purpose. The King, recognising the jewel, returned 'it may be so, but then am I deceived,' and broke up the game in a temper.[8] This story of superficially light-hearted horse play with a distinctly aggressive subtext does ring true, and suggests something more than mere flirtation between Anne and Wyatt. In January 1527 Wyatt was to leave the country in a hurry, making a last-minute decision to join a diplomatic mission to Italy.[9]

This takes the story forward towards the time, not exactly datable, when the King's serious attention had turned to Anne. Many attempts have failed to establish exactly when that was – and it is likely that it was a process not an event. The sequence of seventeen love letters that Henry wrote to Anne during his courtship of her, and that survive, improbably, in the Vatican, are undated. What they do suggest is that the King had initially been assuming that he could have with Anne the same kind of affair that he had enjoyed with her sister, Mary – a relationship, of some duration, which would be conducted within the parameters of courtly love, but which would confer no status on Anne, and which would have been likely to come to an end within a year or two – probably as and when she became pregnant. If the affair with Bessie Blount, another maid of honour of Catherine of Aragon, can be taken as a model, Anne would probably have found herself married off to a middle-ranking courtier and thereafter remembered with a New Year's present every year. Anne would certainly have been fully aware of these precedents, and clearly had no desire to follow them.

It is, of course, impossible to be sure what Anne did, or did not, feel for the King in their courting days. At this time he was in his mid thirties, and while it is likely that he no longer had what one observer had once described as the face of a beautiful girl, he was still tall, athletic and had a full head of hair, probably no longer red–gold but ginger. By now he had sustained, while jousting, at least one of the serious leg injuries that were to contribute to his years of chronic pain and ultimately to his death – but he was not yet slowed down by it and had as yet put on only a moderate amount of the excess weight that was to contribute to his decline. He was also charming, musically talented and at least passably learned. He was far from being an impossible object of love. However, his most notable charm must surely have been his crown. We do not know when and in what way Anne came to realise that the King's interest in her was something more focused than the passing moves in the courtly love game. She could hardly have failed to be flattered. She may also have felt wary and, given the likelihood that the King had recently tired of her sister, she may have felt angry. What seems reasonably likely is that she did not fall in love – or not enough to cloud or influence her judgement.

It is clear that, on his side, Henry was susceptible, and that he also went with the fashion of conducting flirtations within the parameters of courtly romance. Everyone at Court did so, and it is highly likely that his attraction for Anne began in this way. Certainly Henry must have met Anne when she first came to the English Court in late 1521. So, it took him at least four years to work his way round to her. We do not know exactly how many people lived at court – estimates vary between 1,000 and 1,500, with about half the full complement going on summer progress each year. Perhaps half of these people were servants of yeoman status or below. Therefore, the King and Anne were inhabiting a social sphere far smaller than a modern campus university. Granted, there were comings and goings between the palace and the outside world, but it is clear that everyone knew everyone and everyone watched everyone. The closest modern parallel in social terms might be with Parliament – often known as the Westminster Village – or the headquarters of a large company. The story of the King, Wyatt and the two rival jewels discernibly belong in this world of watchfulness and gossip.

By the time of the beginning of the King's serious interest in Anne, which Eric Ives dates as Shrovetide 1526,[10] there is evidence that the King had already begun to consider whether he had grounds for ending his marriage to Catherine of Aragon. By now Catherine had passed the menopause – ironically, this may have been brought on early by her constant fasting, which in turn was part of her campaign to convince God to send her a son who would live. Her multiple pregnancies had produced a healthy daughter, Mary, but her son, born in 1511, had lived only a few weeks; other babies had been still born or died within hours or days. Henry appears to have gone on sleeping occasionally with Catherine until 1524, by which time her periods had ceased, and with them all hope of further children. There had been rumours as long ago as 1522 that the King had begun to question whether his marriage to his dead brother's wife had been lawful, or whether there might be grounds for setting Catherine aside in favour of a woman who might bear sons. In 1525 Henry Fitzroy, the King's 5-year-old son from his relationship with Elizabeth Blount, was brought to court and created Duke of Richmond and Somerset. We are told Catherine was outraged at this – but by this time her influence was reduced to the point where it appears that Henry simply ignored her protests.

However, even after he began to think seriously of a way out of his marriage to Catherine, Henry was apparently still trying to secure Anne as his mistress, now with some kind of official status, rather than his wife. One of the letters asks her 'to do me the office of a true, loyal mistress and friend and to give yourself up, body and soul to me who will be and have been your loyal servant' and promises in return to 'take you for my only mistress, rejecting from thought and affection all others save yourself, to serve you only.' This was more, one suspects, than he had ever offered Bessie Blount or Mary Boleyn, but still not a good long-term prospect. Most historians agree that Henry and Anne's agreement to marry took place sometime in 1527. Already their relationship had travelled a great distance from the early days. There is a letter from Henry in which he thanks Anne for the gift of a jewelled trinket in the shape of a ship with a woman on board and with a pendant diamond. This, evidently, was a present with a meaning – in Tudor times a ship was a symbol of protection. And Anne was accepting the protection of the King, who wrote an ecstatic letter of thanks:

'For so beautiful a gift, and so exceeding (taking it in all) I thank you right cordially; not alone for the fair diamond and the ship in which the solitary damsel is tossed about, but chiefly for the good intent and too–humble submission vouchsafed in this by your kindness.'

He goes on to make it clear that their relationship is now on a new footing:

'Praying you also that if ever before I have in any way done you offence, that you will give me the same absolution that you ask, ensuring you that henceforth my heart shall be dedicate to you alone, greatly desirous that so my body could be as well, as God can bring to pass if it pleaseth Him, whom I entreat once each day for the accomplishment thereof, trusting that at length my prayer shall be heard....'[11]

The term Henry uses for the present is '*une etrenne*'. David Starkey has argued that the only meaning of the word is a very specific one – a New Year's gift. And so he believes that the promise to marry dates from January 1527 (the story of the relationship was well known to the outside world before 1528). Eric Ives maintained that the term '*etrenne*' could signify other kinds of present, including a novelty, and that it was also acquiring a secondary meaning, that of virginity. Ives put forward an alternative date of June 1527 for the letter, arguing that Anne was not the catalyst for the King's seeking an annulment to his marriage with Catherine of Aragon. Whatever the truth of the timing of the present and its reception, it may well be true that the first public indication of the King's love for Anne was at the Shrovetide joust in early 1527. At this time Catherine of Aragon was still in official – and probably real – ignorance that the King was seeking advice as to how he could repudiate their marriage, although she may have been aware of the change in the political climate at court. However, as Henry took his first steps with discretion, it may be that she felt too secure in her position to suspect such a devastating attack was even a possibility.

The road to the final end of the marriage between Henry VIII and Catherine of Aragon, and to the start of that between Henry VIII and Anne Boleyn, lasted for six years, was convoluted, painful for all concerned and involved much of western Europe. The story could fill, and has filled, many books – this is not the context to retell it in detail. The King's aim was to convince the Pope, and the whole of Europe, that the dispensation allowing him to marry his brother's widow had been granted erroneously. Canon lawyers were divided on the issue, but he would probably have got his way if it had not been that the power play of European politics went against him when the Pope fell into the power of the Emperor Charles V, nephew of Catherine of Aragon, whose troops have over-run Rome in May 1527. Although the King did not realise it, once that had happened, the chances of the Pope finding in his favour had reduced to vanishing point. Many of those concerned, including the Pope, hoped that Catherine would agree to retire honourably to a convent, a course of action which had been followed by other discarded queens. However, it was not for nothing that Catherine was the daughter of two fighting sovereigns – she was sure she was the true Queen of England, and compromise was not in her nature.

Cardinal Wolsey had the unenviable task of trying to achieve the feat of securing the annulment. Opinions differ as to whether, firstly, he ever believed it was possible, and secondly, whether he wanted it to be possible. It may be that both the Pope and Wolsey believed that, given enough time, either Henry's passion for Anne would cool, or she would accept second best and become his mistress, possibly a very high status mistress, but would not insist on the ultimate commitment of marriage. If so, they underestimated both the intensity of the King's love for Anne and the intensity of her determination. Her casting as Perseverence in the masque of the Storming of the Chateau Verte was proving to be a prescient one. Already in February 1528, when Stephen Gardiner and Edward Fox were being sent to Rome in the latest stage of negotiations, they were instructed to call in at Hever to give Anne an update. The King sent a letter to be delivered by them, counselling her to accept that the business would take some time. In 1527 the King appears to have thought the matter could be resolved in months; and, if Catherine had been prepared to go quietly into a convent, she would not have been the first superfluous queen to do so. In fact, this was the preferred option, not only of the King and Wolsey, but of the Pope too. But they had not considered Catherine's temperament and self-belief – and as the daughter of Isabella of Castile, who had ruled in her own right, she was never likely to accept that her own daughter, Mary, could not also rule England in her own right. This was to become a story, not only of international politics and of religious change, but a highly personal one. It was also, of course, a very common human story – powerful man, entering middle age, seeks to trade in the wife of his youth for a younger model.

Through the summer of 1528, opinions were split. By this time, although 'The King's Great Matter' was still officially a secret, it is clear that it was a fairly open one. In London, there was much sympathy for the Queen. It has become received wisdom that Catherine was universally loved by the common people, especially the women, and there are a number of stories that suggest there were demonstrations in her favour. On examination most of these turn out to be hearsay, and are to be regarded with some scepticism. At this stage of events, however, it is likely that most people who knew something of what was going on, were still assuming that the King was conducting an affair that would finish in time. Catherine of Aragon was still in her place as Queen for all official purposes, and, like many another wandering husband, Henry remained on pleasant terms with her. In fact, he did this in all his marriages, treating his wives with courtesy to their faces, and employing others to do the dirty work. It is possible, too, that he had not completely made up his mind about continuing to pursue the aim of the annulment once the difficulties became obvious. Late in 1528, Henry made a speech at the Bridewell Palace to a large group of London notables at the time of the arrival of the Papal envoys who were to investigate the case. It did not go well – Edward Hall said in his 'Chronicle' that before the speech:

> 'The common people being ignorant of the truth, and in especial women and other that favoured the queen, talked largely and said that the king would for his own pleasure have another wife, with many foolish words, insomuch that whosoever spake against the marriage was of the common people abhorred and reproved.'[12]

In his speech Henry maintained that, were he to have his time over, he would choose Catherine again, and it was only scruples of conscience that were making him question the legality of the marriage. The reception was mixed: 'Some sighed and said nothing, other were sorry to see the king so troubled in his conscience. Other that favoured the queen much sorrowed that the matter was now opened.'[13]

At this time Anne was, by agreement, staying away from court so as to demonstrate that the proceedings were nothing to do with her. Clearly unnerved, Henry went off to visit her, and appears to have pleaded with her to accept that the divorce was unachievable, and that she should accept the position of his official mistress.[14] By the end of the visit the divorce was back on, and Henry went to Wolsey to ask him to come up with a way of lodging Anne appropriately but not too near the official Royal apartments. This incident is strong evidence that the King was indeed highly indecisive, and likely in at least some situations to go with the prevailing wind, hoping that it would blow him something acceptable. He wanted to be rid of Catherine, but he wanted to do it in a way which at least looked honourable. Anne was then given a suite of rooms in London, possibly at Durham House in the Strand, one of the properties under Wolsey's control – it was later made available to Thomas Boleyn as his London house. And at Greenwich that Christmas, Anne was again in evidence, in a separate suite of rooms. From henceforward, the Royal household essentially contained a king, a queen and a queen in waiting. The Christmas of 1528 must have been a curious one – the Pope's envoys were present, and Hall noted that the Queen 'made no joy of nothing, her mind was so troubled.'

Now Anne was back at Court and everything was out in the open. We do not know how Anne and Catherine behaved to one another – the likelihood is that, by mutual tacit consent, they kept out of each other's way. Wolsey's biographer Cavendish reports that they treated one another with courtesy. George Wyatt goes further and suggests that Anne was loyal to the Queen, who tried to shield her from the King's advances. This seems unlikely, but Wyatt also tells the story of a game of cards between Anne and Catherine, during which Anne picked up a king, and Catherine observed: 'My lady Anne, you have good hap to stop at a king, but you are not like others, you will have all or none.' As with so many of Wyatt's stories, it is impossible to know whether, after half a century, this one is accurate – but this tale of well-bred malice sounds very possible, especially if it is true that Anne did indeed have a deformed finger that would have been impossible to hide while playing cards.

This stand-off must have been extremely hard on the nerves of everyone concerned. Most, although not all, historians agree that at this stage Anne entered the political arena on her own behalf. Victorian commentators regarded Anne as the victim of the ambition of her father and uncle, the Duke of Norfolk; some modern writers think that Anne had little real influence other than, as one ambassador put it, 'the English King's lust, and her eyes, which are black and beautiful'. At least one[15] believes that the two had a physical affair for a while, but that the King decided it should cease until they could marry, and that Anne had neither the personality nor the drive to operate politically in her own right. But Cavendish recorded that at this time it was her influence that 'might work mysteries with the king and obtain any suit of him for her friend'. An example of this was to bring Anne into direct conflict with Cardinal Wolsey. It came about when the Abbess of Wilton, a rich and fashionable nunnery, died. This kind of appointment, although officially a religious one, was high profile, influential and lucrative – and in the gift of the King. Anne and Wolsey put forward rival candidates – Anne's being Eleanor Carey, the sister of her brother in law, William Carey, and Wolsey's being the Prioress, Isobel Jordayn. All was looking good for Eleanor Carey until it was revealed that she had had children by two different priests. As this hardly made her the ideal candidate as an Abbess, Henry hastily agreed with Anne that she should withdraw her support, and instructed Wolsey that, as a compromise, the job should go to some as yet unnamed third party. For whatever reason, Wolsey went ahead and confirmed the appointment of Isobel Jordayn, which in turn offended both the King and Anne – Wolsey sent a grovelling letter of apology. In this instance Wolsey's candidate won, but it is clear that by this time Anne in person was an influential player in the crucial world of appointments. In Tudor England any kind of advancement depended on who you could get to speak for you.

It was during this period that Anne began to build up her network of influence at court.[16] Up until now her parents and brother, all courtiers of long standing, had been her chief allies, and it appears she was skilful in securing more. As others have pointed out, for everyone at court, alliances were pragmatic and conditional, even, and sometimes especially, those based on family. There was little about them that was ideological or even religious – if your 'good lord', or lady, was not in a position to do enough for you and yours, then you were off in search of a better patron. Only a very few connections turned out to be more visceral and more enduring. It is almost certainly a mistake to regard court factions of this time as in any sense being forerunners of modern political parties, since, as will be shown, self-interest almost always trumped ideology – the rare exceptions almost always turn out to concern individuals whose mutual affection outweighed any other consideration. Given that the price of being identified with the wrong faction at the wrong moment was often death, the brutal pragmatism displayed by lovers, friends and close family members at the time of a fall from power becomes all too understandable.

For now, Anne's star was in the ascendant. The only question was just how far it would rise – and what those close to her felt about it. Neither do we know how far Anne herself really believed she would rise. She was playing for the very highest stakes now, but there is evidence that she was playing her hand with some caution. Through the first half of 1528 she went to great lengths to be on almost theatrically good terms with Cardinal Wolsey – she dropped heavy hints, via Thomas Heneage, a Wolsey hanger-on now in place at court, about how nice it would be to have some fish from Wolsey's famous ponds, to cheer up her Lenten fare. The request was duly passed on, and a parcel of carp and shrimps arrived for her. During that year, Anne fell ill with the sweating sickness, as did so many others. This was the epidemic that claimed the life of her brother in law William Carey, and had the King fleeing in terror from palace to palace through that summer, abandoning any member of his household who might be an infection risk and issuing increasingly ferocious instructions intended to ensure his personal safety, no matter what might become of anyone else. Wolsey sent Anne a kind letter and present to mark her recovery. If Anne was anxious to ingratiate herself with the Cardinal, then he too was more than willing to play her game – certainly to the extent of thank you letters and shrimps.

Meanwhile, both Campeggio, the Pope's envoy, and Wolsey colluded in a game of prevarication intended to conceal the almost total lack of real progress towards ending the King's marriage to Catherine. Campeggio had instructions to play for time, evidently hoping that the King, and Anne herself, would get tired of waiting and either settle for the second best of giving Anne an official status without making her Queen, leaving Catherine with her status intact, or else, even better, that Henry would tire of Anne. It is almost certain that Wolsey shared these hopes – it is just that it took the King longer to lose trust in him. Opinions differ as to whether Anne had ever trusted him, or whether she had simply needed to go along with pretending that she did, and giving Wolsey, as the King's chief minister of over fifteen years, a fair chance of proving her mistaken. In the early days of her relationship with the King, firstly, she may have believed in Wolsey's ability and desire to arrange the divorce, secondly, she would not have been likely to have been able to turn the King against him and, thirdly, there would have been little point in doing so, as there was no alternative candidate of sufficient stature to set in the Cardinal's place. Whether Anne recognised this last point is something of an open question – she was to go along with, and may well have shared in, the decision to send her own father and brother as envoys during the negotiations. Although both were, in different ways, men of ability, the messages that were being sent out by their appointment were less than helpful.

However, as the diplomatic process continued, one step forward, another sideways and sometimes two steps back, some influential people began to declare their support for Anne – probably having decided that hers was likely to turn out to be the winning side. One of these was Stephen Gardiner, a protégé of Wolsey, future Bishop of Winchester and a past friend of Catherine of Aragon, who began a friendly correspondence with Anne. As 1528 wore on, however, and the reports from the English envoys in Rome made it abundantly clear that the Pope was not going to quash the dispensation allowing Henry and Catherine to marry even though they were brother and sister in law, any optimism about an early settlement drained away. So this meant that, back in England, the heat was on Campeggio, who, under orders to prevaricate for as long as possible, managed to put off opening the legatine court in London until May 1529. The deal was that the case had to be tried by Campeggio and Wolsey jointly. By this time, there is strong evidence that Anne was proposing to move against Wolsey unless, against the odds, Campeggio gave judgement in favour of the annulment. Famously, the hearings at Blackfriars Palace were a fiasco, as Catherine made just one appearance, during which she addressed Henry directly, kneeling at his feet, begging him to take her back and reminding him of her loyalty as a wife, maintaining that theirs was a true and legal marriage. She then walked out of the court and refused to return, instead applying for the case to be heard in Rome – the outcome that Henry and Anne were trying at all costs to avoid.

In the light of this failure, Wolsey's position was increasingly vulnerable. Over the summer of 1529 his enemies, including Anne, her friends, and the Duke of Norfolk, had made at least one attempt to overthrow him, but it took a series of his own mistakes to remove him. Part of the problem was that he had been kept away, at the King's insistence, from the negotiations for the latest international peace treaty. Wolsey was made to stay in London so as to be free to attend the hearings at Blackfriars, while over the Channel in Chambrai, crucial negotiations were taking place. The English envoys, Bishop Tunstall and Thomas More, appear to have been out of their depth and were being kept on the sidelines, and the French came away with everything they had set out to achieve, having double crossed Henry's delegation. This meant that the French and Charles V were now on good terms, which in turn meant the support of the French for Henry's divorce was now in question. The Treaty of Chambrai was signed in August, and the English envoys had had precious little influence over what was decided. Unfairly, but inevitably, Wolsey got the blame for this. By this time it was early autumn, and Wolsey's position was so weakened that his enemies were able to keep him away from the King until it was, essentially, too late. The King no longer fully trusted him.

It could still have gone either way, however. Wolsey was fighting back over the summer, and in September asked for a meeting with the King so as to be able to pass on highly sensitive information. At this time the King, accompanied by Anne, was on summer progress, again planning the route with a wary eye to where there were outbreaks of sweating sickness. Henry, probably at Anne's insistence, asked Wolsey to indicate what he wanted to talk about.[17] This resulted in a stand off which was broken only when, according to Cavendish's account, Campeggio insisted that Wolsey should accompany him when he went to take his leave of the King before leaving England. At this point the court was at a comparatively small house, Grafton, where there was no space for many courtiers to sleep, the overspill having to be put up elsewhere. Wolsey was pointedly not allocated a room at Grafton, but he did get in to see the King, who greeted him kindly. They then went on to have a friendly meeting, during which Wolsey appears to have allayed some of his master's suspicions. Over dinner in Anne's chamber, at which Wolsey was not present, Anne tried unsuccessfully to turn the King's mood once more against Wolsey. All that happened was that the King spent the rest of the day in a secret tête à tête meeting with Wolsey, and arranged to meet him again in the morning.

Overnight, Anne is said to have moved quickly, arranging a picnic for the next day and ensuring Henry and the Cardinal did not meet again.

Eric Ives questions the detail of this,[18] maintaining that there was no picnic and that Wolsey and the King did in fact meet the following day, and that Anne's triumph was less decisive. Certainly up until early October, Wolsey retained all his offices, was still dealing with administrative matters and was chairing council meetings in the usual way. We are told, too, that Anne had extracted a promise from Henry that he would never again allow Wolsey into his presence.[19] On 9 October Wolsey was charged with praemunire, the crime of allowing foreign influence into the country. He was then dismissed as chancellor – and very sensibly resigned all his offices, admitted the charges, surrendered all his property and threw himself on the King's mercy (it is likely that he was, probably accurately, thinking that Henry would be made more inclined to forbearance by the riches on offer). When, in the autumn, Parliament arraigned Wolsey on forty-four charges, the King would not proceed against him, and allowed him to keep several of his appointments, including the Archbishopric of York. At this stage Anne and Henry went to inspect York Place, beginning to make plans to turn it into a royal palace – at last a London base fit for the new royal couple. Technically the property belonged to the archdiocese of York, but the King did not allow this to stand in his way. Knowing this, Wolsey had ordered the sumptuous contents to be laid out ready – trestle tables covered with rich hangings, stacks of gold plate, and a stock of precious books. Not least among the charms of the place was the fact that, as a bishop's palace, it had no queen's apartments. Therefore the King could visit, officially on his own, and accommodation was prepared, less officially, for Anne and her family. Meanwhile, at Hampton Court, a major building scheme was well underway – this featured a new private lodging for the King, including a jewel house and library as well as a bedchamber and a bathroom with hot and cold running water.

Again, according to Cavendish, Wolsey himself acknowledged that it was Anne who had brought about his downfall – calling her 'a continual serpentine enemy about the king'[20] – and prepared to leave for what amounted to internal exile in his archbishopric of York. Once there, he began to campaign at a distance, both to be restored to the King's favour and to regain some part of his immense possessions. A deal was reached in February 1530 – this allowed Wolsey to retain not only the archbishopric of York, but a pension of 1,000 marks a year and £6,000 worth of possessions to be returned by the King. Far away in London, the Duke of Norfolk, foremost among those who had rejoiced at Wolsey's departure, manoeuvred energetically to prevent his return. And, just as determinedly, Anne was in the background blocking Wolsey's friends' attempts to gain access to the King. Thomas Cromwell, formerly of Wolsey's household, was a key contact in London at this time, and it was he who received the instruction 'If the displeasure of my Lady Anne be somewhat assuaged as I pray God the same may be, then it should be devised that by some convenient mean she be further laboured, for this is the only help and remedy. All possible means must be attempted for the attaining of her favour.'[21] Plainly Wolsey had identified the source of the most effective opposition to his return to power – and there is plenty of evidence that Anne was working hard to keep the Cardinal well away from London. Towards the end of 1530, Anne and her friends were positioning themselves for a counter-coup in the likely event that the Pope would find in favour of Catherine and order Henry to return to her. At this time Wolsey was beginning to prepare the ground for getting back into favour with Catherine, who was still at Court and still acknowledged as Queen. He also put out feelers for a renewed alliance with Charles V, and it was news of this that provoked Henry into having Wolsey arrested, soon after which he was taken ill. It was when he was on his way, by slow painful stages, to imprisonment in the Tower of London that Wolsey died at Leicester – despite many rumours, almost certainly of natural causes. His last words were apparently such a vitriolic warning to the King about his current conduct that the Council prudently decided not to pass them on.

The Pope's edict came – for Anne, and for Henry, the worst possible news from Rome, ordering the King to return to Catherine. Anne responded by flying into a rage with Henry and threatening to leave him. Wolsey was out of the way, but there was no one of comparable stature who could, or in some cases would, take his place. The King was looking about for competent theologians to speak for him, and it was at this time that the academic Thomas Cranmer was recruited and sent off to stay with Thomas Boleyn while he wrote a treatise in support of the King's position. At this time, too, Anne was introducing the King to what many would have regarded as subversive religious material – William Tyndale's *The Obedience of the Christian Man* and Simon Fish's *The Supplication of Beggars*. The first attacked the idea that the church possessed any separate power, and argued that everyone was under the same secular authority. The second was a petition addressed to Henry, and contained a scathing attack on what it characterised as the avarice and immorality of the English clergy. It appears that Fish sent a copy of the pamphlet to Anne, who read it, showed it to her brother and, by agreement with him, then passed it on to the King. The next practical step was to organise a great petition to the Pope from most of England's ruling class, asking him, in the national interest, to reconsider his refusal of an annulment. It contained, too, an implied menace, as it stated that, although a continued refusal on the Pope's part would make the lot of the English 'more miserable', they would still have the option 'to find relief some other way'. The Pope was being warned – a radical solution was no longer out of the question. Meanwhile, Thomas Boleyn was overseeing the research that was being undertaken in universities throughout Europe to look into both the specifics of the case of the marriage of Henry and Catherine and, more generally, into what authority the Pope should really be acknowledged to have. Heartened by this, in late 1530 the King proposed to the new parliamentary session the idea that the Archbishop of Canterbury should be allowed to decide the divorce suit. The next step was to accuse the clergy collectively of complicity in Wolsey's offences.

At this stage, the cobbled-together alliance that had worked together to ensure Wolsey's downfall began to become unstitched. The somewhat ill-assorted group, insofar as it can be regarded as that, began to realise the extent of the radicalism of Anne and her friends, and some of them took fright. The Duke of Suffolk, whose wife, the King's sister and Anne's former mistress, had been forced to give precedence to the queen in waiting, was among the first defectors from her cause. Another was the Duchess of Norfolk, Anne's aunt by marriage and an old friend of Catherine of Aragon – who may have been motivated, at least in part, by a desire to spite her husband, who was living openly with his mistress, Bess Holland, who was one of Anne's ladies. Chapuys, by now in place as Imperial Ambassador, claims that the Duchess was briefly banned from court for her noisy espousal of Catherine's cause.[22] A third was Nicholas Carew, one of Henry's Gentlemen of the Privy Chamber, a cousin of Anne and a known Francophile. On the face of it, he was an unlikely ally for Catherine, but we are told that during a diplomatic mission to the imperial court in 1529 he spoke up in her favour and, on his return, lost no time in setting up friendly relations with Chapuys. It is unclear what his motivation was, but thereafter he was unswerving, although moderately discreet, both in his loyalty to Catherine and his hostility to Anne.

So by Christmas 1530 there was little movement in any direction. Anne took out her feelings by ordering new livery for her servants, embroidered with the motto '*Ainsi sera, groigne qui groigne*' ('that's how it's going to be, no matter who grumbles'). A song of the time may or may not be by or about her:

> 'Grudge on who list, this is my lot:
> Nothing to want if it were not...'

And on for seven more verses – it is easy to imagine the song being performed by Anne herself, with the 'If it were not' refrain referring to the marriage of Henry and Catherine. This had been a year of stalemate in terms of the Great Matter. Anne had fewer and fewer allies at court, and the state of what may have seemed like suspended animation evidently grated on everyone's nerves. There continued to be three households within the court – the King's, the Queen's and Anne's.

There began to be reports of Anne's increasing abrasiveness. She and the King quarrelled frequently, but always made it up. One of their quarrels came about when Anne discovered that Catherine was still making shirts for Henry – a custom he had evidently never seen reason to change. She fell out, also, with her father, who remained loyal to her, and her uncle, the Duke of Norfolk, who did so with increasing resentment. Norfolk was heard to mutter that Anne would prove to be the undoing of the Howard family[23] – and was almost certainly out of sympathy with the radical religious line he found his niece expected him to accept. Amid all this, Catherine tried to go on as if Anne did not exist, continuing the custom she had had, since their marriage, of writing to Henry every three days. By midsummer 1531, however, after several months during which the King showed every sign of continuing to hedge his bets, he had broke with Catherine. This appears to have been precipitated in part by her refusal of an appeal by a delegation of nobles and councillors to agree to the repatriation of the divorce case to England. The decisive action came after Henry and Anne had been on a series of hunting trips, taking with them very few attendants. Then came the start of the annual summer progress, due that year to start at Windsor. Catherine and her household duly went to Windsor – but on 14 July Henry and Anne left suddenly for yet another informal hunting trip, leaving a message to Catherine to stay where she was. When Catherine sent one of her usual messages, Henry flew into a rage, replying that he wanted no more letters. Catherine's accusing reply provoked a formal response telling her not to contact him again. They were never to meet again, although her household remained unchanged for the time being.

Christmas 1531 was the first at which Catherine was absent. Anne was now living in the queen's lodgings at Greenwich, but may well have felt very far from secure. At New Year Anne and Henry exchanged gifts as usual – a set of decorated boar spears for him, a sumptuous set of cloth of gold and silver hangings, enough for a whole room, for her. Catherine sent Henry a gold cup – he had evidently not forbidden her to send presents – but received nothing in return. Although this may have been a less than entirely festive Christmas for Anne, 1532 was to be a far better year for her. It seems that former friends were returning, recognising the change in her status, and she was now being courted as one in a position to give favours – the Lisles began to send her presents, including a peewit and a bow. More significantly, much of the year was spent in setting up a summit meeting with the French. The rapprochement between France and England was holding, and there was now a serious possibility of negotiating some kind of settlement with the Pope, with the French acting as intermediaries. At this time the marriage between François's son, Henry, and the Pope's niece, Catherine de Medici, was being discussed, and there is evidence that François was prepared to help Henry in this. The plan was for the King and Anne to visit Boulogne or Calais, and there meet with the King and Queen of France. This would, of course, have meant an immediate international validation of Anne's position as Queen in Waiting. Unsurprisingly, in view of the controversies surrounding her, it was not as simple as that. The Queen of France Anne had known, Claude, had died, and François had remarried, this time to a niece of Catherine of Aragon, who could not be expected to agree to meet Anne Boleyn. The second choice was Marguerite d'Angouleme, accompanied by other French royal and noble ladies. However, this too proved difficult to agree, and in the end it was agreed that the French delegation would be a men-only affair.

If Anne was to go to France and be convincing as an official consort, her status had to be built up. If she could not yet go as a queen, she could at least go as a noblewoman. Since Thomas Boleyn had been made Earl of Wiltshire, Anne had had the courtesy title of Lady Anne Rochford. But now she needed status of her own, and this the King could and did provide. On 1 September, Anne was created Marquess of Pembroke in her own right, taking part in a glittering ceremony at Windsor. The new Marquess, in ermine trimmed crimson velvet covered in jewels, her long dark hair worn loose about her shoulders, was conducted into the King's presence by two countesses, her coronet carried by her cousin, Mary Howard. The Dukes of Norfolk and Suffolk took part in the ceremony, which was followed by High Mass and a banquet. So, the former lady in waiting to a Queen of France could meet the King of France on near-equal terms. Interestingly, however, the letters patent granting Anne the title stated that she could be succeeded by any child she bore, without the usual proviso that the heir should be born in wedlock. It is impossible to know if this was a mistake or represents Anne and Henry providing themselves with an insurance policy.

On Friday, 11 October, Anne and Henry embarked at Dover, had a good crossing and reached Calais at around 10 in the morning, They were accompanied by an entourage of nearly 2,000 men of all ranks – Anne herself was accompanied by only some twenty or thirty ladies, most of whom were from the Boleyn faction. But amidst the royal salute of guns, the parade of the garrison and the official welcome, this can hardly have mattered. After ten days of official partying at Calais, the King and some of his male entourage left for four days at the French court in Boulogne, returning to Calais with François on 25 October. One of François' first actions on arrival was to send Anne a diamond worth £3,500 in the currency of the day – but she did not appear until the time of the feast Henry gave on the Sunday night. It seems likely that Anne herself planned her first appearance as the King's official partner on the international stage – and her sense of theatre, and her timing, were impeccable. The room was hung with cloth of silver ornamented with gold wreaths and lit by 100 candelabra – and in this sumptuous setting, a supper of 170 dishes was served, with French and English recipes alternating. Anne and her entourage of six did not appear until after the meal, and when they did, it was in theatre costumes and masks. Her supporters were her sister Mary, her aunt Dorothy, Countess of Derby, another aunt, Elizabeth Lady Fitzwalter, her sister in law Jane Parker, Lady Rochford, Lady Lisle, the wife of Lord Lisle the Governor of Calais and a Boleyn client, and Lady Wallop, the wife of the ambassador to France. The selection is interesting as it is made up entirely of relatives and political allies, with no one from elsewhere in the nobility – and the King's sister Mary was, of course, very conspicuous by her absence (there is a story she had made insulting comments about Anne the previous year, and since the ensuing uproar had withdrawn to her country house in Oxfordshire).[24] However, no one would have been surprised, as she had long made her hostility to Anne extremely clear. But even in the absence of royal princesses, this must have been a glittering, and probably a glamorous, troupe. They wore cloth of gold overdresses, with crimson satin, silver ornamented sashes, and full-face masks, and were escorted by four maids of honour in crimson satin with cobweb-fine cypress lawn tabards. Each lady chose one of the French party to dance with – the King of France was, of course, claimed by Anne. After only two dances Henry rather spoiled the fun by personally removing the masks – although François evidently played along and declared himself overwhelmed by Anne's beauty. François can hardly have been cast into the sartorial shade by Anne, as we are told he was wearing a doublet covered in jewels. The dancing then continued for another hour, but Anne and François spent much of the time in private conversation – impossible to know whether or not they talked over old times or whether Henry was within earshot.

The party broke up two days later, after a meeting of the Order of the Garter and a ceremonial wrestling match involving French and Cornish fighters. Some of the English party then appear to have rushed back to London – with someone evidently briefed to pass on to Wynkyn de Worde the information that went into the adulatory newsletter describing the event that was on sale on the streets within days. 'The Manner of the triumph at Calais and Boulogne' reads very much like a prepared press release – it would be interesting to know how many copies were sold in London. The narrative stops as the two Kings parted company, and at that point the trip departed from its intended schedule. Until that point the autumn weather had been kind – but now it became stormy. Henry and Anne stayed on in Calais until the storms subsided and they could set sail with less risk of being forced back to port. They did not reach Dover until 11 November, and then took a very leisurely twelve days to travel back to Greenwich – as others have said, this was probably a honeymoon journey through Kent. Certainly at some point late that year, Henry and Anne finally became lovers. Some sources suggest, too, that they went through either a betrothal or a wedding ceremony that November. Edward Hall claimed that the couple married 'on St Erkenwald's Day, which marriage was kept so secret that very few knew it' – 14 November. It may well be that the couple did exchange vows on that day. At that time, an exchange of vows before witnesses, and followed by sexual intercourse, constituted a binding contract of marriage.

In December both the King and Anne visited the Tower of London, where there was building work underway in preparation for her coronation. The King visited several times, travelling from Greenwich by boat; he appears to have given the French ambassador a somewhat curtailed guided tour of the Jewel House. A few days later, he was ready to show Anne round, taking in both the building work and the Jewel House. The French ambassador turned up again, bringing some dispatches as an excuse, was allowed to join the party and was given a fine gold cup, either as an early New Year present or to please Anne. One of the purposes of the visit appears to have been so that Anne could make a choice of silver and gold plate for use in her household as Queen. A list of the choices she made survives,[25] and includes several dozen items, with a weight totalling some 5,000oz of plate. Many of the items had been the property of Cardinal Wolsey. It is likely that Anne viewed the crown, sceptre and rod she would wear and carry at her coronation at the same time.

Christmas 1532 was again celebrated at Greenwich. It was almost certainly a time of happiness for both Anne and Henry – and, early in the new year, Anne discovered she was pregnant. Events then moved fast. If the child was to be born in wedlock, there was no time to wait for a deal with the Pope, even if it had turned out to be possible to agree a solution acceptable to all, which would have been one that allowed both sides to claim they had won. So, on 25 January 1533, the couple went through a very private wedding ceremony. None of the details are known for certain, but it probably took place in the gatehouse of Whitehall Palace, very early in the morning and with only half a dozen people present. The priest who celebrated the wedding was probably Dr Rowland Lee, who was later the Bishop of Coventry, and the only witnesses, Henry Norris and Thomas Heneage, two of the Gentlemen of the Privy Chamber, with Anne's sole attendant being Anne Savage, later Lady Berkeley. This description came from Nicholas Harpsfield in an account written some twenty years later,[26] who also claimed that the King lied to Dr Lee, telling him that permission had been obtained from the Pope. The secret was kept so well that for several weeks neither the French government nor Chapuys had any idea of the truth. As Eric Ives has pointed out,[27] it is likely that, in England and elsewhere in Europe, many people found it difficult to believe that the King of England would really remarry without the Pope's approval. But the day before the wedding, the news got out that Thomas Cranmer was to be the next Archbishop of Canterbury; two days later, Thomas Audley was appointed as Chancellor, and, in that week, Anne began to talk freely in Court circles about appointments to her household as Queen. Thomas Cromwell was hard at work on the final draft of the Act of Appeals that would break the judicial link with Rome, and was sounding out – and in some cases browbeating – contacts about whether they would vote for the legislation.

At Court, Anne's pregnancy became known before her marriage did. This was because she could not resist dropping hints herself. By February, Chapuys was reporting that she had said to the Duke of Norfolk that if she were not pregnant by Easter she would go on a pilgrimage to pray to the Virgin Mary. Later in the month, a famous incident took place in which she asked Thomas Wyatt for an apple, saying that she had developed a craving for the fruit, and that the king had said it meant she was with child. She said she had denied this was so, but left the room laughing loudly – leaving the assembled courtiers to exclaim, speculate and pass on the news.[28] On 24 February Anne gave a party for the King in her own rooms, which were decorated for the occasion with rich tapestries and gold plate. Henry was heard to ask Anne's step grandmother, the Dowager Duchess of Norfolk, whether she agreed that Anne had made a good marriage. No one at court can have been in much doubt by now as to what had taken place. On 30 March Cranmer was consecrated Archbishop, the Act of Appeals was passed in both houses of parliament, and Anne's household at Queen was formed. A message was sent to Catherine of Aragon that she was now to be known as Dowager Princess of Wales, and her household reduced accordingly. By now few people would speak up for Catherine in public.

On Easter Saturday, 1533, Anne Boleyn attended mass as Queen of England, wearing a gown of cloth of gold, with her cousin, Lady Mary Howard, carrying her train and attended by sixty maids of honour. And so the six-year courtship ended in marriage. This news spread like wildfire, first to London, then to the wider country and across Europe. Chapuys wrote an immensely long letter to Charles V,[29] retailing a stormy audience he had had with the King, during which Henry had essentially said he would do as he wished. Chapuys was doing his best to fight a rearguard action to defend Catherine of Aragon's status, and was outraged to learn that she was no longer to be known as Queen. Chapuys claimed that Anne's supporters were almost as stunned as everyone else, and 'did not know whether to laugh or cry'. At court, most people had been prepared for the news – and sometime during the first half of the year, they had been treated to a performance of John Heywood's *The Play of the Weather*, an allegorical piece featuring a none-too-subtle story of a leaky old moon that could not contain its water being replaced by Jupiter with a fine new crescent moon, to the benefit of all. And most courtiers were by now used to the idea that Anne would be queen, and, if not happy with her advent, then certainly prepared to take advantage of it. There was no shortage of applicants for appointments in to her household.

Chapuys was, of course, determined to believe that virtually the whole country hated Anne. He reported in his April letter that the King intended to 'forbid anyone speaking publicly or privately in favour of the queen' (meaning Catherine – he was to stick determinedly to referring to her as the Queen, and to Anne as the lady or the concubine). From this time his position with regard to the two of them was personal, to the point where his genuine affection and loyalty to Catherine may well have clouded his judgement along with his ability to report impartially about what was happening in England. The difficulty is that, in many instances, Chapuys is the only source of the time who mentions a significant event. All too often, it is difficult to know if he is telling the exact truth, giving an exaggerated version, or passing on an invented story that had been fed to him and that he wanted to believe. It is highly unlikely he included deliberate lies in his reports, and he was certainly no fool. However, he spoke limited English, and his instincts were so partisan that it is very possible that he accepted anti-Boleyn propaganda without asking enough questions. Whether we should do so is another matter. It is perhaps safest to draw a distinction between his reports of the many events he personally witnessed and took part in, and the equally many occasions on which he was writing about occurrences he had been told about. Chapuys, like all other diplomats of his time, had paid informers in all departments at court and in London. The potential problem for us is partly that he often did not name them, and partly because it is likely that many of the people who were happy to work for Chapuys were the ones who were highly sympathetic to Catherine of Aragon, and likely to interpret and report on events from that standpoint.

On 9 April, Norfolk headed a delegation to inform Catherine that the King was now married to Anne. The even more unenviable task of informing Catherine that she would henceforward not be known as Queen, but as Princess Dowager of Wales, was left to her Chamberlain. This began a conflict that was to last for the rest of Catherine's life, as she refused to speak or communicate with anyone who addressed her as anything other than Queen. It was a battle she fought partly to try to protect her daughter's position, but it achieved nothing other than the increased misery of both of them. Meanwhile, the newly consecrated Archbishop of Canterbury, Thomas Cranmer, undertook yet another examination of the circumstances and legality of Henry and Catherine's marriage. Cranmer sent a summons to Catherine to appear as a witness at a hearing on 1 May at Dunstable Priory, near Ampthill, where she was now living. Chapuys claimed that this location had been chosen because it was out of the way, and far from London where the people might rise up in Catherine's favour. In the event, Catherine refused to appear, enabling the hearing to go ahead without her. In fact the proceedings appear to have been ill organised, with witnesses failing to appear, papers not being to hand and the expert legal statements in the King's support from the various universities not being in order. However, neither Catherine nor many of the other interested parties bothered to send observers to Dunstable. So, despite what appears to have been little short of administrative chaos, Henry's marriage to Catherine was declared null and void, and his union with Anne good in legal and religious terms.

Meanwhile, at Court, after six years of struggle, the newly married couple began on the journey towards 'happily ever after'. It would, in any circumstances, have been a formidable enterprise.

Chapter 4

The White Falcon Crowned: 1533

Anne Boleyn's coronation followed the pattern laid down for this grandest of ceremonies. However, this particular coronation was a great public event planned in a hurry – Anne was first prayed for as Queen on Easter Saturday, 1533. By this time it was widely suspected at court that she was pregnant – she was dropping unmistakable hints, and the rumour had reached Chapuys. That day the newly proclaimed Queen Anne went to Easter Eve mass at Greenwich dressed in pleated cloth of gold, heavily jewelled, her long gauzy train carried by her cousin, and accompanied by sixty maids of honour – given the reputation for eye-catching grandeur she had already acquired, this promised to be just the first taste of her personal style as queen. And the elaborate nature of the clothing suggests some time to plan ahead – although the cloth of gold dress may possibly have been the one in which she had danced with the King of France the previous October.

During Easter week Chapuys had a long and stormy meeting with the King, during which he told Henry straight out that he had no grounds for divorcing Catherine, and that he should be content with his daughter rather than seeking to marry again, as he might not have any sons, even by another wife. Understandably, perhaps, Henry lost his temper and turned on Chapuys, asking 'Am I not a man like other men? Am I not?' In the very long report he wrote after this, Chapuys was clear that Henry and Anne were married, Anne was probably pregnant, and a coronation likely in the next few weeks.[1] In the same report, Chapuys added that people were coming to him every day asking if he knew anything, and if he were being recalled – which he then recommended that the Emperor should do. He went on to claim that no one he spoke to could believe that the King had actually gone ahead and married Anne without permission from the Pope, and that:

'All the world is astonished at it, for it looks like a dream, and even those who take her part do not know whether to laugh or cry. The King is very watchful of the countenances of the people, and begs the lords to go and visit the new Queen, whom he intends to have solemnly crowned after Easter.'

The Dukes of Norfolk and Suffolk, with others of the Council, had already been sent to Catherine of Aragon to tell her the King had married Anne, and to ask her to withdraw her appeal to Rome, putting forward the argument that in doing so she would be helping to avoid war – and implying that the King would be much more generously inclined towards her if she complied. Catherine turned them down flat, and the Councillors appear to have withdrawn hastily, rather meanly leaving it to Lord Mountjoy, her Chamberlain, to break it to Catherine that she was no longer to be addressed as Queen. That was the beginning of a series of standoffs that were to last for the rest of Catherine's life.

So, as of the middle of April 1533 there were two rival Queens in England – and at this stage, it is clear that a great many people still considered Catherine to be the genuine article. It was, of course, true that Anne was by now around four months pregnant – her daughter was born in early September. It was, therefore, an urgent necessity in political as well as personal terms that Anne should be crowned Queen. The coronation needed to be a high profile, magnificent success, demonstrating to the whole world that she was indeed Queen of England, the true and beloved wife of the King – and that the court and the country had accepted and were loyal to her. If a fitting coronation was to take place before Anne was too heavily pregnant to take part, there was no time to be lost.

The wedding had been kept secret – so secret that the details are still uncertain today. It is sometimes claimed that Henry and Anne were married twice, first on 14 November on their return from France, and for the second time early in the morning of 25 January at Whitehall. The only contemporary source for the November date is Hall's 'Chronicle'[2] – although not corroborated in this instance, Hall was on the spot, contemporary, and is likely to have had good information to back up what he wrote. The likelihood seems to be that the first ceremony was a handfasting. At that time it was possible for a couple to exchange vows in front of witnesses. If the marriage was then consummated, it counted as a binding contract, but could then be followed by a wedding ceremony. If this is correct, and the actual wedding did indeed take place in January, in a pre-dawn ceremony in a room over the gate at Whitehall, we do not even know who officiated. The newly created Archbishop Cranmer, one of Anne's closest allies, claimed in a letter written that winter that he did not know of the wedding until a fortnight after it had taken place. There are two possible candidates for the role of officiant – in recusant circles later in the century Rowland Lee, later Bishop of Lichfield, was identified, while two years after the event, Chapuys was claiming it had been George Brown, Prior of Austin Friars. Similarly, reports vary as to who else was present. It may have been Henry Norris and Thomas Heneage of the Privy Chamber, with Anne Savage, later Lady Berkeley, as Anne's sole attendant.

In March 1533, although the court was rife with rumour, Chapuys was still writing in March about gossip regarding an imminent ceremony and, although the court (which was mostly at Greenwich at this time) was seemingly buzzing with a new story almost every day, it was not until Anne herself began to drop proud hints about being pregnant that it became clear that there must have been a wedding: no one who knew her believed that, after six years of waiting, she would have begun to sleep with the King outside marriage. (This was despite the fact that, in Europe, she and Henry were credited with having had several children together already). It was in February that the now famous incident in which Anne asked for an apple took place; she carefully explained that the King had told her the craving must mean she was pregnant, but that she had said it could not be so. She then left the room, laughing loudly, leaving the assembled company to enjoy (or not) the sensation she had caused.[3] Anne also said to her uncle the Duke of Norfolk that if she were not pregnant by Easter she would go on a pilgrimage.

Early modern coronations were demanding affairs. A four-day series of public spectacles, beginning with a water pageant, continuing with a procession through London, interspersed with entertainments and culminating in the religious ceremony at Westminster Abbey and followed by a great feast, was involved. On this occasion all this had to be achieved with a lead-time of little more than six weeks from the day Anne was proclaimed Queen. Nothing could be taken on trust – given how controversial a figure she was, everything had to be planned and agreed at the highest level at court. The eyes of the whole of Europe would be watching, and it was crucially important for the newly married couple to weigh up and control the messages given by each aspect of the ceremonial, as well as to impress friends and enemies alike with its erudition, sophistication and luxury. Political spin is no modern invention. There is evidence that both Thomas Cromwell and the Duke of Suffolk had important roles in the planning of the event. Cromwell was an obvious choice, but Suffolk was being put in a difficult position – his wife, the King's sister, Mary, had already let it be known that she would not accept Anne Boleyn as Queen. She had refused to take part in the visit to France the previous autumn and, a few weeks before, after a fight between some of her household and that of some of Anne's supporters, during which one person was fatally stabbed, the Suffolks had left court, beating a hasty retreat to their country home.[4] But Suffolk was not allowed to get away with this, and back he came to London, where he was on duty until after Anne was crowned. Mary may well have already been ill by Easter 1533 – she was to die at the end of June, which could of itself explain her absence from the coronation. It does not, however, explain the absence of her daughters, Frances and Eleanor, the elder of whom was by now 16 years old. Frances Brandon was married to Henry Gray, Marquess of Dorset, in London in the spring of 1533 – there are few records of the wedding, and we do not know if either her mother or Anne Boleyn were present.

There were, of course, a great many people and agencies involved in the coronation. In terms of the City, there were traditions and precedents to call on, but even so the schedule was tight – the Lord Mayor only received the order to prepare a water procession to escort the queen from Greenwich to the Tower of London on 13 May, just over a fortnight before the event. This was a demanding schedule –

when Catherine of Aragon arrived in London in 1501 there had been two years to prepare, and even the state visit of Emperor Charles V was planned some ten weeks in advance. In 1533 the City Aldermen and the King's Council joined forces to plan all aspects of the procession through the City, with some moderately courteous squabbling about who was to finance which aspects of the day (between them they managed to secure some funding from London's resident German merchants). Thomas Cromwell, the Duke of Norfolk and the King's Council agreed to make the royal musicians available, and the King's Works were to provide painters and materials. The final cost is not recorded, but the Milanese ambassador speculated that the City's share alone came to an incredible £46,000 (multiply by about 500 for an indication of early twenty-first century equivalent values). In order to get some idea of both the significance of the event and the size of the budget, we may think in terms of an Olympic opening ceremony and add a royal wedding. The burden of finding the money for the City's share of the funding fell on the individual livery companies, with a major part of the cost landing on the shoulders of Stephen Pecocke, the current Lord Mayor, and his own livery company, the Haberdashers. This was, however, among the accepted responsibilities of livery companies – display and splendour were an integral part of maintaining status in the Tudor world.

The first, and absolute, necessity was that the coronation should take place in a London that was at least peaceful, and preferably enthusiastic. As with so much else relating to Anne Boleyn, there is conflicting evidence about just how big a challenge this presented. As so often, Eustace Chapuys is an important, if sometimes questionable, source – on this occasion he was determined to believe that London hated Anne Boleyn, and that the coronation would be at the very least a farce, and preferably a disaster. Chapuys reported that, when Anne was prayed for as queen on Easter Saturday at St Paul's, 'almost all left the church in high displeasure and with sad countenances without waiting for the rest of the sermon.' Chapuys then reports that the King sent for the Lord Mayor of London to warn him that nothing like it must happen again, and the Lord Mayor must personally ensure that no one spoke out against the new marriage.

The Lord Mayor then apparently sent for the senior members of all the livery companies to warn them to keep quiet and look pleased.

There are some other pieces of evidence to back Chapuys up. A scattering of reports from all over the country concern ordinary people in trouble for criticising either the King for breaking with Catherine of Aragon, or, slightly less riskily, disrespecting Anne Boleyn herself. It may well have felt better to blame 'the other woman' not only for luring the King away from his faithful wife of twenty years, but for all the changes that were taking place. A new mother in Gloucestershire was denounced by her midwife for having said, in the throes of labour, that the midwife's services were good enough for 'good Queen Catherine' and too good for Anne Boleyn. As early as 1530 the Venetian Ambassador was speculating that the people of London might rebel if the King were to marry Anne Boleyn. It seems, too, that London was rife with rumours. Early in 1533 a woman called Elizabeth Amadas became notorious as she spread stories centring round a prophecy of a ruler called the Mouldwarp, a tyrant bearing a strong resemblance to Henry VIII who was due to be overthrown that year. As Amadas was the wife of the King's own jeweller and had been left by her husband, she may have had a personal agenda when it came to abandoned wives – however this may be, her stories appear to have spread like wildfire. The evidence is too sparse to be sure whether the mood of London in 1533 was genuinely and consistently hostile to Anne. What appears certain is that both the King and Anne herself were afraid that it might be, and were determined to take no chances. So this was yet another reason for planning every detail of the coronation with as much care as the limited time available allowed. Doubters and detractors were to be overwhelmed with her magnificence.

The first part of the coronation took place on Thursday, 29 May when the Lord Mayor of London and the Masters and senior members of all the Livery Companies went by barge to Greenwich to collect the queen-to-be and bring her to London in her barge (which was, in fact, the one that had belonged to Catherine of Aragon, newly painted with Anne's coat of arms and colours). At this time the river Thames was London's greatest thoroughfare, and the great and the good made as many journeys as they could by water – far preferable to the mostly appalling roads. Anyone of high status would own a barge, and these were richly decorated and rowed by liveried oarsmen (part of any great household). The livery companies' barges were seen every year when the new Lord Mayor took office – the Lord Mayor's Show was then a river pageant. So this part of the coronation would be easy to arrange – apart from the dragons spitting fireworks. An eye witness to the event, the chronicler Edward Hall, was to claim there were over 300 boats in the procession, which was almost as long as the route to Greenwich. As the cavalcade returned to London, the dragon boat was joined by one with a white falcon superstructure – the Queen's personal badge, which was to be an important motif throughout the celebrations. All along the route guns were fired in salute, and boat loads of musicians played. Once arrived at the Tower, the Queen and her ladies were greeted by the King – the Lord Mayor and a few senior officials went in to be entertained, but most of the procession stayed on the water, where there were more fireworks and music.

It was traditional for the new King or Queen to sleep the night before the coronation in the Tower of London, which was still as much a palace as a fortress, so it was there that Anne Boleyn disembarked, to be greeted by the King and conducted to the newly refurbished Queen's house within the Tower. It is on record that Anne disembarked, and was greeted by the Lieutenant and Constable of the Tower, the Lord Chamberlain and other officials, and finally by the King, who kissed and embraced her. Although Henry VIII deliberately planned to take little part in the festivities, leaving his new queen to be the unchallenged focus of everyone's attention, he left no one in any doubt that he was watching closely. However, it was only during the next, relatively quiet day of private ceremonial within the royal apartments of the Tower of London that he played a part. One of those ceremonies was the creation of eighteen Knights of the Bath – a notable honour, and the beneficiaries were Anne Boleyn's relatives and supporters, now publicly honoured after all the years of waiting. A total of fifty new knights belonging to a number of orders of knighthood, were made – a graphic demonstration, if a further one was needed, to the assembled court and country of just who was now in favour. The ceremonial involved a very literal immersion in a bath, and eighteen of these were set up in the White Tower. The newly made knights, in their violet gowns and hoods trimmed with miniver fur, took part in the procession the following day – and if Cranmer's comments are anything to go by, by that date, the whole ritual appeared somewhat archaic: an example of what care was being taken to demonstrate that everything was done properly. It is, however, on record that the same ceremony had taken place at the coronation of the King and Catherine of Aragon, so it may well be that this was one of the ways of demonstrating the importance given to the coronation of the new Queen.

The next public ceremonial was planned for 31 May, when Anne was to ride through the City of London, entertained as she went with plays, music and special effects. The final agreement among the organisers was for twelve 'pageants' – set pieces to take place at specific points through the city. Of these, six were identified as major 'devices', and John Leland and Nicholas Udall were commissioned to design and script them. Both were court officials known to be Boleyn supporters. Udall, an Oxford man and a reformer, was to go on to be a somewhat scandalous headmaster of Eton, while Leland was a scholar with an international reputation. They had all the resources of the King's works and London's guilds at their disposal, and they used them, involving several hundred people in the preparations and finally staging a series of entertainments that combined political and religious imagery and spectacle to what most observers conceded was good effect. To a modern audience the mixture of saints, characters from classical mythology and heraldic devices, with continuing emphasis on the crowned white falcon might seem curious. However, to Tudor Europe this was the expected form – the references were known to their audience. It was part of the political language of the time, at court and in London and further afield, that political and religious messages were conveyed by means of drama.

At court there were frequent musical and theatrical entertainments staged on festive occasions through the year. It was expected that any high-status person would be able to act, dance, sing, play a musical instrument and make elegant and witty conversation This applied to both sexes and these accomplishments were a necessity for anyone who hoped to make a good impression (or indeed to obtain a place at court at all). Certainly the King could do all of these things, as well as being something of a composer (several songs of his writing survive, the most famous being *Pastime with Good Company*). Anne Boleyn was also an accomplished dancer and singer, as well as a writer of poetry. So although the most important entertainments were written by professional writers such as Leland, Udall and John Heywood, the performers included the courtiers themselves, joined by professional musicians, actors and, often, the choristers of the Chapel Royal. Court entertainments were often more than merely a pastime. Just a few months before, in the autumn of 1532, a performance of a piece entitled *The Play of the Weather* had announced the imminent marriage of the King and Anne Boleyn in allegorical form – the king of the Gods, Jupiter, is about to bring about a change in the weather, exchanging an old, leaky moon for a new, 'tighter' one. Nothing very subtle about the allegory, but it was of a kind understood and expected by its audience.

Outside the world of the court, Londoners too were used to drama with a message. In London, as in several other English cities including York and Coventry, the ruling guilds staged annual cycles of mystery plays telling the main events of the Old and New Testaments. These were performed on temporary wagons and stages, and featured livery company members and school boys. Just a few years after Anne Boleyn's time the London plays were suppressed and all copies of them destroyed, but it is highly likely they were similar to the ones at York that survived the rigours of the Reformation, offering a combination of religious imagery, spectacle, mechanical contrivances such as fireworks and flying machines, and local in-jokes. Each livery company took charge of a particular play, often one on an appropriate theme – for example, at York, the Bakers staged the play depicting the Last Supper, while the Butchers staged the Crucifixion. The guilds took their responsibilities extremely seriously and were highly competitive with one another as to the standard of the presentations, which took place annually at Corpus Christi. The London crowds certainly turned out to watch the Mysteries, and so were used to entertainments of the kind they were offered as part of Anne Boleyn's coronation.

Each pageant was to take place on its own stage along Gracechurch Street, Cornhill and Cheapside, with the houses in between along the processional route being hung with cloth of gold or crimson, and with other 'diversions' including a fountain running with three kinds of wine at once. Because of the shortness of time, only one of the pageants featured the spectacular mechanical effects that were often a feature of both coronations and mystery plays. It is notable that many of the pageants that formed part of this ceremony owed much of their ancestry to mystery plays – it is even possible that they featured some of the same actors and costumes. The themes, script and music for all the entertainments had been written by the Leland and Udall, and the fact that the scripts were preserved and still survive in the Royal collection speaks volumes for the attention and care with which the events were planned – it is highly likely that both Henry and Anne had some input. Some of the motifs repeated some of those that were used during the coronation of Queen Claude in Paris, which Anne had almost certainly witnessed and may well now have chosen for herself. No records have come to light of how the playlets were rehearsed, who directed or who acted in them, but it is likely that the actors and singers included choristers from St Paul's, boys from the city's schools and some of the liverymen who took part in the mystery plays, with the addition of court employees. The authorities in London did employ a group of six professional musicians, the Waits, whose responsibility it was to play at official events, and they were almost certainly involved in proceedings alongside the Court musicians.

It is tempting to imagine fraught last-minute rehearsals and frayed tempers – certainly, given the timescale, the preparations must have been rushed. On the day, the procession began at least three hours late – whether because something had gone wrong or because Anne herself was not ready on time we shall never know. At least one participant mentioned waiting in position for several hours, while the judges mistimed their arrival and had to scramble into place after the procession had started. However, it was not until the late afternoon of Saturday, 31 May, that

Anne finally emerged from her apartments in the Tower to set off to ride through the streets of the city, riding in a horse litter with a canopy held over her head. Observers described her as dressed in white cloth of gold adorned with rubies, and 'in her hair' – this dress and her dramatically dark hair, worn loose to her waist, must have made her an eye-catching figure. Not only her dress, but her litter and the trappings of her horses were white or silver, and she wore a gold, ruby encrusted circlet on her head – not yet, of course, a crown.

The procession was headed by the gentlemen of the royal household and the servants of the French ambassador (a great honour, almost certainly given by Anne herself in recognition of the support of the French king), all in violet, with one sleeve in the Queen's colours of violet and blue, followed by the judges, the Knights of the Bath, the royal council, the bishops and the Lord Mayor of London. The queen came next, surrounded by her chief ladies, some in carriages and some on horseback, all dressed in crimson or black velvet. Those chief ladies included many of Anne's own closest relatives, including her mother and sister, and her step-grandmother, the dowager Duchess of Norfolk. There were at least two notable absentees, however – the current Duchess of Norfolk, and the king's sister, Mary, the Duchess of Suffolk – both opponents of Anne and of sufficient importance that the King had been unable to force their attendance. It is true, however, that the Duchess of Suffolk was known to be ill, and was to die only a few weeks later, and the Duchess of Norfolk was on acrimoniously bad terms with her husband, who was present. The ladies were followed by the King's guard in two lines. In all there were perhaps 700 people involved in the procession, which stopped each time a new pageant was due to be performed. Anne's father, now the Earl of Wiltshire, was present, with new honours and in magnificent clothes. Anne's brother, George, was in France, where he had been sent some weeks previously to let King François I know of his sister's marriage and pregnancy, and had to be content with a description of the day from his sister's chamberlain, who reassured him that everything had been done 'honourably and according to tradition'.

The route of the coronation procession took the new Queen all through the streets of the city, starting at Tower Hill, going on through Gracechurch

Street and Cornhill, using the Leadenhall as one of the performance points, on to St Paul's and then down Fleet Street and along the Strand to Westminster. It is on record that the streets were newly gravelled so that the horses could not slip (the city authorities had to exercise constant vigilance at all times to try to keep the streets from becoming clogged up with mud and worse, and becoming impassable). The livery companies and rich individuals whose halls and houses were along the route decorated them and hung out tapestries and flags. Looking at the scripts of the plays and descriptions of the other entertainments, the whole procession must have taken perhaps three hours to complete – in late May it would have been light until late enough in the evening to allow for this.

So far as is known, each entertainment was performed only once, so the proceedings must have been somewhat tedious to all those who were too far away to see them. Anne appears to have played her part with the expected grace and good humour, knowing of course that her every move and expression was being watched by observers from all over Europe. As with so much relating to Anne Boleyn, it is impossible to be sure which of those eye witnesses, most with a personal agenda, to believe with regard to how she was received. One of the 'Anne Boleyn myths' is that she was hissed by the London crowds as she rode through the city. There is no contemporary source for this. A city lawyer, Sir John Spelman, reported that all went according to plan.[5]

Perhaps the most memorable part of the scripts is one of the songs. *The White Falcon* was written by Nicholas Udall as the final item in the pageant performed on a stage at the Leaden Hall in Gracechurch Street, on the corner with Cornhill. A structure had been set up in the shape of a castle, with a cupola painted inside with clouds, planets and stars. The floor represented a green field and hill, with a tree stump growing out of it. The action included the blessing of the new queen by St Anne and the 'three Blessed Marys', followed by a series of mechanical wonders – the tree stump began to spill out roses, whereupon a white falcon swooped down out of the cupola to land on the flowers. Finally, an angel appeared and crowned the falcon, while a child recited a blessing. The white falcon representing Anne recalls the dove representing the Holy

Spirit in the iconography of the day, which is often shown in images of the Annunciation – so the queen is given a quasi-saintly status. It is worth quoting the lyrics in full, as they give both a strong sense of what may have been the atmosphere of the occasion and demonstrate the political and religious messages intended:

> This white falcon
> Rare and gaison
> This bird shyneth so bright
> Of all that are
> No bird compare may
> With this falcon white.
>
> The virtues all
> No man mortall
> Of this bird may write
> No man earthly
> Enough truly
> Can praise this falcon white
>
> Who will express
> Great gentleness
> To be in any wight
> He will not miss
> But call him this
> The gentle falcon white.
>
> This gentle bird
> As white as curd
> Shineth both day and night
> Nor far nor near
> Is any peer
> Unto this falcon white.

Of body small,
of power regall
She is and sharp of sight
Of courage hault
No manner fault
Is in this falcon white

In chastity
Excelleth she
Most like a virgin bright
And worthy is
To live in bliss
Always this falcon bright

But now to take
And use her make
Is time, as troth is plight
That she may bring
Fruit according
For such a falcon white

And where by wrong
She hath fleen long
Uncertain where to light
Herself repose
upon the Rose
Now may this falcon white.

Whereon to rest
And build her nest
God grant her, most of might!
That England may
Rejoice alway
In this same falcon white.

Neither the imagery nor the political commentary is subtle: the falcon is to provide 'fruit according' for England, now that she can come to rest on the (Tudor) rose. A further layer of allusion to the royal family is provided by the tree stump – a 'Woodstock' was also a royal badge. The description of the bird/Anne is interesting – she is little, 'of body small', but fierce – 'of power regall', and, despite the emphasis on her 'gentleness', the impression is of a formidable creature. The first line of the eighth verse alludes to the long delay before the marriage could take place – 'by wrong/she hath flean long.' But now all will be well, and she will 'build her nest' and provide England with the long-awaited heir. The whole is reminiscent of the many hymns in praise of the Virgin Mary – a precursor of the adoration of Anne's daughter, Elizabeth, as Gloriana. Curiously, it is almost certain that the music used for the occasion comes from a secular song from the King's own music book. This was identified by Tamsin Lewis in 2013, and the song was perfomed, probably for the first time since the 1530s, at the 2013 Lord Mayor's Show. The use of an existing melody adds to the evidence of the speed with which the coronation had had to be prepared.

All this religious iconography was interspersed with classical allusions. Mount Parnassus (the mountain outside Delphi considered sacred to Apollo and the Muses) made an appearance, complete with a fountain gushing wine, a mechanical eagle (the imperial bird associated with Zeus) and actors representing Apollo and the muses, each of whom recited, sang or played in praise of Anne, using a somewhat eclectic mixture of snippets from Greek myths to swell the chorus of praise. This tableau was the one at Gracechurch Street, paid for by the German merchants and designed by Hans Holbein. At Cornhill the Three Graces waited to greet the Queen, their names anglicised to Hearty Gladness, Stable Honour and Continual Success – this bringing a flavour of both the chivalric entertainments of Court and the names given to characters in mediaeval plays such as 'Everyman'. So, traditional religious imagery alternated with the new humanism – but in both, the message was the same – Anne was ushering in a new and hopeful age. At the end of the day's celebrations, after singing from the boys of St Paul's, the Recorder of London presented the

Queen with a purse made of cloth of gold containing 'a thousand markes of angell nobels' as a gift from the city (this was about £600 – serious money in 1533). She was then escorted through Ludgate, up Fleet Street and on to Westminster. Thomas Cranmer, taking part, as Archbishop of Canterbury, in the day's celebrations, described the moment when she finally went off duty for the day:

'She was conveyed out of the backside of the palace to a barge and so unto York Place, where the King's Grace was before her coming.... for this you must ever presuppose that his Grace came always before her secretly in a barge, as well from Greenwich to the Tower, as from the Tower to York Place.'[6]

The next day was that of the religious ceremony in Westminster Abbey, when Anne finally achieved the status of an anointed queen. Dressed this time in purple velvet and ermine, and with a gold canopy held over her head, she walked along a carpeted route, followed by her ladies, who were dressed in crimson robes, and watched by the whole court, the lord mayor and judges, and by the King from behind a screen. The great and the good occupied specially constructed stands in the abbey – it was crucial for them to be seen to be present, and to take part in the acclamation of loyalty. The new queen was supported by the bishops of London and Winchester, and the dowager Duchess of Norfolk carried her train. However, it was Thomas Cranmer as Archbishop of Canterbury who crowned and anointed her, and was to write a detailed report of the day.[7] The usual ritual for a queen consort was followed – Anne was first anointed with holy oil on her head and breast, and then she was invested with the crown, ring, sceptre and rod. We are told, however, that she was crowned first with the Crown of St Edward, usually reserved for sovereigns, but that this, being extremely heavy, was then exchanged for a smaller, lighter crown, which had been specially made for her.

Then it was on to Westminster Hall for the coronation banquet – another procession, on foot, and this time led by her father on her right hand and Lord Talbot, deputising for his father the Earl of Shrewsbury, on her left. All the nobility, judges and bishops, the Lord Mayor and aldermen attended, as well as Thomas Cromwell in a specially designed crimson outfit trimmed with miniver fur. The Duke of Suffolk presided in his role as high steward, from the back of a horse and in a jacket dripping with pearls. Anne sat alone at a high table under a cloth of estate, with the Archbishop some way to her right. Nothing and no one must be allowed to take the focus from her on her day of triumph – this time the King, with a couple of ambassadors for company, watched proceedings from a screened viewing platform. The chronicler, Edward Hall, reporting on the event, was struck by its good organisation and by the 'costly' food – he does not mention how good it was, but that was hardly the main point,[8] which was, of course, magnificence – there were three courses, each of between twenty-five and thirty dishes. It is curious to note that two ladies sat on the floor under the table, close enough to the Queen to attend her in any way she might need – presumably so that their presence did not disrupt the theatrical elements of the event. There were also two visible ladies who stood one on each side of her as she sat at table – the Dowager Countess of Oxford and the Countess of Worcester. As at the abbey, when at last she rose to leave, all the most influential people in the land had to be seen to be present. They were to stand as she washed her hands and drank a final draught of wine from a gold cup offered by the Lord Mayor, then kneel, with everyone else, to Anne as she left Westminster Hall, smiling and saying 'I thank you all for the honour you have done me this day.' By this time it was late at night – the day's ceremonies had begun at 9 in the morning: an exhausting day for a woman six months into pregnancy.

All this is recorded by the official herald. Chapuys, grudging as ever, described the day's events as 'cold, meagre and uncomfortable'. But there was evidently no disruption – if there had been, it seems highly likely that Chapuys would have heard of it and reported every detail with glee. As it was, he had to be content with implying that the atmosphere, as in the procession the previous day, was one of sullen acquiescence. The Venetian ambassador, one of those invited to observe alongside the King, reported that the coronation had been celebrated:

'with the utmost order and tranquillity, all the streets and the houses
being crowded with persons of every condition, in number truly
marvellous'.

Whatever the truth of the matter, the celebrations continued into the
following week – still the new Queen could not rest, and Monday, 2 June
was devoted to jousting, dancing and a banquet in the Queen's Chamber.
The jousts were the first to be held in the newly built tiltyard at Whitehall,
and were somewhat marred by technical problems with the stands. But
this was not allowed to spoil the day.

By this time the official reports from the various ambassadors were
being sent out. Chapuys, as we have seen, went to great lengths to make it
sound as if the coronation had been, if not a disaster, then at the very least
an embarrassment and an anti–climax. The French ambassador, given,
of course, that his countrymen had had such an honoured place in the
coronation procession, was hardly going to share this view.

Not even the most hostile witness could claim that anything had gone
spectacularly wrong. What they could and did say, however, is that the
London crowds were sullen and even mocking. An anonymous report,
the original of which is now lost, was sent to Brussels,[10] saying that Anne
rode in a litter so low the ears of the mules appeared to be hers, dressed
in a robe suitable for the Witch of the West, as it sported embroidered
tongues pierced with nails and a high neck to hide a huge swelling
in her neck. The account continued that the crowds did not cheer or
take off their hats as she passed, and that the Lord Mayor, when she
complained, said he could not command the people's hearts. We are
then told that Anne's fool said they were keeping their caps on to hide
their scurvy heads, and that some people in the crowd started shouting
out 'ha, ha' when they saw the decorations with Henry's and Anne's
initials intertwined. The *Cronica del Rey Enrico*, written two decades
after the event, tells a similar story. These stories may have some basis
in fact – or they may be the result of wishful thinking on the part of
Anne's enemies. We may be fairly sure that there was no sustained or
overt hostility, or the Venetian ambassador, who was present throughout,

would have witnessed and reported on it. Neither, however, was he reporting anything resembling public acclaim – 'order and tranquillity' do not go with public enthusiasm, let alone affection.

However, if the London crowds were silent, the ruling classes, at home and abroad, were not. The next days saw the arrival of presents from all over Europe, including a magnificent litter from François I of France.[11] Lancelet de Carles, writing in 1536, was to claim that most courtiers were falling over each other to honour their new Queen – 'everyone strove to be as attentive and solicitous as possible to their new mistress',[12] not from regard for her, but in order to please the King. This applied to many of those who were most hostile to Anne – for example, Nicholas Carewe, who was to become a great supporter of the Seymours, took a prominent part in the coronation jousts. At the same time the King was issuing a proclamation threatening penalties against anyone according royal honours to anyone but himself and Anne – this was, of course, a public warning to Catherine of Aragon, her daughter, Mary, and their supporters. Henceforth they were no longer queen and princess, but Princess Dowager of Wales and the Lady Mary. This marked a new round in the battle to deprive them of status. Catherine was the first target – Mary could wait until Anne's child was born. Predictably, Catherine continued to maintain she was Queen, and countered by ordering new liveries for her servants showing her initial and the King's entwined. But while orders and angry letters chased each other round southern England, the King and Queen settled down to spend most of the summer months at Windsor, allowing the King to go on hunting expeditions and the Queen to spend a few relatively restful weeks before the birth of her child, expected in early September.

Anne Boleyn's daughter, Elizabeth I, was to become the arch exponent of political spin. The Virgin Queen, Bel Phoebe, Gloriana, Good Queen Bess – her myth abides still. However many historians may suggest her reign did not represent the golden time that myth suggests, the aura still clings. Elizabeth Tudor was to be very clever as to how she presented herself to the people she sought to rule – and some of the methods of presentation had been used by her mother before her. It was not until Elizabeth's own coronation, more than a quarter of a century after that of her mother, that Anne Boleyn was again to be mentioned, let alone celebrated, on the streets of London. Anne's effigy was placed beside that of Henry VIII along their daughter's triumphant route through London. At that time both mother and daughter took what turned out to be enduring places in the history and myth of England.

Chapter 5

Earthly Powers: London

In the sixteenth century as in the twenty-first, London represented a number of different worlds, some interconnected and some barely aware of one another. As we have seen, geographically it covered an area scarcely bigger than the present-day City of London, but with a population that was in the process of quadrupling in the century between 1500 and 1600, from perhaps 50,000 to around 200,000. This was a city of the young, and of migrants. According to one estimate, in the region of a fifth of all English people spent some part of their life there, arriving in their teens or twenties to seek work. The dream of Dick Whittington attracted the ambitious, the hopeful and the desperate. Part of that desperation was born of the enclosures that were driving country people off the land that was being increasingly given over to wool production that needed far fewer workers. Most of the successors of the real, historical Dick Whittington (a fourteenth-century mercer who made an immense fortune, gave much of it to charity and who was not just three but four times Lord Mayor of London) arrived with the contacts without which it was virtually impossible to get anything but the most menial work.

One of Tudor London's identities was as a commercial city. Perhaps a quarter of the working population was involved in producing food, and another half, with the production of clothes and cloth.[1] Ninety per cent of England's exports at this time were of cloth, and while little of it was produced in London, much of it was finished there – these were the occupations of the members of the large and influential Clothworkers' Company. The other main categories of work were construction, metal, wood, a somewhat bewildering variety of skills relating to leather, from saddlers to glove makers, and a small group of professionals, including barber surgeons and stationers. In theory, all those occupations were totally controlled by the Livery Companies, which operated as trainers, trade unions and friendly societies. Only the members could work in any given occupation within London, and the companies protected their closed shops with ferocity. At this time, for the most part the members of each company really worked in that particular trade, but already there was some diversification. This appears to have been particularly true of the companies where members were essentially traders rather than manufacturers, for example the Mercers, Vintners and Skinners.

While they mostly took care of their own people first, many of the companies had wider charitable purposes, generally with a specifically religious aim, and often under the auspices of a particular saint. They operated strict quality control policies – no one could enter the trade at the end of their apprenticeship until they had demonstrated their competence. This often involved producing a 'masterpiece' which was judged by a panel of freemen of the relevant company. Once this hurdle was past, the new freeman was entitled to set up in trade on his own account – if he had the money do so. Outsiders were rigorously excluded from trading within London – incomers who tried to bypass the rules would have their stock and tools confiscated. Dishonesty and poor standards were also severely dealt with – company records show that everything from bad carpentry, to rotten fish, to underweight loaves of bread were complained of and the culprits dealt with. The companies were as keen to maintain standards as they were to maintain their closed shops.

The companies were also an integral part of the government of London. Their members elected the sheriffs who were the city's magistrates, and influenced the election of the Lord Mayor, who, then as now, changed each year and was, among other things, the chief magistrate. There was keen competition for precedence among the various companies. This was virtually established by about 1515, with the highest status going to the richest, of whom the Mercers were, and remain, the wealthiest of all. Companies built up their riches as members made them presents and legacies. One of their functions was to provide funerals for members who had fallen on hard times, as well as to care for widows and orphans. Rich freemen often left property to be rented out and the proceeds used for charitable purposes – it was in this way that the Mercers now come to own most of Covent Garden. The more entrepreneurial companies also became involved in new initiatives, in particular exploration. Some companies, for example the Skinners, had had international links for centuries – Skinners had built up links with traders in the Baltic countries and were involved in the Hanseatic League as they sought to secure the best furs for import. In the sixteenth century, the Mercers had close links with the newer Merchant Venturers' Company.

As time went on, the companies became integral to most aspects of life in London – anything for which the church was not responsible, a livery company generally was. Each company had strong links with a specific London church, usually the one in which their hall was situated. Rich and successful liverymen left money to build elaborate tombs, and even entire memorial chapels, in their company's church, and helped to fund both building work and priests' salaries. The religious characters of the companies was important – most of them had an affiliation to a patron saint as well as to a church, and the charitable work they did was always significant, although it was often limited to company members and their dependents. By the sixteenth century the members of individual trades were less certain to live in the immediate area of their hall, although many still did so. For example, the Goldsmiths' Hall of Tudor times was on the same site as the one that now stands, and the immediately surrounding streets of Foster Lane and Cheapside were the locations of many goldsmiths' shops. This was to go on being the case for at least another hundred years. The same applied to Smithfield, where the Butchers' Company had, and still have, their hall (although they lost their mediaeval site to the Underground system in 1883), where there have been butchers' shops since before the Norman Conquest. The Butchers have had links with the neighbouring church of St Bartholomew the Great for much of the last millennium.

It should be remembered that for centuries a significant number of women were company members. For example, it is recorded that in 1495 there were a number of 'freemaiden' members of the Cooks' Company. And in the sixteenth and seventeenth centuries, there were female members of the Goldsmiths' Company, working usually as burnishers. Some of these took on apprentices who then joined the company themselves – one study has shown a small but significant number of girls being formally apprenticed in the fifteenth and early sixteenth centuries.[2] In addition, it was very common for both widows and daughters of company members to take on the family business. During the 1530s and 40s, Elizabeth Pickering married, and outlived, no fewer than three members of the Stationers' Company, finally becoming a printer in her own right. There are enough similar examples on record to make it clear that, early in the sixteenth century, it was perfectly usual for a woman of independent status – that is a 'femme sole', a single woman or a widow – to operate in London in her own right. It is clear, however, that there was a 'glass ceiling' preventing female company members from achieving any significant seniority – there are no records of women members of any livery, that is, the senior level of the company, let alone a woman master or sheriff. Everyone concerned appears to have been more comfortable if influential women kept a relatively low profile. In the 1540s a number of livery companies, including the Carpenters and Bakers, were to pass rules forbidding women to 'work openly' – they could continue to work, but were to be as low profile as possible.

For married women the position was different again. In theory, in the sixteenth century a wife was totally subservient to her husband, to whom she owed unquestioning obedience. The husband was supposed to be the head of the household, whose word was law to his wife, children, apprentices and servants, and any man who was unable at least to look as if this was the case was an object of disapproval and perhaps ridicule. It was also important for a woman to look as if she had a husband who could maintain his status, and for them both to appear to be part of a contented and functional family. A woman's virtue was supposed to be fragile, and she had to maintain modesty, decorum, piety and, preferably, silence in order to maintain it. The reality was, unsurprisingly, often very different. It is very clear that, in many London households, the husband and wife worked together to run a business. If that had not been the case, it would hardly have been possible for a widow to have taken on the running of a business in the way that did so often happen. It is clear that there were many women Londoners at this time who were both capable and confident.

In terms of public life, again, women were supposed to play no part. Certainly there was no suggestion a woman could hold any public office, or vote in any kind of election. However, the same applied to most men. There is evidence that London women had ways of making their feelings known. During the years when Anne Boleyn was a queen in waiting, there are several claims that women Londoners demonstrated against her, and later, after she was Queen, there is evidence that a number of London wives joined prominent courtiers in some kind of public demonstration in favour of the King's daughter, Mary. The reporting on these occasions indicates that, because these were 'things done by women', there was official reluctance to take action against those involved. The degree of this semi-immunity varied according to the status of the person concerned – poor women were likely to be able to remain under the official radar, while in the case of the demonstration in favour of Mary, we are told that two of the ringleaders were briefly imprisoned in the Tower.

So, in official terms, the governance of London was undertaken by high status men, mostly connected to livery companies. It was this elite who also provided the Members of Parliament for London – there were four, two elected by the aldermen and two by the sheriffs. Parliament did not, however, sit very often. During the thirty-seven-year reign of Henry VIII, nine different parliaments sat for a total of 183 weeks: less than four years. London operated in some respects like a self-governing city state, but in others, was subservient to the King, who took a close and highly personal interest in its affairs. The mayor, sheriffs and aldermen were expected to be responsible for law and order, and were to contribute to the security of the realm. Successive kings relied on the companies for a significant amount of their income, especially in times of any unusual expense. In many respects this appears to have been a symbiotic relationship, and in principle the companies accepted their role in bankrolling foreign policy. The connections between the livery companies themselves, their senior members, and the royal court were very close. In part these were commercial – the King, his family, individual courtiers and the court as an entity, were all highly lucrative customers for everyone from mercers and goldsmiths to tallow chandlers and carpenters. Regarding the direct custom of the King and Queen, there was of course strong competition, especially as this often led to becoming a usual supplier. It should be noted that, although the Livery companies fought hard to maintain control over all aspects of their particular trade, this was quite often trumped by the crown. For example, in 1520 Louis de Fava of Bologna was granted a Royal licence to import 1,200 sacks of wool.[3] In theory, duty was levied on all imports, of cloth as well as other goods, and in the 1530s there was trouble when Thomas Cromwell discovered that the Common Packer, a city appointee, had been colluding with foreign merchants to smuggle in imported cloth in return for a bribe. The balance of power between court and city was not always either stable or good tempered.

A striking example of a lasting connection, and perhaps even friendship, between a London merchant and the King is the story of William Lok. By 1507 Lok, a mercer, was providing cloth of silver to Henry VII. By 1527, by now an alderman and sheriff, Lok received an 'exclusive licence to import silks, jewels and mercery wares for Court revels'. Over the preceding twenty years, he built up an international trade, importing not only silks but items such as wine and currants. As he married four times, and had nineteen children, of whom twelve survived him, he become the centre of a wide and influential family, almost tribal, network. This was international in scale, as Lok himself made many trips to Antwerp and to other places in Europe, including Crete. At some stage Lok became interested in the 'new learning', and by the end of the 1520s he appears to have been importing religious books into England. A few years later he was sending reports to Thomas Cromwell from Antwerp, passing on information and commenting on what was being said and done there. In 1534 Lok gained the King's gratitude in a very public way. It was at this time that the Pope finally issued a public declaration, or Bull, excommunicating Henry VIII from the Catholic Church and releasing his subjects from loyalty to him. Copies of the Bull were posted on every church door in mainland western Europe, seeking to humiliate and to stir up rebellion. William Lok, visiting Dunkirk, tore the Bull down from the door of the local church. This was duly reported to the King, who, delighted with Lok's loyalty, rewarded him with an annuity of £110. He was also made a gentleman of the Privy Chamber – a good example of someone of mercantile rather than gentle background being given direct access to the King.

After this, Lok and his family were in even higher favour. His daughter in law, Anne, nee Vaughan, was appointed a silk woman to Anne Boleyn, as was Joan Wilkinson, the widow of another mercer and a member of Lok's circle. Rose, one of Lok's daughters, was to record her memories of the King inviting himself to dinner at her father's house[4] in Bow Lane – this was just one of the many properties he owned locally. Rose herself, who lived to a great age, was to share and further the Protestant sympathies of the family. She went into exile during the reign of Mary I, and wrote her memoir when she was in her eighties so as to place on record her memories of the great changes that took place during her early years. This one example is a clear indication not only of how close and personal were the connections between court and city, but of the extent to which London was a melting pot for anything new. The authorities were fully aware of this, and also of the fact that, once anything new had reached London, it was only a matter of time before whatever it was – fashion, idea or invention – would spread. Thomas Bedyll was to write to Thomas Cromwell: 'London is the common country of all England from which is derived to all parts of the realm all good and ill occurrant there.'[5] The security of London and that of the whole country were dependent on each other – but that did not mean that peace on the streets of the capital was necessarily easy to maintain. Tudor London was evidently a sporadically violent place at the best of times. In less good times, that sporadic violence became something more sustained and more serious.

1516 and early 1517 saw a crescendo of unrest in London, rooted in Londoners' endemic dislike of the many foreign merchants who were resented for the competition they represented. Graffiti appeared on church doors attacking the King and Council for supporting foreigners to take part in the wool trade; the Mercers' Company records claim that a promise was made to 'subdue all strangers that be breakers of the privileges of the city'.[6] By Lent 1517 there were fairly consistent and well-documented attempts to rouse the citizens against the alien merchants, and it is likely that the disturbances that took place on Mayday, the day when a certain amount of misrule among apprentices was accepted, were well planned in advance. The rumours reached the council the day before, and a curfew was declared. What actually took place is described in Hall's 'Chronicle' – a total of up to 1,000 young men, mostly apprentices, thronged through Cheapside and St Paul's churchyard. At St Martin's churchyard, where the usual city regulations did not apply and foreigners had workshops, they broke up buildings and their contents, going on to attack the home of a French merchant, who was able to escape before they could carry out their stated intention of murdering him. In the event, no one was killed in the rioting. However, the King and Council cracked down viciously on the troublemakers, and thirteen, some only children, were executed. The mayor and aldermen, too, afraid of losing their privileges, made anxious apologies. Subsequently there was an elaborately staged charade of penitence by the survivors, and forgiveness by the King. But for the rest of his reign, Henry was to regard London with suspicion.

As it was to turn out, Evil Mayday was the most serious unrest on the streets of London for at least the next half century. However, there was some basis for the nervousness of the King and the council. One cause for concern was the number of beggars and vagrants on the streets. Then, as before and since, London was a magnet for the dispossessed, who came looking for work. Some did indeed find employment, but very many ended up homeless, jobless and on the streets. The authorities accepted that there would always be beggars, and responded, not by organising food or shelter for them, but by giving out an allocation of begging licences for use by those who were 'so impotent, aged, feeble or blind that they be not able to get their livings by labour and work', who 'may not live but only by alms and charity of the people'.[7] In 1518, 821 of these licences were made available for distribution by the aldermen to those in their particular wards who they considered to be deserving. However, no one pretended that this figure represented the total number of the homeless poor, and at intervals efforts were made to clear the streets of London of 'vagabonds being might of body and able to get their living, but live by begging and other men's labour, contrary to the pleasure of God and to diverse Acts of Parliament'.[8] These able-bodied poor were to wear a yellow cloth 'v' to mark them out, and, in September 1518, efforts were made to get them out of London and send them back to where they came from, to help get in the harvest. At intervals the city authorities authorised house-to-house searches for able-bodied vagrants – an indication of how much trouble-making power was ascribed to them.

The foreigners who were so unpopular with many Londoners were certainly present. One estimate[9] is that there were five or six thousand foreign nationals living in London by the mid-sixteenth century. Most of these were 'Dutch', the term given indiscriminately to anyone from present-day Germany or the Low Countries, with significant numbers from France, Spain and Italy. Most of these people lived in separate communities, often around the outskirts of London, generally in the less desirable areas. They were subject to a number of restrictions, especially with regard to what they could buy and sell. The only Londoners who had the full rights of citizenship, allowing them to take part in all aspects of political and economic life, were those who were freemen of a livery company. Next down the pecking order were 'foreigners', who might come from elsewhere in England, and lastly 'aliens' from overseas. So the livery companies, by right of a statute granted by Edward II in 1319, controlled who was, and could become, a Londoner in all senses. The statue ordained that 'every freeman shall be of some mystery or trade,' so citizenship and economic activity went together. Only perhaps half of adult male Londoners were in that position. There is strong evidence that this elitism was bitterly resented by those outside the charmed circle. There is evidence, too, that the King and his Council were also attacking the city's privileges, mostly quietly and by attrition – a request for a Freedom of the City for a Royal appointee here, a Crown grant of rights that cut across that of one of the Great Twelve livery companies there. It did not make for a happy life.

The 1520s was a less than easy decade for London in other respects, as these years featured two appallingly bad harvests (1520 and 1527), with consequent food shortages and sharp price increases. The war with the Holy Roman Empire closed vital international markets to English traders. On top of this was a series of epidemics of plague and of sweating sickness. Bubonic plague was an accepted part of life – there were some cases in most years, and no one knew how or why it was transmitted. Few people recovered, and the disease was regarded as an affliction sent by God. Sweating sickness had appeared only in comparatively recent years; it may have been a particularly virulent form of influenza, probably similar to the Spanish Flu of the 1918-19 outbreak. In each epidemic, a high proportion of those who died were healthy people in their twenties – possibly because the virus caused such a strong immune response that the victims were killed by the resulting catastrophically high temperature. Ironically, those older and younger, with weaker immune systems, were more likely to survive, probably because their bodies took longer to fight the infection. During the 1520s, on several occasions the court, led by the King, fled from the London area so as to avoid disease – in London, infection spread from house to house and hundreds died. The court, too, had its share of cases, and when in June 1528 one of Anne's ladies went down with the illness, Anne went into quarantine at Hever, where she did fall ill, but soon recovered, and the King set off, with a small entourage, on a round of visits to country houses in what were considered safe areas.

By the time the news of the 'King's Great Matter' began to reach the ears of Londoners, probably in the early summer of 1527 when the early annulment hearings were being held in secret, the relationship between sovereign and capital city was already strained. And news of the rumours had in turn spread back to the King, who called in the Lord Mayor and instructed him to 'see that the people should cease of this communication upon pain of the King's high displeasure.'[10] At this point it was being suggested that the plan was for Catherine of Aragon to be discarded in favour of a French princess. If most Londoners had heard of Anne Boleyn at all, they would certainly have assumed she was the latest in the line of Royal mistresses. But as the season wore on, the gossip grew. In July a letter from the King, threatening action against those who spread 'seditious, untrue and slanderous rumours'[11] was circulated to the livery companies.

Sometime around that time, the King wrote to Anne wondering when they would next meet, 'which is better known at London than with any that is about me'.[12] Two things are clear – the Great Matter was the chief topic of conversation in London; and the King had excellent channels of communication to let him know what was being said.

The King should not have been surprised by Londoners' response to the long-delayed opening of the hearing in front of Cardinal Campeggio, the Papal Envoy, in the summer of 1529. According to the chronicler Edward Hall, he had already held a meeting of significant London citizens at the Bridewell Palace late the previous year, only to find his reception less than enthusiastic, ranging from total silence to expressions of concern that the King was so troubled in mind.[13] There was, therefore, nothing secret about the fact that the hearings were going to happen. The return to Bridewell may have been in order to demonstrate beyond doubt the openness of the judicial process and the genuineness of the King's doubts as to the validity of his marriage to Catherine of Aragon. This was the relatively new, but not very large, palace, which stood by the side of the River Fleet, between Fleet Street and the Thames, and which until the mid-1520s had been the King's main residence in what was then the centre of London, and on which he had spent the equivalent of several million pounds. After the fall of Cardinal Wolsey, Henry had lost interest in Bridewell in the excitement of the newly acquired York Place and Hampton Court. However, Bridewell was well appointed and useful – it was the location for the preliminary discussions with Campeggio and his retinue. On 21 June 1529 both the King and Queen attended a hearing in the Great Hall of Blackfriars, which was next door. Famously, this was the occasion on which Catherine of Aragon made a powerful speech, going on her knees before the King and pleading that she was, and always had been, his true and faithful wife. She then rose and walked out of the court, never to return. It is on record that a large crowd had gathered outside the palace to cheer her on – Cardinal Jean du Bellay wrote that the women of London 'did not fail to encourage the queen at her entrance and departure by their cries, telling her to care for nothing and other such words'. This, in addition to her outspoken courage, placed the King at a great disadvantage. However, it did nothing either to reignite his past love for Catherine or to reduce his mistrust of London crowds.

The occasion of this hearing must have become well known in advance, and it is understandable that a crowd gathered and was able to make its collective feelings felt. On many other occasions, significant but almost certainly unscheduled events took place in front of similarly large crowds. For example, when Cardinal Wolsey left York Place for the last time, he was watched by several hundred people. Cavendish, who was an eye witness, described how he:

'took his barge at his privy stairs and so went by water into Putney, where all his horses waited his coming. And at the taking of his barge there was no less than a thousand boats, full of men and women of the City of London waffeting up and down in Thames, expecting my Lord's departing, supposing that he should have gone directly from thence to the Tower, whereat they rejoiced.'

Commentators of the time agree that news travelled at great speed in the city – and this must have been door to door, as friends, neighbours and colleagues told each other what was going on. Inns and alehouses, too, served as information hubs, as of course did shops. That this rapid spread of news is the usual pattern is made clear by the eyewitness accounts of virtually every significant occurrence that took place during this period, including those that cannot have been planned in advance. That news was spread by word of mouth is not surprising in a society where only perhaps half of the population could read, and where printing had been known for only a few decades. However, by the 1530s it had become common for printed pamphlets to appear recording significant events – for example, in 1536, just before they married, the King was to warn Jane Seymour that:

'There is a ballad made lately of great derision against us, which if it go abroad and is seen by you, I pray you to pay no manner of regard to it. I am not at present informed who is the setter forth of this malignant writing; but if he is found he shall be straitly punished for it.'[14]

That the offending ballad was printed, not just being sung on street corners, is made clear by the reference to the possibility of Jane Seymour's seeing, rather than hearing it. This was one of the first of the printed street ballads and pamphlets that were to become highly significant for more than two centuries. Already these forms of dissemination were playing an important part in spreading the views of Martin Luther to a wider audience, in a process that at least one modern writer has likened to that of present-day social media[15] – a writer would present a new idea in the form of a pamphlet, which would be sold and then reprinted by other printers in other towns. This would often be accompanied by news ballads – a famous tune would generally be given new words written to publicise a person or event. It is highly likely that such pamphlets and ballads telling versions of the story of the King and Anne Boleyn went the rounds of Europe in the late 1520s and 30s, and that at least some were circulating in London. Within a few years the pamphlet and ballad, with attendant sellers and singers, had become a familiar part of London life. Within a decade of the ballad about the King and Jane Seymour (alas that the text does not appear to survive), Anne Askew's own account of her life, arrest and torture in the Tower of London was smuggled out of her prison and then published – Askew, a protestant, was the only woman who is known to have been tortured in the Tower, and was then condemned and burned for heresy. Her story had become famous long before the publication of Foxe's Book of Martyrs later in the century.

Although the unrest of Evil Mayday was never repeated on anything like the same scale, there are references to, and rumours of, at least two public demonstrations against Anne Boleyn. They appear to have been very different in character, but share the important characteristic that both involved women only. As long ago as late 1528 when the King met with a group of influential citizens to talk about the Great Matter, Edward Hall reported that 'the common people, being ignorant of the truth, and in especial women and other that favoured the queen, talked largely.'[16]

The first of the reported demonstrations is said to have taken place in November 1531, and to have taken the form of an attack by a group of women on a 'pleasure house' where Anne Boleyn was dining with friends, somewhere in London. The rumour, by the time it reached the Venetian ambassador, Ludivico Falier, was of 8,000 women, and possibly some men dressed as women, storming the house with murderous intent, and of Anne only escaping because she was warned just in time. The second, at Greenwich and after Anne become Queen, happened while she and Henry were away on summer progress, and apparently took the form of a public but non-violent demonstration against Anne in favour of restoring Mary as heir presumptive to the throne. It was led by, among others, Anne's sister in law, Jane Rochford, and her aunt by marriage, Lady William Howard, as well as a number of unnamed wives of London citizens (which makes them wives of Freemen or men of higher status). The two ringleaders were briefly imprisoned in the Tower and then banished from Court, but Chapuys, reported that the whole matter had again been hushed up as being 'a thing done by women'. As neither the Venetian ambassador nor Chapuys had witnessed the occurrence on which they reported, it is impossible to be sure how seriously to take either report. The first could be anything from a small group of women shouting abuse in the street to a coherent and organised attack; the second, anything from, again, a small group cheering Mary Tudor to some form of mass picket, possibly of a church service.

Subsequent commentators have based a great many suppositions about the hatred of the London population for Anne on these two uncorroborated reports, adding to them by taking at face value Chapuys' disparaging comments about how Anne was received by the crowds at her coronation. However, while a certain degree of scepticism is probably in order, it does seem likely that these particular puffs of smoke did represent fire of some sort. Earlier in November 1531, the Venetian ambassador had already been reporting that there was a possibility of an uprising in favour of Catherine of Aragon, 'her majesty being so loved and respected that the people already commence murmuring'.[17] There is, however, no indication as to whether this 'murmuring' was directed gainst Anne personally. We also know of a small assortment of prosecutions of people who spoke against Anne – for example, the Abbot of Whitby was indicted in March 1532 for calling her a 'common stewed whore' (meaning he regarded her as a professional prostitute). In 1533, two unnamed women were beaten and banished from London for life for saying that Catherine, and not Anne, was the true Queen[18] And, most persuasively, there is strong evidence of the King's, and his Council's, efforts to eliminate even a whisper of public opposition. When Anne was first prayed for as Queen at Easter 1533 and, at Austin Friars, many of the congregation left in protest, both the Venetian ambassador and Chapuys were told that the King sent for the Lord Mayor and ordered that there was to be no more trouble, on pain of 'extreme punishment'.[19] All over the country, but especially in London, there were rumours of antagonism to the King's divorce and remarriage, and consequent hostility to Anne. It should be acknowledged that these events were taking place before Thomas Cromwell's spy network was quite as pervasive and as effective as it was to become in the next few years. By 1533, and for the rest of the decade, we may be reasonably sure that Cromwell was aware of most of what was being said and done, certainly in London and usually at court.

Thomas Cromwell, who was one of those best placed to discover the truth of such reports, is probably more talked about at the time of writing than he has ever been since his lifetime. One of the most divisive of historical figures, his reputation has ranged from the somewhat chilly respect accorded by those who have acknowledged his abilities as a policy maker and administrator, to the contempt of the historians who regard him as a political thug and serial destroyer. Famously, it has taken the nuanced and attractive figure portrayed by Hilary Mantel in her historical novels *Wolf Hall* and *Bring up the Bodies* to reinvent him as a thinking and feeling man, a view reinforced by Mark Rylance's television portrayal. However, any doubt as to the width of the gap between the character evoked in these excellent works of fiction, and the Thomas Cromwell who lived and died nearly five centuries ago, is soon removed by comparing the sensibilities suggested by the candle-lit close-ups of Mark Rylance with the Holbein portrait of the real man. Thomas Cromwell was born in what was then the village of Putney, the son of a man who is variously described as a blacksmith and a brewer. Many of the more aristocratic members of the King's Council were to claim he had risen from the gutter, and there were many rumours about the violence, drunkenness and the general undesirability of Cromwell's father. In reality, however, the family was middle ranking, originally from Nottinghamshire; Thomas' grandfather, John Cromwell, had moved south in about 1460 to take possession of a fulling mill. John Cromwell settled down to a life in the wool processing business, married and had children, among whom was Walter, who was to become the father of Thomas.

Although Walter Cromwell, like many men of his time, was involved in an assortment of court cases, he was also a man of some standing in his local community, holding the office of parish constable. He kept sheep, probably continued with the wool fulling business and kept at least one alehouse. It is true, however, that Thomas, who was born around 1485, left home at the age of fifteen or sixteen, probably running away and possibly stowing away on a ship, and spent a number of years in Italy and the Low Countries, first as a mercenary in the French army. He arrived in Florence in 1503, a penniless fugitive, but was taken on by a member of the Frescobaldi banking family. In later years he was to describe his youthful self as a 'ruffian' – but when he returned to England it was with invaluable experience of military and mercantile life. He may also have brought back an interest in, and perhaps a sympathy with, religious reform. At some stage along the way Cromwell had acquired legal knowledge and possibly training, and by around 1518 he was practising as an attorney in London. He had married a lady named Elizabeth Wykys, who came from a gentry family, and with whom he was to have three children. By 1522 Cromwell was being referred to as a gentleman, and his most important client was Cardinal Wolsey. By the next year Cromwell was an MP – we do not know for which constituency, but it is likely that his election had been engineered by Wolsey. He was also a man of some wealth, having interests in the wool trade as well as in the law, and also seems to have operated as a money lender.

In 1523 Thomas Cromwell and his family were living in the substantial house at Austin Friars that was, by now, his main home. The house was part of a large monastic complex in Broad Street, close to what is now the Bank of England. The friars' lands covered some 5½ acres, and they followed the very common practice of raising extra cash by leasing some of their property for building purposes. The Cromwells' was one of several houses in the site, and was fairly substantial, including two parlours and a large kitchen – it was built on three floors, and had a total of fourteen rooms. The garden is still in existence, and now belongs to the Drapers' Company. An inventory taken in 1527 provides a vivid picture of the luxurious style in which Cromwell lived – his possessions included a generous supply of expensive furniture, textiles, household goods and jewellery, with the most impressive items on display in the hall that was the main reception room. The focal point must have been the 'great gilt chair' on which, as master of the house, Cromwell himself sat, arrayed in one of the sixteen doublets he is listed as having owned. Even by this date, some years before he came into prominence at court, Cromwell was operating at the centre of a highly successful personal empire. He entertained friends very frequently, and his household accounts show that he made regular payments to a group of musicians as well as a theatre company – 'Lord Cromwell's Players', as they were subsequently known, went on tour as well as entertaining his own guests.[20]

Among the immediate neighbours were the philosopher Erasmus, Eustace Chapuys, the Imperial Amasssador, and the father of John Stow, the author of the *Survey of London* that was published in the 1590s. We know little of whether Cromwell and Erasmus saw anything of one another, but his relations with both Stow and Chapuys are enlightening. In the case of Stow, if the story is true, we are seeing Cromwell at his worst. According to the account written by Stow's son, Cromwell had begun to buy up leases on other properties near his own, including a large plot of land so that he could extend his garden as well as build extra rooms onto his house. However, not satisfied with what he had purchased, Cromwell ordered his servants to move the fences of his neighbours' gardens back by twenty-two feet so that his own holdings should be increased – evidently he gave neither warning of, nor compensation for, this. He then followed this up by ordering for the house of Thomas Stow to be put on rollers, and began to build an extension of his own on the land thus vacated. John Stow was to write that all this had taken place:

> 'ere my Father heard thereof: no warning was given him, nor any other answer when he spake to the surveyors of that work but that their master Sir Thomas commanded them so to do.'

Stow also wrote that his father and his neighbours could get nothing done in the matter, and ended up having to pay their original rent for the reduced amount of land left to them. As Stow observed, 'The sudden rising of some men, causeth them to forget themselves.'[21] This occurrence was in 1532 – by then, Cromwell was of high enough status to inhibit those around him from arguing with anything he might choose to do.

Cromwell's relations with Eustace Chapuys were more amiable – over the succeeding years, the two saw a good deal of each other, and although their respective political allegiances and agendas meant they could never be friends, it is clear they developed a mutual understanding and respect. This was before the days of official residences for ambassadors, who had to make their own arrangements for lodgings in whichever city they were posted. An experienced lawyer as well as a professional diplomat, Chapuys was chosen for his new role in 1529 when the 'Great Matter' was nearing its height, owing his appointment to Charles V's hope that he could provide Catherine of Aragon with useful legal advice to help stop the King from finding a way to end their marriage. In this Chapuys failed, although hardly by his own fault – it would certainly have taken something more powerful than diplomatic or legal advice to have made any difference by this stage in events. This did not, of course, stop Chapuys from doing his best – and, hampered by the fact that he spoke almost no English and had a limited budget, he settled down and began to set up a network of informers to keep him up to date with events at court and in London. In order to do this, he needed an insider in each significant household. This was well within the parameters of how information was obtained at this time. However, Chapuys was also hampered by his own prejudices – he quickly became very fond of Catherine of Aragon, who came to trust and regard him as a loyal ally. Chapuys took up the position that the King was 'not ill natured', and that everything he was doing with regard to ending his marriage was being brought about by the influence, mostly of Anne Boleyn herself, and to some extent of her relatives and allies. Although, when he arrived in London in September 1529, Chapuys sent detailed reports about his reception at Court, he says only that he has taken up residence in London – there is no mention of how the accommodation was found and by whom. It seems very possible, however, that, even at this relatively early stage of Cromwell's rise in the world, he may have had a brief to oversee Chapuys' movements. This is speculation – but that the newly appointed and highly influential ambassador came to live virtually next door to Cromwell by coincidence, seems unlikely.

This possibility is reinforced by the fact that there is strong evidence that while he was first working as a lawyer and then working virtually exclusively for Wolsey, Cromwell was building up the network of informers that were to stand him, and the King, in such good stead in later years. He was also building up a substantial property portfolio, buying a house in Stepney and another in Hackney – most of his acquisitions were in London, the furthest afield being a house and estate at Ewhurst in Surrey. When, in 1534, he was appointed the Master of the Rolls – one of the highest legal appointments in the land – he also acquired an official residence, the Rolls House in Chancery Lane. While he does not seem to have lived there, he certainly filled it with his staff, and the place operated like a mini court, filled all day with Cromwell's people and a constant population of place seekers, supplicants and ambassadors. Like Wolsey before him, Cromwell worked phenomenally long hours, helped by his small personal staff, headed by Ralph Sadleir. It is often said that Cromwell was universally hated, but this may not have been true in London – the author of the (admittedly often unreliable) *Spanish Chronicle*, records that Cromwell was greatly loved by the people of the city. There is also at least one letter which acknowledges that he made regular gifts to London charities.[22] After his execution in 1540, all but one of the extant ballads commenting on the event mourn him as a friend of the common people. There is a case to be made for arguing that Cromwell died in part because he never managed to become a courtier. It is evident that London was his home water, and that he swam there far more easily than at court.

It would be unfair to claim that the reverse was true of the Boleyns – but there is a possibility that the lack of a real power base in London caused Anne Boleyn difficulties. Geoffrey Boleyn, Anne's great grandfather, made a resounding success of his London career. Although he almost certainly had London contacts to start him off, Geoffrey rose several social and economic notches on his way from Norfolk hatter to Lord Mayor of London. As part of this he certainly acquired a London powerbase – he would not have been elected Lord Mayor by his fellow Aldermen without one – and London property to go with it. In the fifteenth century, as long after, Lord Mayors were expected to use their own homes for official purposes. Sadly we do not know exactly where that house was, but as Sir Geoffrey was buried in London, it is likely that he died there. This, in turn, suggests that he was spending a significant amount of time in his London home. As Geoffrey's son, William, spent most of his life in Norfolk, leaving instructions that his body was to be buried in Norwich Cathedral, it is likely that, for William's son Thomas, London was a relatively unfamiliar place. The Boleyns may, of course, have maintained contact with London friends and relatives, but they do not appear to have had any London-based family or close friends.

The Howards, the family into which Thomas married, had a London home, Norfolk House, in Lambeth. It was a large property set in extensive gardens, and there were a number of Howard family tombs in the local church, St Mary's, now the Garden Museum. That Elizabeth Howard maintained close links with her own family after she married Thomas Boleyn is demonstrated by the fact that she was one day to be buried in the Howard Chapel at St Mary's, Lambeth. If Anne Boleyn spent time in London as a child, it was probably at her mother's childhood home. However, it is probably more likely that she spent most of her time at Hever, where the Boleyns appear to have made their main home after the death of Anne's grandfather, William, in 1505. For aristocratic and gentry families, it was usual to keep children in what was regarded as the healthier air of the countryside, even if this was far from their parents.

The Boleyn children would certainly have been looked after mostly by servants, in a nursery presided over by Mrs Mary Orchard, who was to remain a part of Anne's life right through to the end. Although women of the status of Lady Elizabeth Boleyn were not expected to be quite such long-distance mothers as queens (who often spent months without being under the same roof as their children), neither would they necessarily expect to undertake much of the day-to-day care of their families.

When Anne Boleyn returned to England in 1522, it is quite possible that she had never before visited London. As we have seen, she was now a professional courtier of many years' standing – which naturally stood her in good stead for her new life at the English court. She was clearly more than capable of operating in that world, having all the necessary skills and instincts. However, when she became a figure of significance beyond court, and as soon as there was a serious possibility she might become Queen, Anne needed to be able to communicate with people and networks outside her own circle. This, of course, if we are to accept the view that she was actively involved with the Great Matter rather than waiting, patiently or otherwise, for the King to determine her future. In this she was in some respects hampered by the fact she was a woman, and there were some places which were male preserves. For example, in Parliament she was dependent on the official channels. In and around London, however, Anne and her family and supporters needed to network, and to do so effectively. Some things she could do herself; other kinds of work needed other hands.

From the sources available – and in this, as in so much else, the evidence is sketchy – the Boleyn faction was stronger at court than it was in London. As we have seen, the Boleyn family was relatively small, and the nature of Thomas Boleyn's international career meant that his contacts were largely either at court or overseas. So far as is known, it was not until Thomas was given the use of Durham Place, one of the greatest of the mansions that fringed the south side of the Strand, that the family had a London base. This one had started life in the thirteenth century as the palace of the Bishops of Durham, and technically, this is what it still was – but Cardinal Wolsey had negotiated the use of it, and on his fall the bishop had failed to secure its return. So, in 1529 Foxe tells us that Thomas Boleyn had the use of the house, where he was hosting Thomas Cranmer, then still an academic on sabbatical, while he had peace and quiet to write a paper telling 'his minde concerning the kings question'. This has given rise to a suggestion that Anne herself was chairing regular meetings of a 'think tank' at this period, devoted to finding ways through the divorce crisis. The idea of Anne in such a position of intellectual leadership is, of course, very attractive in the present day – but without further evidence we do not know if it has any basis in fact. What we do know is that the house, in effect, became the Boleyn faction's headquarters, and that Anne spent time there between 1529 and her marriage.

Anne's brother, George, was certainly her chief ally throughout both their lives. As already discussed, the brother and sister may well not have met at all between 1514, when Anne left the country for the court of Margaret of Austria, and June 1520, when the Field of the Cloth of Gold almost certainly provided a rare opportunity for Thomas, Elizabeth, the newly married Mary, Anne and George to be together. Whether that opportunity was welcome to all of them we have no way of knowing. At the time of Anne's return, George, then aged about eighteen, had probably just returned to court after putting in some time at Oxford but without taking a degree (not unusual at the time). In 1522 George and his father shared the grant of some minor official appointments in Kent,[23] which probably marked the beginning of his independent career – and in 1524 he acquired the manor of Grimston in Norfolk, giving him a country home. From 1525 onwards George appears regularly in the records, receiving a series of court appointments plus a small additional annuity. As Anne's relationship with the King became closer, so more favour came George's way. He became Keeper of the Palace of Beaulieu in Essex and, in 1529, was appointed Keeper of Bedlam, (St Mary's Hospital).

At this time the Hospital of St Mary of Bethlehem had been in existence for some 300 years. It had been founded by the Bishop of Bethlehem, with the help of the Mayor and Sheriffs, as a centre for fundraising for the Crusades and as a hospital in its mediaeval sense as a place of hospitality. Its use as a specialist hospital for the insane appears to have evolved over time – the first definite mentions of this function date from the fifteenth century, and by the time Tyndale was writing, the term 'Bedlamite' was synonymous with 'lunatic'[24] By the time of George Boleyn's appointment, the Crown had won a series of tussles over who had the right to appoint a secular Master, and the main official purpose of the place was to house and restrain (certainly not treat) the insane. A visitation in the mid-fifteenth century mentions around a dozen inmates, most of whom were restrained with manacles. The hospital occupied a site in Bishopsgate Street, close to what is now Liverpool Street Station – maps of the time show a series of stone buildings and a church on a spacious site including what may be gardens. It is sometimes said that the appointment was a sinecure, and it is almost certainly true that George did not have to involve himself in the administration of the hospital. However, it is also true that his position would have certainly given him an excuse, and possibly a need, to be on the premises.

We know that George Boleyn lost no opportunity of discussing religious reform – Chapuys complained bitterly about this.[25] George's various overseas diplomatic missions gave him ample opportunities to make overseas contacts and to bring back books that would have been risky for a lesser person to import. As we have seen, the cheaply printed French evangelical books, which George translated, had decorated, rebound and then presented to Anne, are probably an example of his imports, and certainly of their mutual interests. We know, too, that these interests were well known in reformist circles in London, which, in the late 1520s, were still operating at least semi-illegally, with frequent prosecutions for heresy, enthusiastically pursued by Thomas More. When Simon Fish, at that time in hiding in London, published his *Supplication for Beggars* in 1528, he knew that by sending a copy to Anne he was choosing the surest route to place his ideas before the King. Ever since the time of the Lollards, those who wanted to discuss new, and possibly subversive, religious ideas, had done so in secret, in the houses of sympathisers – and now, very possibly, at Bedlam. George Boleyn himself was already a privileged person, but this did not extend to many of those with whom he would have been in touch. When Thomas More was appointed Chancellor in 1529, his highest priority was to protect the Church from what he perceived as heresy – and he pursued his policy of persecution with added vigour because he knew the new ideas were gaining ground in London. However, like most sensible persecutors, he attacked mostly those who could not fight back – the poor and the simple. Although More's appointment related to the whole country, he seems to have concentrated his energy on seeking out London-based heretics, and joined with John Stokesley, the newly appointed Bishop of London, to do so.

More, Stokesley and their allies concentrated much of their energies on destroying religious books, especially Tyndale's New Testament in English. On one occasion their agents bought up a whole edition of the Testament, and the books were ceremonially burned at Paul's Cross, outside St Paul's Cathedral. The net result of this was to provide Tyndale with the money to print another, larger edition, much of which evidently found its way to London. It is clear that, if you had the right contacts, it was quite easy to buy imported religious books at this time. Although for obvious reasons people who were bringing them into the country were not doing so openly, it is a fair inference that certainly George Boleyn, and possibly Thomas, were promoting this trade. It is probably fair, too, to assume that certainly Durham House and possibly Bedlam were being used as meeting places by those interested in the New Learning. This had to be done very quietly – More and his allies were doing all they could do stop the spread of what they regarded as the ruin of the Church. For example, after the King and Anne Boleyn had read and discussed his work, Simon Fish was arrested and kept in prison for over two years in appalling conditions. Neither the King nor the Boleyns were prepared to be seen to help him.

Not everyone interested in the New Learning was necessarily a Boleyn ally – for example, Tyndale himself published an article making it clear he did not believe there was any theological reason that the King's marriage to Catherine of Aragon should be regarded as invalid. However, it was in these circles that many of the Boleyns' allies were to be found. At this time they were also the circles where Thomas Cromwell operated, and, for the most part, their interests were the same. It used to be assumed the

Boleyns and Cromwell were friends by choice and, that once she became Queen, Cromwell was loyal to Anne because he owed at least some of his rise in the world to her. More recently some historians have suggested that this was much more of a pragmatic alliance of shared interests. We can certainly be sure that Cromwell's London network of places and people was deeper rooted and more extensive than anything available to Anne. London was home territory to Cromwell in a way it could never be to Anne; the reverse was true at court. In order to survive for long in the pitiless world of Tudor power politics, you needed to be able to operate effectively in these two disparate worlds – that, of course, in addition to pleasing the King without annoying or boring him. An impossibly tall order.

Chapter 6

Earthly Powers: Court

The Tudor court was not just a place, or even several places – it had more the nature of a planetary system, constantly on the move, with the King at the centre, and with the courtiers and hangers-on circling him in different orbits, some closer, some further out, some elliptical. Court was not only where the King was, but was the centre of government, of influence and of favour. Monarchy was highly personal, and much, if not everything, depended on the monarch as law-giver, head of the household, centre of every client and factional network, and arbiter of behaviour. In theory the Queen's orbit and influence were of a different kind – but that depended on the queen. A queen consort had her own 'Queen's Side' of court, with a separate parallel household, not only of ladies in waiting but of male officials, too. No one knows exactly how many people had court appointments, but one recent estimate[1] gives the figure at around 1,000 – this at a time when the population of London was less than 100,000, and that of York, probably around 10,000. This vast group of people moved house several times a year – partly because no neighbourhood could keep them in food for long, partly, too, because of the strain placed on the water supply and sewage disposal systems in each palace in turn. In addition, the King needed to be seen, in all his magnificence, by as many of his subjects as possible.

The Tudors were sophisticated exponents of political spin. This is famously so of Henry VIII and his daughter, Elizabeth I. That this applies also to Henry VII is beyond doubt. The evidence survives – one piece has been recently rediscovered, in the shape of the so-called Bed of Roses, which reappeared in 2014 after years in a Chester hotel. After initial doubts, it now seems that this really is the marriage bed made for Henry VII and Elizabeth of York in 1486. The intricately carved oak bed head, originally brightly painted, features two figures – Adam and Eve, Christ and Mary, Henry and Elizabeth – who are joining right hands. Between them the Serpent presides, but they are surrounded with the imagery of salvation. Christ is represented by a daisy, Mary by a marigold. The bed also includes the coats of arms of the bride and groom, together with a wide variety of emblems that held iconographic significance at the time. The theme is, of course, salvation – the Biblical fall has already been redeemed by Christ and His mother, but the people of England now need Henry and Elizabeth to save them from civil war. There is just enough resemblance between the carved figures and the known portraits of the royal pair to give everyone the idea. And any question as to whether a marriage bed was a public enough object to be an effective place to depict propaganda of this kind is answered by the consideration that the bed apparently spent several years during their marriage on view in the Painted Chamber at Westminster. Sixteenth-century ceremonial royal bedrooms were rarely very private places. Apart from the personal attendants of the King or Queen, the rooms were used for entertaining high status guests. This one piece of furniture, which appears to have survived because of a series of unlikely lucky chances, demonstrates that the royal preoccupation with image existed in an advanced stage before the turn of the sixteenth century. In the present day, Henry VII does not have the reputation for taking much care over how his regime was perceived – evidently that should change. It was a preoccupation he was, of course, to pass on to his successor.

Henry VIII had had, for a prince of his time, a fairly sheltered upbringing. As the second son he did not figure at Court as his elder brother, Arthur, did. There is some evidence that Henry was intended for a career in the Church;[2] whatever the truth of this, he continued to spend much of his time with his mother, Elizabeth of York, and sisters, Margaret and Mary – Margaret married James IV of Scotland in 1503 and thereafter was no longer part of the family picture. Henry was still only eleven when Arthur died in 1502 at the age of fifteen, a few months after his marriage to Catherine of Aragon. Elizabeth of York then undertook the risk of a pregnancy in her late thirties – at that time considered an advanced age for a new mother – and died the next year along with her newborn daughter. Henry VII's response to these personal and dynastic tragedies was to keep Henry, his only remaining son under close supervision. The Prince's academic education had not been neglected – when Erasmus was taken to visit the Royal children at Eltham in 1499, he was much impressed by their attainments, and in later years he was to call Henry a 'universal genius'. Even deducting something for well-aimed flattery, this suggests the future King was no fool in academic terms. He also had tutors in music and in sporting and athletic fields – but even when he was fifteen, which according to the ideas of his day was close to adulthood, observers noted that he spent most of his time in a room that led off his father's bedchamber, was not allowed out except in the company of a few designated persons, and was discouraged by his father from speaking when there were outsiders present. This did not mean his father was not training him to take over in due course; he was, however, keeping his son on a very short rein.

As time went on the young Henry began to appear on selected public occasions. One of these was in 1506 when the Archduke Philip of Burgundy and his wife, Juana of Castile, made an unplanned and involuntary visit to England. Their ship was caught in a storm as they were on the way to Spain and they took refuge on the English coast near Portland. Henry VII greeted them with lavish hospitality, preparatory to driving a hard bargain over a treaty in which the two monarchs agreed an alliance against the French. Prince Henry was sent to Winchester at the head of the party to greet Philip and Juana and escort them to Windsor, and thereafter took part in, or was at least on display at, the summit conference interspersed with lavish entertainment that ensued. On one occasion the two kings and the prince dined alone so that they could continue their discussions without witnesses. However, it appears that Prince Henry was still not allowed to take part in the dangerous sport of jousting, with which he appears to have been obsessed. He was allowed to take part in the practice version, running at the ring,[3] but it appears that the King was not prepared to risk his only son in the tournament, during which participants, in full armour, rode full-tilt at each other with lances. There were regular casualties, and some deaths, so this caution is understandable, but equally understandable is that the Prince's participation in jousting was merely postponed: one day he would make up his own mind.

Perhaps Henry VII believed he would live longer than he did – until a few weeks before his death he was talking of recovery. He had suffered a severe throat infection in early 1507, and, although he was able to resume most activities, he was never really well again. In the final months of his life, Henry VII appears to have kept his son closer than ever – it seems likely his intention was to train his successor in statecraft. The Prince had some attendants of his own, including the learned Lord Mountjoy, and in the final months of his father's life there is some evidence he was allowed contact with a wider circle. But when the King lost his hold on life in April 1509, he left a successor who, although he was nearly 18 years old, tall, handsome, well educated, musical and athletic, had been allowed comparatively little opportunity to learn the statecraft and judgement he would need as King. Given this, and given how little the younger Henry had been able to see even of the court, let alone the outside world in which he would have to operate, he did remarkably well. He ensured the support of much of the nobility by the immediate arrest of his father's two most hated councillors, Empson and Dudley, who had been responsible for taxation policies that amounted to extortion in the last years of the reign. It was his Council, inherited from his father, that made the suggestion he issue a General Pardon, helping the accession of the new young king seem like a liberation from tyranny.

It is perhaps surprising that Henry did not go further out of emotional control than he did in his early years as King. A late adolescent, freed, after years of over protection, of all restraint, might well have gone totally off the rails: Henry VIII appears to have confined himself largely to high-risk sports, drinking and a certain amount of sexual roistering. Some of the credit for this probably belongs to his early marriage to Catherine of Aragon. Henry and Catherine had been in an on-again, off-again betrothal ever since Arthur's death. A Papal dispensation had had to be obtained, as Catherine and Henry counted as brother and sister in the eyes of the Church – marriage ties were considered the same as blood ones. In the case of high status people this could be, and was, negotiable, but there were questions about whether the marriage had been consummated – several witnesses attested to the fact that Arthur and Catherine had often shared a bed during their three months of marriage, but Catherine swore she was still a virgin. Equally importantly, Henry VII had hesitated when negotiations over the financial settlement proved difficult and because Catherine's mother had died. Catherine, the daughter of the King and Queen of both Aragon and Castile, was a much more eligible bride than Catherine, the daughter of Ferdinand of Aragon only. The younger Henry had, under instruction, repudiated the betrothal that had been negotiated in his name as soon as he was of an age to do so; negotiations had been somewhat half-heartedly resumed thereafter, and the matter was unresolved at the time of the death of Henry VII. Some sources claimed that it was the old King's dying wish that his son should marry Catherine, but it is much more likely that the wishes were the new King's own. At the time of the marriage there were some doubts as to its legality, but the final negotiations between the Spanish ambassador and the Council took place before the old King's funeral.[4]

Henry and Catherine were married, with only two witnesses, in June 1509. The celebrations were reserved for their joint coronation, which took place later that summer. To begin with, the marriage was happy. Catherine was small, pretty, auburn haired, educated, intelligent and devout. She was 23 years old to Henry's 18, but at this time, when they were both so young, the age gap neither showed nor seemed especially significant – and each of them had siblings, so no one doubted that they would soon have children. Catherine appears to have settled happily into her new role as Queen. Henry VII's mother, Margaret Beaufort, had laid many of the ground rules of Court protocol; she had been omnipresent all through her son's reign. Known as 'My lady the King's mother', her status had been very little below that of the Queen, her daughter in law – when her son became King, Margaret began to sign herself 'Margaret R' – and, in the early years at least, her influence had been considerably greater. Margaret died only a few days after her grandson's coronation, but among her legacies was her rulebook covering the etiquette of most occasions of Royal life, from the proper way to organise the confinement of a queen to shopping lists. Her directions were to be observed for the whole of Henry VIII's reign – but it may well be that the lives of both her grandson and his wife were made easier by her departure. There is no evidence about how Henry felt about his grandmother – but with her passing, the break with his childhood was complete.

No matter where the Court was, there was provision for a separate King's and Queen's side. There is more specific evidence about the way that of the King's worked – but that, as others have pointed out, is mostly to do with the sexism of history. In fact, the Queen had a set of rooms, and of staff, that mirrored those of the King. The Queen too had a sequence of chambers, beginning with a public room where anyone who appeared decently dressed could go, passing on to a presence chamber and thence to a bedroom and more private rooms, usually including a private chapel, beyond. The King and Queen shared use of a privy kitchen in most Court locations – this meant that they could eat in private at whatever time suited them. The Queen also had her own wardrobe arrangements, accounting system, barge and stables. Her household included a significant number of male servants, headed by her own Lord Chamberlain, and including ushers, grooms and pages of her Privy Chamber, which operated independently of that of the King. The Eltham Ordinances of 1526, as well as the earlier ordinances issued during the previous reign, make it clear that the two sides operated separately, with many functions being duplicated. The closest modern parallel is probably to departments within a campus university.

'The Queen's ladies' is a term taking in women of many different kinds of status and levels of commitment to a life at Court. Soon after her coronation, Catherine of Aragon had thirty-three aristocratic women in her household, of whom eighteen were the daughters of peers. These included the ladies who were making a career of serving the Queen as well as some who were there more occasionally because of the status of their husband or father. Catherine herself chose the women she wanted to have around her – unsurprising given the long hours they all spent in each other's company. As there were far more willing ladies and young girls of the right status than there were places, the Queen, like other queens, could afford to be selective. On the face of it, the rewards were modest and the outlay in clothes and equipment vast. However, the Queen's women were amply repaid in both goods and influence. The Queen, and sometimes the King too, would often give presents, generally of expensive fabric, to her women. And they were on hand to secure the favours that usually went to those close to the sovereign.

After Queen Catherine, the lady of highest status in the early days of the reign was Mary, the sister of the King. The two remained very close, and were in some respects quite similar; both had musical ability, red-gold hair and a ruthless determination to have their own way. However, as Catherine of Aragon already knew at first hand, it was the destiny of the female relatives of kings at this time to be pawns in the game of international diplomacy, their marriages bargained over in terms of both political and financial advantage. Mary had been destined for marriage with the Emperor Charles V, who was understandably furious when Henry backed out of the agreement in favour of an alliance with the French. The price of this was marrying the teenage Mary to the chronically ill fifty-something King Louis XII of France. It appears that Henry and Mary came to an arrangement over this ill-assorted match: Mary would go through with this marriage, and in return, when her almost inevitable early widowhood came to pass, she would choose her next husband for herself.[5] Along with a stock of magnificent jewels, eighteen dresses in the English style, five in the Milanese and £10 13s 4d worth of stockings, Mary took with her to France a suitable complement of ladies. The Venetian ambassador reported that the English court was full of people learning French in the hope of a place – and Thomas Boleyn was doubly successful, as both of his daughters were among those chosen. Indeed, it was reported that Mary had specifically asked for Anne Boleyn because of her linguistic abilities. After a proxy marriage, the new Queen of France and her party set out in great splendour in November 1515. After a horrendous winter Channel crossing, Mary's coronation and its attendant celebrations were an international success. As she and her entourage made their way into Paris, they were presented with a series of welcoming mini-performances and tableaux, from a presentation featuring King Solomon and the Queen of Sheba being blessed by God to a model walled city enclosing a rose bush with mechanical stems growing towards a lily. The highly elaborate and expensive displays were calculated to impress not only the young Queen and her entourage, but the whole of Europe too, as indeed they appear to have done. Evidently, too, the French were equally impressed with their glamorous new Queen; and the increasingly frail King wrote ecstatic letters to his new brother in law about his happiness with his bride.

However, most of that entourage were back in London after only a few weeks, as the King of France dismissed all but six of his wife's ladies, replacing them with French women so as to reduce English influence over his new wife. The Boleyn girls were among those allowed to remain, but there is some evidence that the young Queen felt out of her depth without any trusted older women to advise her. How she would have adapted can never be known – at Christmas 1514 all appeared well, and King Louis wrote yet another letter describing how happy he was with her. On New Year's Day 1515, however, he died suddenly. As soon as the news crossed the Channel Henry sent three ambassadors, including Charles Brandon, Duke of Suffolk, to comfort his sister, who was going through the mourning ritual expected of French Royal widows, who remained in isolation for forty days in a darkened room, with only their women for company. Part of the point of this was to establish if the widow was pregnant. Once she could emerge from strict isolation, Mary lost no time in marrying Suffolk, with whom she had already been in love, consulting no one and informing the world only after the event. In doing this she showed considerable ruthless good sense, as her brother's promise might well not have held good had he had the chance to consider what a very useful matrimonial prize his sister again represented.

Thereafter, once they had made their peace with Henry, Mary and her new husband were important figures at the English Court. The new Duchess of Suffolk continued to be known as the French Queen; still only in her teens, she was famed for her looks as much as her high status. Although Henry was seriously annoyed with both her and the Duke for marrying in such a scandalous fashion, he allowed himself to be mollified – and bought off. Part of the price of reconciliation was a share of the jewellery that Mary had been given as Queen of France and that she quietly brought home with her – a vast diamond, known as the Mirror of Naples, now became the property of Henry. Additionally, the Duke was required to hand over large sums of money to buy the goodwill of his old friend and new brother in law. The French Queen had a household of her own at Court – she also had a large household at her main country home, Westhorpe Hall in Suffolk. It was laid down in ordinances issued at various times just how many attendants a courtier of a particular status was allowed – for the sister of the King, the number is likely to have been considerable, and in this may lie the answer to the mystery of where Mary Boleyn, sister of Anne, was in the years after Mary Tudor returned to England and before we hear of the marriage to William Carey. We know Anne stayed in France in the household of the new Queen, but there is no mention of her sister, Mary, having done so. Records of the time are incomplete, and it is very possible that Mary Boleyn returned home the way she had arrived. Another possibility is that Mary Boleyn was a member of the household of another court lady. Aristocratic women were allowed a staff of waiting gentlewomen of their own.

By the 1520s, the King's favourite homes within reach of London were Greenwich and Richmond, with some time also spent at Windsor. Henry VII had renamed the Palace of Sheen as Richmond after his own title when he came to the throne – the area that is now known as East Sheen was not so called until the nineteenth century. By this date the Royal apartments at the Tower of London had fallen out of favour as too old-fashioned, and the centrally-situated Bridewell Palace, near Blackfriars, was considered too small. At Westminster, the mediaeval Privy Palace (of which the Jewel Tower still survives) was badly damaged by fire in 1512, leaving the King with effectively no adequate accommodation in that area. It was not until the fall of Cardinal Wolsey in 1529 that Henry was able to acquire York Place, which historically had been the London home of the archbishops of York – when it fell into the hands of the King, it had been the London base of Cardinal Wolsey, who had spent vast sums of money on improving it and on acquiring superb furniture, paintings and tapestries. Henry acquired at a very early age what was to be a life-long preoccupation with acquiring and improving property.

To the south there was Eltham Palace, which was somewhat small and not accessible by water. As the reign went on, this and other less-favoured houses were used as nursery palaces for the King's children. There were a number of these at a similar distance from London – far enough away to be regarded as healthier, close enough to be accessible. There was also what might be termed a third layer of smaller properties, such as Beaulieu in Essex, where the King and a few favoured courtiers could make unofficial visits. These were too small to accommodate the King and Queen's whole retinue, and it was a sought-after honour to be chosen to go on one of these visits – some of them were hunting trips, which might take in, for example, the small but exquisitely decorated hunting box at what is now Bromley by Bow. This house belonged to a local monastery until 1531, but was let to Sir John Blount, father of the King's mistress, Bessie Blount, and expensively refurbished.

Court was also used to mean its people. By this period there had come to be a class of people who were career courtiers rather than simply being among those whose status made them appropriate servants for the King or Queen, and whose presence would, indeed, add to the Royal prestige. Such people were most certainly still present, but they had been joined by a considerable number of the new careerists, and it was to this category that the Boleyns belonged. As we have seen, Thomas Boleyn was very far from being a nobody at the beginning of his court career, and he would not have been able to secure the early appointments that he did, without some pre-existing importance. However, despite his aristocratic mother and grandmother, Thomas was very largely dependent on the Royal favour to maintain his status and his income. Although the Boleyn family already owned Hever and Blickling as well as a number of additional smaller properties, these were not nearly enough for Thomas, especially once he was married. When, later in life, he wrote that his wife 'gave him every year a child', this was in order to demonstrate how poor he had been before his father died and he inherited Hever Castle and the rest of the

estate. It should be borne in mind that this poverty was comparative –
Thomas and his wife and (probably) five children had an annuity of fifty
pounds a year. This was not a vast sum, but, as a comparison, a working
carpenter would be lucky to bring home four pounds a year, while in the
1520s a Vicar earning £20 a year was considered enviable.[6] But Boleyn
was aiming high, as were others round him. And he was, of course, in
exactly the right place to add to his fortune. Those unable to be at court
themselves were dependent on the client network by which preferment
was handled in Tudor times. There was an elaborate system of giving and
receiving favours and presents, with people higher up the chain of status
and influence being expected to help those behind them – to be 'good
lord' to dependents and others who were useful to them and to whom
they could be useful in return. And ultimately, and with a few exceptions,
most preferment began and ended with the King.

Court also meant a set of manners and expectations. In 1517 the
Venetian Papal Nuncio wrote that:

'The wealth and civilisation of the world are here and those who
call the English barbarians appear to me to render themselves such.
I here perceive very elegant manners, extreme decorum and great
politeness, and amongst other things there is this invincible King,
whose acquirements and qualities are so many and so excellent, that
I consider him to excel all who ever wore a crown.'[7]

A few years later, the Eltham Ordinances drew up a detailed list of the
behaviour expected of everyone at Court. In part this rule-book was an
attempt on Cardinal Wolsey's part to limit the influence of the Privy
Chamber, over which he had no control, so he sought to limit the numbers
of those employed there. It also served also to formalise the expectations
made of everyone in this vast household. Some of the requirements are
somewhat basic – those working in the kitchen must be properly dressed,
despite the heat; no one is to spit anywhere on the premises. Some of the
rules related to controlling the amount of waste, especially of food – no
one is to have meals served except in the dining room designated for them;

no one is to bring extra people to court; the number of servants and horses a courtier can maintain is regulated according to rank. Indeed, much of the document is devoted to making clear the distinctions between people of different ranks, most importantly to control who is allowed close to the King. For example, the King's clothes are to be delivered each morning by the Grooms of the Chamber, but only as far as the door – a Gentleman of the Privy Chamber must hand over those clothes. The King's barber was of yeoman, not gentle, status, so several rules are set specifically for him – he must be clean, not hungover, and keep away from bad company.

Court had a symbolic, as well as an actual meaning. This was sometimes illustrated very clearly, such as in the wake of the Evil Mayday riots of 1517, when several hundred apprentices and others rampaged through London, burning any property they thought belonged to a foreigner. This apparently came about because of ill feeling caused by the number of French and Dutch immigrants living and working in London. No one was killed, but the authorities took a very serious view of the matter, as it was a potential threat to the foreign trade on which London depended. So a number of the ringleaders were executed, and several hundred others made to appear in Westminster Hall in their shirts, with halters round their necks, and to beg the King for mercy. The Queen, Catherine of Aragon, and Cardinal Wolsey interceded on their behalf, and the King duly let them go after making an improving speech. This somewhat heavy-handed piece of political theatre made its point very effectively – the King was the fount of both mercy and justice. It appears that this was an isolated piece of popular unrest at the time, as nothing like it is recorded for the rest of the reign.

Moving the whole Court was no joke. The complexity of the exercise was added to by the fact that each palace was left virtually unfurnished in between visits. Not only clothes and personal possessions, but hangings, furniture and pots and pans were taken on the road, leaving bare walls and a skeleton staff in place. The frequent moves were necessary partly so as to be able to clean each house – food and water supply and sanitary arrangements were put under strain by several months of occupation. This restless, semi-nomadic life was what Kings and courts were used to

– certainly it was replicated at European courts. So professional courtiers, such as the Boleyns, were used to being mobile. Anne Boleyn, leaving home at twelve and not returning until she had reached her twenties, was an extreme case. It could be argued, however, that a princess making a foreign marriage was an even more extreme case of a similar kind – in each instance, a young woman was required to leave everything she knew to seek her own advancement and that of her family. And, in all probability, none of the young women had much choice in the matter.

All this was, of course, made possible by a vast number of servants of lower status who did the physical work involved in keeping the court on the road – from perhaps 400 cooks and kitchen helpers to cleaners, laundresses (washing and ironing have always been among the few activities men have generally been more than happy to leave to women), grooms, ushers and pages. The domestic side of Court was controlled by the 'Board of Green Cloth', which was supposedly a separate world. The term had been in existence for several hundred years, and was called after the cloth on the table at which the heads of department sat to have their planning meetings and to examine the accounts. Although there were rigid distinctions in terms of status, the way the Tudor domestic world worked meant that in physical terms, courtiers of supposedly totally different spheres came into close physical contact. Attempts were made to control this – the example of the delivery of clothes to the King is far from being the only one. The mental and emotional, as well as the physical worlds of the court depended on everyone involved agreeing to believe that proximity to the sovereign was everything. And theoretically, the closer you were allowed, the more important you were. However, this was a world without corridors, in which rooms opened into each other, and the bell to summon servants from a distance was nearly three centuries into the future. At Court as elsewhere, this was a world where the inhabitants lived in close proximity to each other.

At the beginning of the reign of Henry VIII, the King's official lodgings, no matter where he found himself, were divided into three zones – the first, where anyone who looked respectable could gain access, was the outer, or 'watching' chamber. This led into the Presence Chamber, over whose doors there was some control, and thence into the Privy Chamber, where only the very privileged were allowed – in theory, at least, there were supposed to be lists of who was allowed in. However, as the very privileged could number several dozen on any day, the King was still on semi-public display. As the reign went on, Henry began to redesign his lodgings at a number of palaces, with extra rooms added beyond the Privy Chamber, making a Privy Lodging, with a smaller private bedroom, a library, private closet and chapel. There was also often a Privy Kitchen, so that the King could have meals at different times out of the public gaze. There was also a private accounting system for this private space, so that the King could gamble for money, buy anything he fancied and go on expeditions without the rest of the Court knowing.

The Privy Lodgings were run by the King's Groom of the Stool – early in the reign this was William Compton. The holder of this office was the closest of the King's personal attendants, in charge of the Gentlemen of the Privy Chamber, and had the opportunity of becoming highly influential as he was in attendance on the King when no one else was allowed near. This included accompanying the King to the close stool (hence the name of the office) which served him as a lavatory, and handing him lambs' wool cloths with which to clean himself when he had used it. The duty to give such very personal services, however, should not distract attention from how very influential this office was – for example, the Groom of the Stool administered a large, and semi-secret budget and several houses as well as looking after all the furnishings, plate and other contents of the Privy Lodgings and, to some extent at least, controlled who could get to see the King, certainly when he had retired there. Self-evidently, there must have been many secrets known to the Privy Chamber gentlemen that never found their way into the outside world. It is notable that the men who obtained these appointments were of a different kind from other senior court officials. They were generally of roughly the same age as the King, and, although they were gentlemen, were not necessarily of the highest rank. William Carey, the man who was to marry Mary Boleyn a decade into the reign, seems to have been typical of the kind of man favoured – of gentle birth, yes, but a younger son of a younger son, of slender means but

HEVER CASTLE.
From a Drawing by G. L. SEYMOUR.

A nineteenth century drawing of Hever Castle, still largely as it was when Anne Boleyn spent much of her childhood there. It was later extended by the Astor family.

The small memorial brass in St Peter's Church, Hever to Anne's brother Henry Boleyn, who died young.

Margaret of Austria, the '*très redoutée dame*' in whose cultivated household Anne Boleyn began her career as a courtier. From a portrait by Bernard van Orley.

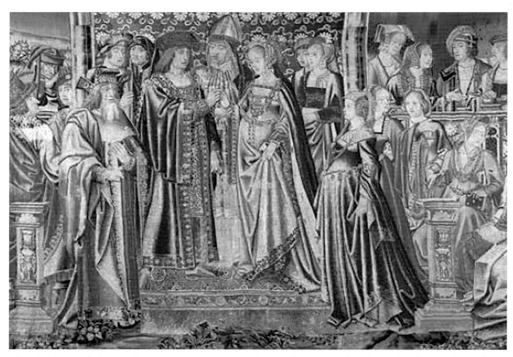

Mary Tudor marries Louis XII of France. There is a tradition that the figure third from the right in the back row of this tapestry represents the teenage Anne Boleyn.

The Bed of Roses, the recently rediscovered marriage bed of Henry VII and Elizabeth of York – with religious and political images in every exquisitely carved inch. (©*The Langley Collection*)

Henry VIII in 1509 – the not-quite 18-year-old king, whose charm and good looks had ambassadors running out of superlatives. (*From a portrait by an unknown artist, now in Denver Art Museum*)

Anthony van Wyngaerde's precise and detailed drawings of London give us a sense of the buildings and perhaps the atmosphere of the city Anne returned to in 1522. This image shows the Billingsgate area.

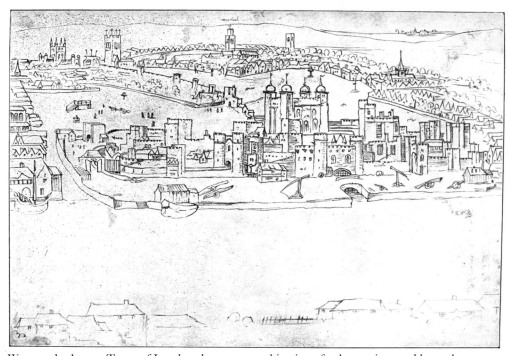

Wyngaerde shows a Tower of London that was a combination of palace, prison and barracks.

Early Tudor home security. This is the original front door of Sutton House in Hackney, which dates from 1535.

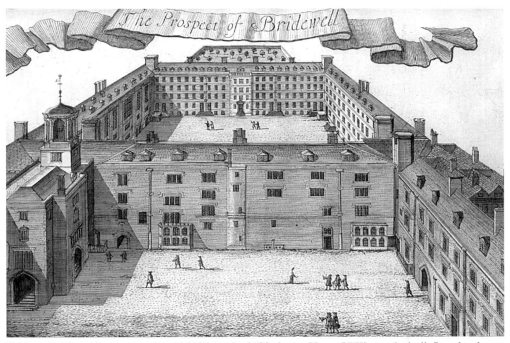

Bridewell Palace, from a drawing of 1720. In the 1520s it was Henry VIII's newly-built London home and latest acquisition, but he soon started to find it too small, especially in comparison with Wolsey's York Place.

By the 1790s, when this drawing was made, only the gatehouse remained of Durham House, once the London home of Thomas Boleyn.

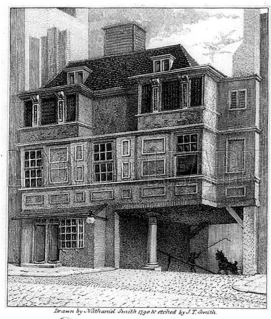

Drawn by Nathaniel Smith 1790 & etched by J.T. Smith.

Durham House, Strand.

This music manuscript almost certainly belonged to Anne Boleyn. It bears her signature and her father's motto, 'Nowe thus', suggesting it dates from her earlier years. (© *The Royal College of Music / ArenaPAL*)

This drawing by Hans Holbein may be of Anne as Queen, although there is doubt about this, especially as the arms of the Wyatt family appear on the reverse. (*Royal Collection Trust / © Her Majesty Queen Elizabeth II, 2016*)

'The Moost Happi'. This portrait medal, issued in 1534, is the only fully authenticated image of Anne dating from her lifetime. (© *The British Museum*)

This ring, now at Chequers, belonged to Anne's daughter Elizabeth I, and contains miniatures of them both. The portrait of Anne closely resembles The British Museum medal.

The familiar portrait type of Anne – there are many versions, all dating from the later sixteenth century, and may be derived from a lost original.

Henry VIII painted by Holbein in 1536. Although not yet the grotesque figure of his later years, by now the King was balding and beginning to gain weight. (*Portrait in the Thyssen-Bornemisza collecton in Madrid*)

The modern Royal barge, Gloriana, is built to a pattern close to those of the sixteenth century. (*Photograph courtesy of Daren Clarke*)

The mythical and religious figures along Anne's coronation route would have been in the style of these female saints, which appear in a stained-glass window in King's College chapel, Cambridge.

The seating plan for Anne's coronation banquet in Westminster Hall, showing the new Queen seated alone under her canopy. (© *The British Library*)

Anne's badge as Queen. The white falcon alighting on a tree stump, which then bursts into bloom with Tudor roses. This was also one of the motifs in her coronation procession.

Thomas Wyatt, by Hans Holbein. He was fortunate to survive Anne's fall, after he was one of those arrested with her. (*Royal Collection Trust / © Her Majesty Queen Elizabeth II, 2016*)

Mary Tudor, daughter of Henry VIII, champion of her mother Catherine of Aragon, shown in her teens. (*Portrait by an anonymous artist*)

Henry Fitzroy, Duke of Richmond, the son of Henry VIII and Elizabeth Blount. He died of TB only weeks after Anne's execution. (*Royal Collection Trust / © Her Majesty Queen Elizabeth II, 2016*)

Thomas Boleyn's magnificent memorial brass in St Peter's Church, Hever. The King had masses said for his soul.

Thomas Cromwell by Hans Holbein. The subject's shrewdness, intelligence and ruthlessness are unmistakable here. (*Portrait in the Frick Collection, New York*)

Anne Boleyn's memorial tile set into the pavement of St Peter ad Vincula, within the Tower of London, at the time of its Victorian restoration. The image shows the roses sent anonymously on 19 May each year.

A voluptuously romantic, early nineteenth century take on Anne's story: 'The Banquet of Henry VIII at York Place' by James Stephanoff. (*The Royal Collection Trust/© Her Majesty Queen Elizabeth II, 2016*)

'Anne Boleyn in the Tower' by Edouard Cibot. The doomed Queen is shown as a beautiful and innocent victim, with an open Bible to provide comfort.

The Tower of London. This drawing of 1873 shows serious-looking Victorian tourists absorbing history.

The Queen's House at the Tower of London in 1898. It is often pointed out as Anne's place of imprisonment, but it was built a few years after her lifetime.

The White Falcon uncrowned. The carving made in the wall of the Beauchamp Tower by one of Anne's 'lovers'.

The White Falcon returns. Part of Clio's Company's float in the 2013 Lord Mayor's Show, photographed against the backdrop of the Gherkin, now a famous London landmark.

able to offer youth, energy, a certain knowledge of the world, and musical and athletic prowess. The Privy Chamber gentlemen were expected to join the young King when he wanted an adventure. Given the constant surveillance of his adolescence, and his early marriage, it is less than surprising that the first years of his reign appear to have featured some questionable nights out. Viewed with sympathy and with an awareness of his age, these may seem harmless – there are, however, indications that the King and his friends' idea of fun may have included a vein of the misogyny and casual violence displayed by at least some of the other men of their time.

As time went on and the King's Lodgings in some of the palaces were redesigned, private doors to the Privy Lodgings were included, and, where possible, a discreet exit so the King could come and go unobserved. It appears that Compton also organised very unofficial jaunts for the King, including visits to friends in the City of London, parties at secluded 'safe houses' as well as at his own house in Thames Street, well away from the rest of the Court. In later years, Elizabeth Amadas, as part of a statement in which she denounced the King for leaving Catherine of Aragon, gave details of an earlier affair she said she had with him, claiming:

> 'The King had often sent her offerings and gifts, and that Mr Daunsy had come the bawd between the King and her to have had her to Mr Compton's house in Thames Street.'[8]

If this is true (and we only have her word for it), it may well be there are a number of women whose relationships with the King have successfully been kept quiet for nearly five centuries – that some historians believe that Henry VIII only ever had two mistresses may be in part a tribute to the discretion of his Groom of the Stool. That Henry and Compton had a complicated relationship is demonstrated by the fact that Compton appears to have facilitated an early affair between Henry and Lady Anne Hastings, the sister of the Duke of Buckingham – we only know about this because the enterprise became embarrassingly public, the lady's husband removed her to the seclusion of a nunnery, and both her brother, the

Duke, and the Queen, Catherine of Aragon, got to know, and to resent the relationship. There was, however, a sequel to this story – Anne Hastings soon returned to court, and began a relationship in earnest with Compton, who left her a generous bequest in his will – he died, as did so many other courtiers, of the sweating sickness in 1528.

Less romantically, all through the years of Henry's reign there are pieces of evidence that the King was not above preying on low-status women who would have had little choice other than to have sex with him. The King's probable daughter, Etheldreda Malte, may well have been the offspring of just such a fling. This little girl was fostered by John Malte, the King's tailor, who provided for her in his will out of lands granted by the King, naming her as the daughter of Joan Dingley, who was a Royal laundress. This, of course, may have been a consensual relationship – the fact that the King provided, even if at one remove, for Joan's child, suggests so. Many years later, Etheldreda and her husband were to be among the servants of Elizabeth Tudor while she was imprisoned in the Tower. In 1535, a London merchant was to complain that the King and a group of his friends had snatched his wife while she was out riding, taken her to a private house where she appears to have been raped, and later released her. If such tales are true of the King, it has to be said he would not have been the only one of his contemporaries to have behaved in this way. To give just one example, Thomas Culpeper, one of those who was to be executed for having an affair with Henry's fifth queen, Catherine Howard, was almost certainly guilty of raping a park-keeper's wife and murdering a villager, but was exonerated, perhaps because of his court appointment and influential connections.

More decorum was expected at court itself, and Henry's only early affair for which there is much evidence, was certainly conducted, in public at least, within the rules of courtly romance. Elizabeth Blount was part of a minor gentry family from Staffordshire – her father, John, was a member of the elite company of King's Spears, whose fifty or so members served as bodyguards to the King, so was at Court himself. This alone would have been unlikely to have been enough to overcome the ferocious competition to get a place as Maid of Honour to the Queen for his daughter. The explanation may be that Sir Henry Guildford, who was a relative and who held the influential appointment of Master of the Revels, recommended Bessie, as she was usually known. If so, this would be an excellent example of the Tudor client system at work. The first we hear of Bessie is when she went on the payroll as a Maid of Honour in 1513 – as they were paid in arrears, she was probably appointed the previous year, at the minimum age of twelve. The salary of 100 shillings a year, or £5, would certainly not have covered all the new clothes she would need, and at this time her father received an advance on his salary, perhaps to make up the short fall. Evidently Bessie had impressed Catherine of Aragon as someone she wanted to have around – the Queen approved all such appointments herself. This was understandable, as the Queen's ladies were in very close attendance on her. Not only were they expected to dress her, but to wash her, including washing her hair, dress her hair, anticipate her every mood and wish, watch her health, pray with her, sew with her, and take turns to sleep in her room on the nights she was not with the King. Inevitably, the Queen's ladies also saw quite a lot of the King, so it is unsurprising that it was from among them that he found a number of flirts and at least two mistresses. It was also how he met all but two of his six wives.

In theory, maids of honour in particular, as unmarried, and often very young, girls, were considered to be in the care of the Queen, although there was an older lady who had the job title of Mother of the Maids. They were expected to spend a lot of time sewing garments for the poor and attending Mass – and as Catherine of Aragon was devout, this does seem to have occupied much of their time. However, the job description also included providing entertainment for the Queen, and sometimes helping with those for the whole Court. This may have been a factor which helped to win Bessie Blount her appointment. It appears that not only was she pretty and intelligent and reasonably well educated, she could also dance, sing, and may also have written song lyrics and music. To the Master of the Revels, whose concern it was to facilitate and organise entertainments, these talents must have been a recommendation. It was usual for the Queen and her ladies to appear in masques, which were specially written to celebrate holidays such as Christmas. There are a number of recorded instances of Bessie taking part in these (and as the records are very incomplete, there were probably more). Masques at this time were the height of newly imported continental fashion – a piece of musical entertainment, often with a storyline of some kind, where the participants took the opportunity to dress up, dance, and possibly sing or play a musical instrument. Evidently Bessie was an accomplished performer in these, including one on New Year's Eve, 1514, when she danced with the King. During another, she sang a song beginning

> 'Whilst life and breath is in my breast
> My sovereign lord I shall love best
> My sovereign lord, for my poor sake,
> Six courses at the ring did make
> Of which four times he did it take
> Wherefore my heart I him bequest
> And, of all others, for to love best
> My sovereign lord ...'

There are six more verses of this. The song is preserved in a book written during the early years of Henry's reign, and there is a possibility that Bessie may have composed the lyrics herself.

There is no evidence as to when Bessie first caught the King's eye. As appears to have been usual with Henry, the early stages of the affair were conducted with discretion – and if there was gossip at Court, few echoes of it have come down to us. Bessie goes on being mentioned as being at court until 1518, and it appears she was quietly removed when she became pregnant. It is because she had a son by the King that she is still remembered. In the sixteenth century it was completely usual for a man to have a passing affair while his wife was pregnant, and there is evidence that this is what Henry did on several occasions, behaving relatively discreetly out of consideration, perhaps, for all concerned. After Catherine's very public quarrel with the King over his affair with Anne Hastings and its consequences,[9] she appears to have adopted a policy more like that of other Royal wives of her time – that of pretending not to notice her husband's infidelities, and, in return he may well have tried to spare her any further public embarrassment. Catherine had pregnancies each year in 1515–18 (her daughter, Mary, was born in 1516), and so would have been sexually unavailable for most of those four years, as it was considered dangerous to both mother and child for a pregnant woman to have sex. It is clear that Bessie was well known and much admired at Court – one of a number of appreciative contemporary comments describes her as 'eloquent, gracious and beautiful'.[10]

However, in early 1519, still aged only about nineteen, Bessie Blount left Court. She was pregnant with the King's child, and he sent her to live at a small house at Blackmore, Essex – it was known as 'Jericho'. Evidently the King began to spend a lot of time visiting her there, and those around him were warned 'not to enquire where the King is or goeth, be it early or late'.[11] He had a second house, Newhall Boreham, built nearby – it may well be that Bessie was not the only tenant of Jericho who received visits from the King. Their son was born in June 1519. Wolsey was his godfather, and the baby was given the name Henry Fitzroy – this surname had been used by several Kings of England for their illegitimate children. Some historians have claimed that the relationship between the King and Bessie came to an immediate end, but there is considerable evidence that Bessie's second child, a daughter named Elizabeth born in 1520, was also the child of the King, even though she later took the surname of the man her mother married. It was two years after this, in 1522, that Bessie married Gilbert, Lord Tailboys, and the couple received a series of generous grants of land. It is likely that it was at this stage that the relationship with the King finally ended, perhaps at the point he began to be interested in Mary Boleyn. It is clear, however, that he and Bessie parted on good terms and stayed friendly. Their son remained with his mother, as was usual, until he was six, and until then it is likely that few people knew of his existence. We do not know at what stage Catherine of Aragon became aware of the existence of her husband's son, but she was certainly horrified when, around the boy's sixth birthday in June 1525, he was brought to Court and, in an elaborate ceremony at Bridewell Palace, and in the presence of the Duke of Norfolk, most of the nobility, various bishops, Sir Thomas More and his step father Gilbert Tailboys (it is not known if his mother was present) given the Royal titles of Duke of Richmond and Somerset. There is considerable evidence that, at this time and later, Henry gave serious thought to making the boy his heir.

Although the beginning of the story of Bessie Blount took place long before Anne Boleyn returned to England, the ennoblement of Fitzroy happened when Anne was already at Court, after the likely end of the King's affair with her sister, Mary, and at around the time when the King was starting to take an interest in Anne. There are a number of lessons, Anne could have drawn from this – and it may well be that one of them was that Bessie Blount, although she had done better than Anne's sister Mary, had failed to derive much benefit from a relationship with the King, which in Bessie's case may have lasted as much as six years. Certainly Bessie must have been proud that her son was ennobled, but this came at a high price. Although she remained on friendly terms with the King, Bessie now had little or no influence over her son's education. And, although she had made an honourable marriage, she was neither especially rich nor of particularly high status nor in the centre of things, living as she did on her husband's estates in Lincolnshire. Bessie appears to have been docile enough, or perhaps overwhelmed enough, to allow herself to lead the life the King chose for her. We have no way of knowing how much say she had over whether she wanted to have a sexual relationship with the King in the first place; for a teenage girl in the hothouse atmosphere of Court, it would have taken an extremely strong personality to turn him down – there would have been little chance of simply becoming elusive. Perhaps she was indeed happy with the sequence of events – and it may be that her marriage then turned out well and she was content. From what evidence we have, she appears to have been a gentle person who could well have had enough of Court and, perhaps, of the King. When Gilbert Tailboys died, Bessie made another marriage and had three more daughters with her second husband; she returned to Court as one of Anne of Cleves' ladies – evidently she was on good terms with Henry even after the death of their son. Bessie died in around 1541 – she had, of course, also outlived Anne Boleyn.

It seems likely that Mary Boleyn was in some respects similar to Bessie Blount. Both were professional courtiers from an early age and were daughters of fathers who were courtiers themselves. Both were well, if not highly educated. Both were musically accomplished and good dancers, being chosen to take part in high profile entertainments and masques. Each was extremely pretty, and there is evidence that they were both blonde. It is tempting, too, to speculate that they were both of a similar gentle temperament. Yet, in later years, Mary was to have the strength and determination to make a second marriage that she knew would outrage her powerful relations, to come to Court to face them down, and to campaign for her own and her new husband's rehabilitation. It is certain that she married again in full knowledge of the likely consequences, and chose to place her chance of personal happiness ahead of any worldly consideration – not a usual set of choices for a Tudor Court lady. But the Mary of 1522 was undoubtedly very different from the Mary of 1534. In 1522 Mary Boleyn had probably been at the English Court for at most two years, in addition to whatever time she had spent at the French court. She had been married to William Carey for about eighteen months, and was certainly entitled to share the accommodation, service and food he received as a Gentleman of the Privy Chamber. It is not clear whether Mary was officially one of Catherine of Aragon's household at this time, but she was certainly a person about Court. And, although it is not known when Mary's affair with the King started, by the time it did, the two must have been well known to each other. There is absolutely no evidence to support the often-repeated claim that Mary was 'married off' to William Carey so as to facilitate the affair. Neither is there any evidence that either Thomas Boleyn or the Duke of Norfolk did anything to bring the relationship about – Henry, although suggestible, was well able to do his own seducing on his own home ground. Furthermore, we do not know how long the relationship between the King and Mary lasted. It may have been anything from a few weeks to four or five years. But somehow, at some stage, the King transferred his interest from Mary to her sister, Anne.

As we do not know at what point the King's interest in Anne genuinely became serious, even less can we know when it became a matter of court gossip. We can be sure that anything the King did or said was in any case likely to be observed, recorded and speculated over. We can be sure, too, that Anne at least was in no doubt that this would be the case. As a professional courtier she can have been in no doubt about the way the court worked, and, as she and her allies set up what was in effect a sort of second Queen's Side, her hold on events seems to have stayed unerring. It was, however, when she became impatient or angry that she made mistakes. While she was still in the role of beloved mistress she could afford, for example, the kind of outburst that accompanied her discovery that Catherine of Aragon was still making the King's shirts long after their relationship had broken down in most other ways. It appears that Anne chose to make a very public fuss about the question, probably to ensure that no one was in any doubt of her power to ensure that Catherine was no longer seen to undertake any wifely duty for the King. In the early months of 1533 when Anne was in the early stages of pregnancy, she chose to let the court know by coming into a room full of people and asking one of them (probably Thomas Wyatt) for an apple, saying she had a craving for the fruit, and that the King had said it must mean that she was pregnant, but that she had told him it could not possibly be so. She then left the room, laughing wildly, and leaving her hearers to enjoy the sensation she had caused.

As we have seen with regard to the 'Chateau Vert' entertainment in 1522, it was usual for court entertainments to contain allusions to people and events or, sometimes, to be constructed round them. During the months after Anne had been created Marquess of Pembroke but before she was first prayed for as Queen at Easter 1533, a new play by John Heywood was staged – *The Play of the Weather*, which has previously been referred to. It has been the subject of a major new study in recent years; this involved a full-scale staging at Hampton Court,[12] and it now appears likely that its first production was at Christmas 1532 as part of the festivities at Greenwich. The storyline is simple – Jove is determined to make alterations to the weather on earth, but asks for the opinions of various mortals before he does so. The consensus is that Jove should acquire a fine, new, tight crescent moon in place of the old, leaky one that cannot hold its water. The action contains a number of set pieces, opportunities for dance and jokes that were certainly about specific people and incidents. The general effect is of a very expensive pantomime for insiders (although possibly not the inner circle – there is something of the school play about it), and it may be that its first performance was watched by the King and Anne. It is probably reasonable to imagine that this is a chance survival among many entertainments of the time covering similar themes.

As we have seen, there is what some have regarded as conflicting evidence about life in Anne Boleyn's Queen's Side. There are the religious reformer Rose Lok's recollections. This version of Anne was serious, charitable, cared deeply about religious matters, and maintained a serious tone among her ladies, who were expected to share her tastes and sew for the poor. There is also the Anne who partied in her chamber in the weeks following her coronation, at the height of her power and her happiness. Some historians have assumed that only one of these pictures can be a true one – either the intellectual proto-protestant or the febrile party animal. It may well be that the reality took in them both. It may also be, however, that the transition from queen in waiting to queen was as difficult in terms of her household as it may well have been in terms of her relationship with Henry. Given his apparent track record of losing interest in previous loves as soon as they had a child, and of apparently assuming that infidelity during a wife's pregnancy did not count, it is unsurprising to read that the King began to flirt with other women in the early months of his marriage to Anne. Even Chapuys, who would, of course, have liked to be able to report serious trouble, admitted that both the flirtations, and the resulting quarrels, were in the nature of lovers' tiffs. The events leading up to the new marriage had, of course, represented the overturning of not just lives but expectations and assumptions. But after the upheaval, it may well be that not only the King but those around him too, expected life to revert to something resembling normality. Yes, there was a new queen now, but queens behaved in specified ways. Most importantly, of course, they produced children, especially sons. They were also supposed to be models of religion and charity. They could be learned too – supporting poor scholars, and even founding colleges, would earn approval. Beauty and glamour were acceptable, too, but Queens were not supposed to be players, either in politics or socially. Queens presided, and their influence was to be wielded behind the scenes.

Anne Boleyn must have been aware of all the expectations and unspoken rules, but it may well be she had broken too many rules on her way to becoming Queen to be prepared to adhere to a different set. Neither, it appears, did she necessarily become more formal in her dealings with those round her, even though she was now addressed as 'Your Grace' or 'Madam' ('Your Majesty' was a form of address for the King only). Her uncle, the Duke of Norfolk, for example, did not hesitate to quarrel with her, and it is clear that she remained as close as ever to many of the friends she had known for years, and who were now part of her household as Queen. Her informality was combined with an outspokenness and sometimes an arrogance that did not endear her to some – particularly, perhaps, those who resented her quickness of wit and her occasional acidity. According to Chapuys, in particular, Anne was bad-tempered and strident, and he always places on her the blame for the unkindnesses that were inflicted on the King's daughter, Mary. That may not be altogether true, but there is a possibility that her outspokenness and informality made her more vulnerable to attack. It does seem likely that she did not appreciate an equal outspokenness in others.

The conversations between Anne and first Mark Smeaton and then with Henry Norris in the days leading up to her arrest tell us a great deal, firstly about the individuals concerned, and secondly about the ways of Court. The exchange with Mark tends to support the suggestion that he had become obsessed with Anne. Even allowing for the informality that seems to have been the rule in Anne's household, Mark was being outrageously rude, first in replying 'it was no matter' when she asked him why he was sad, and then in leaving her presence without being given permission to do so. It was hardly surprising that Anne reproved him by saying that he could not expect her to speak to him as she would to a gentleman – but it seems likely that Mark the skilled musician may have been a welcome member of the musical gatherings that took place in the Queen's rooms. As we know George Boleyn had passed on at least one book to Mark Smeaton, it may also be that Mark had begun to feel himself one of a charmed inner circle of friends – only to find out there were very precise limits to how far he was accepted. With regard to Henry Norris, much depends on something we can never know – the tone of voice in which the conversation was conducted. Like the kind of joke where 'you had to be there' it may have seemed nothing more than mildly flirtatious and rather silly at the time. However, Norris took fright when Anne suggested, however flippantly, that he might be staying single in the hope she would be widowed soon, and that, of course, changed the emotional key straight away. They were overheard, and gossip spread – and then Anne added the finishing touch by insisting Norris swore an oath in front of a priest that she was a good woman. Certainly by that time Anne had lost control of the gossip machine that was one of the aspects of the court – and if it is true that she was aware she was in danger for several days before that, then it appears that her judgement was impaired also.

Taken together, these two incidents may have been the icing on the cake for Thomas Cromwell, already calculating whether he had enough evidence to move against Anne if he relied solely on what he had gleaned from the Countess of Worcester and other snippets of hearsay. Whatever view is taken of the events of the days leading up to Anne's arrest, there is no conclusion that is neat and tidy and accounts for everyone's known actions and possible motivations. What we do have, however, is an example of the extent to which Court was ruled by gossip, most of it word of mouth. It was not only Cromwell and Chapuys who paid for information, not only in every department and household, but virtually in every room at Court. Some historians have argued that the fact that no one except Cranmer spoke up for Anne indicates that no one was surprised by the charges against her. This is unpersuasive – but what it may well tell us is that her friends knew there was nothing they could do to help her and that they were, unheroically but understandably, afraid for themselves.

Anne and her five 'lovers' died; most of her friends who survived, kept quiet, in public at least. It took the horror surrounding the fall of Anne Boleyn to make Thomas Wyatt write the words

> 'Who list his wealth and ease retain
> Him self let him unknown contain
> Press not to fast in at that gate
> Where the return stands by disdain
> For sure, circa Regna tonat.'

Wyatt, and the many others who shared his ambitions, had always known that thunder rolled about the throne. Henrician courtiers did not use the language of addiction – but most of them knew what a toxic environment they inhabited, yet were unable, and unwilling, to keep away. Wyatt, like most of the other survivors, was soon back for more. Anne would probably have understood.

Chapter 7

Anne the Queen: 1533–36

By 2 June 1533 Anne Boleyn must have been tired out, both mentally and physically. She was entering the third trimester of her first pregnancy, and there is evidence that she was unwell throughout all her pregnancies. She had been on what must have been an emotional precipice for much of the past six years – it had been far from clear, probably until he knew she had had conceived, that the King would go through with the decisive step of a final break with Catherine, and with marrying her, without some form of agreement with Rome. Also, she had just been through the run-up to her coronation, in the planning of which she was fully involved, followed by four gruelling days of ceremonial, during which she was under constant intense scrutiny, much of it hostile.

Neither could she rest even then. Protocol demanded yet more celebrations – the slightest hint of a lack of honour being done to the new Queen would be gleefully leapt upon by those who wished her ill. As it was, Chapuys, clearly disappointed by the lack of overt trouble in London, was taking refuge in reporting that the coronation had been 'cold, meagre and uncomfortable'. If any expected ceremony had been missing, not only Chapuys, but a chorus of other observers, would certainly have interpreted it either as a deliberate slight on the King's part, or as a tacit acknowledgement of Anne's unpopularity. So, Monday, 2 June had to feature jousting, dancing and a banquet in the Queen's rooms. All this took place at Whitehall, with the jousting in the newly completed tiltyard. There appear to have been technical problems with the central barrier (or tilt) in the arena that meant it was difficult for the teams to land hits on each other, as the horses kept veering away. However, honour seems to have been satisfied, especially as Anne's enemy, Sir Nicholas Carewe, was the captain of one of the teams. He was not the only one of those who had opposed Anne to put a good face on her triumph – it was only diehards like Sir Thomas More who were not present. More's friends had clubbed together to send him £20 for a new gown to wear at the coronation: he took the money but stayed away. That, of course, was one of the purposes of the large-scale celebrations. To a great extent the strategy worked – almost everyone who was everyone was there. Later in the week the Court moved to Greenwich, where the merrymaking continued. Edward Baynton, Anne's Vice Chancellor, wrote to George Boleyn, away on a diplomatic mission, that 'as for pastime in the Queen's chamber, there was never more'. The rest of June was also enlivened with the arrival of presents from well-wishers – one of the finest was a wonderfully decorated litter and three mules to carry it from the King of France. The death of the King's sister, Mary, in late June does not appear to have cast much of a shadow on proceedings – he ordered masses to be said for her, but gave no other sign of mourning. By September, Mary's widower was married to his 14-year-old ward.

Much of the next couple of months appear to have been, understandably, given over to Anne's settling into her new role. Back in January both she and the King had been reassuring all those hoping for places in her new household that they would not have long to wait. By the time of her first appearance as Queen at Easter, many of those to be appointed were already in place. Her household was to consist of some 200 people, all approved and vetted by the King, who was present when they took their oaths of allegiance. Many of them were obvious choices as being Boleyn relatives or adherents – Sir James Boleyn, Anne's uncle, was Chancellor, and his wife, Elizabeth (whom in 1536 Anne was to say she had 'never loved') was a lady in waiting. Anne's sister, Mary, sister in law Jane, Lady Rochford and cousin Lady Mary Howard were all among those appointed, as were her cousins, Margaret and Mary Shelton. Other ladies included Elizabeth Holland, the mistress of the Duke of Norfolk, Anne Gainsford, Lady Zouche and Mistress Marshall, the Mother of the Maids, along with Lady Berkeley and Elizabeth, Countess of Worcester. Some of the choices were of people who had previously been in Royal service – the Queen's Secretary, John Uvedale, had previously served on the Duke of Richmond's Council of the North, while her Master of the Horse, Sir William Coffin, was a Gentleman of the Privy Chamber. Her Physician, Richard Bartlett, had previously been in Wolsey's household, while George Taylor, her Receiver General, had worked for her father, Thomas Boleyn. Some of her ladies had previously served Catherine of Aragon – this applied to Jane Seymour, who had lost her appointment when Catherine's household was reduced, and who was appointed now on the recommendation of Sir Francis Bryan. It is likely that both Jane and Bryan retained their loyalty to Catherine throughout, although both were now prepared to go with the prevailing wind. The Queen needed several chaplains – all Anne's were reformers, and included William Latimer, John Skip and William Betts.

When Anne first called her household together, she instructed them in their duties, exhorting them to be honourable, discreet, just and thrifty, to attend Mass every day, and to display a 'virtuous demeanour'. According to William Latimer's later account, the officers were told they must not quarrel, swear or frequent 'evil, lewd and ungodly disposed brothels'. Each lady was given a little book of prayers and psalms that could be hung from a girdle; all were expected to spend much time sewing for the poor – Anne took part in this herself, and the linen shirts and smocks they produced were distributed on summer progresses. We are told, too, that a copy of the Bible in English – probably Anne's copy of Tyndale's translation of the New Testament – was kept on display in her presence chamber, even before this became technically legal, and that she and the King talked about its contents at dinner. John Foxe was to write that Joan Wilkinson, one of Anne's silkwomen, remembered years later that 'she had never seen better order amongst the ladies and gentlewomen of the court than in Anne Boleyn's day.' Anne was clearly very aware that much of Europe and some of England, regarded her as the Scarlet Woman. This did not, of course, stop many of those who disapproved of her from doing their best to obtain places in her household, her help and her patronage. The competition for all three was intense, from people of all political and religious persuasions. To give just one example, Lady Lisle, wife of the Governor of Calais, spent much time and money and ingenuity in devising appropriate presents in her campaign to persuade Anne to appoint one or both of her daughters as maids of honour. This never quite happened, and it was Jane Seymour who later took one of the girls into her household after a charm offensive on Lady Lisle's part that included a series of carefully chosen presents, including fat quails to satisfy the pregnant Jane's cravings.

It is notable that many of the merchants and traders who received much of Anne's custom as Queen were known in London reform circles. This, as we have seen, certainly applied to the Lok family – who had already served the King for many years. William, officially the King's Mercer, was to become a Protestant as soon as the term and the process became meaningful, as did his whole family; his daughter, Rose, and daughter in law, Joan, were silkwomen to Anne Boleyn. That Anne continued to obtain many of her dress fabrics from the Loks is demonstrated by the fact that she died owing Lok for four months' purchases, which included velvet gowns, both fur trimmed and plain, nightgowns, items for her daughter and fabric for shoes. It was accepted practice for bills to be settled quarterly or even annually, so it was unremarkable that items supplied in the first four months of 1536 had not been paid for by May. The fact that Lok's bill is for the clothes themselves, not just the fabric for them, suggests that it was he who was managing the process of having the items for made up for the Queen. There were several merchant tailors whose names crop up in the royal accounts, and who were paid directly for their work – the fact that none of them seems to have been involved with making these items suggests that Lok was either employing, or working with, someone else. Many of the household goods Anne had as Queen were taken over from what was already in the King's possession – as we have seen, Henry and Anne made several visits to the jewel house at the Tower so she could choose the gold and silver gilt items she wanted for her table and cupboards. Once she was Queen, however, Anne began to order items of her own, for example from the jeweller Morgan Wolf, from whom she ordered a pair of silver-gilt bottles bearing her and the King's arms. Much was melted down after her death; a few items have survived.

Along with the people making changes to accommodate her, the Royal palaces were being adapted for Anne. The King had put work in hand at the Tower of London, at Whitehall and at Hampton Court before they married, and now, at Hampton Court in particular, she was able to imprint her own taste. Her time at the courts of the Low Countries and of France had formed this, and the work she commissioned was in the height of the latest European fashion. At Hampton Court work was in progress on new Royal apartments, with sets of first-floor rooms for the King and Queen, built at right angles to each other and joined by a private gallery and with stairs leading down to a new privy garden. Craftsmen from all over Europe were commissioned to provide items from a headboard for the Queen's bed to six chairs of estate. Henry Blankston of Cologne carried out quantities of decorative gilding, Galyon Hone was to spend a decade working on the heraldic glass, and tapestries were imported from Persia to decorate the walls. Elaborate gardens were laid out, with fishponds, several banqueting houses and artificial mounds. Work was also put in hand at Greenwich and Windsor – but the old Bridewell Palace near Blackfriars was now let out as an ambassador's residence.

In physical terms, in each Royal palace the Queen's Side was planned along the same lines as the King's. There was an outer, or watching chamber, a presence chamber and a bedchamber, with more private rooms beyond. As in the case of the King, it was relatively easy to get access to the outer rooms, with each successive room being open to a more and more select group. The Queen's Bedchamber operated as a reception room for Anne's inner circle of friends – there are references to music and dancing going on there, and this is not unusual for the time. Rooms in houses of all social levels were given different uses at different times, sometimes of the same day, depending on need and convenience. No Tudor of any class, including those of Royal and noble status, would expect to spend much time alone, or to have very much privacy. In palaces, as in the greatest households, rooms opened out of one another, and bedrooms were shared, often with many others. For example, the Maids of Honour had what was essentially a series of dormitories in the various royal palaces, and routinely shared beds. In the case of both the King and the Queen, on nights the Royal couple were not spending together, at least one of their close attendants would sleep on a pallet bed in the same room. The King's Gentlemen of the Privy Chamber had a rota for this, with two of the six being on duty each night; the Queen's Ladies of the Bedchamber operated in much the same way. There were chamberers – domestic servants – who performed the more menial tasks, but it was considered an honour to be physically close to the King or Queen.

At some of the best-appointed palaces, including Hampton Court and Whitehall, there were bathrooms available for use by the Queen, with taps with hot and cold running water (the hot water being provided from a stove in the next room). Baths, usually slipper shaped and wooden, were lined with a sheet before use, and the bathroom often contained a day bed so the bather could recover from what was regarded as an exhausting activity, and perhaps have a massage with herbal oils – bathing was believed to be draining to the constitution. Household books included recipes for soap, often including ash, lanolin and scented oils. The water closet was not yet invented, but Royal palaces were provided with close stools – a metal pot, with a seat and a chamber below, the whole sunk into a wooden frame, often covered with velvet. These were clearly designed so as to be easy to clean. There were careful arrangements, too, for laundry. The King's bedchamber contained two chests, one each for clean and dirty linen, and his personal laundress was required to collect, wash, scent and iron his shirts, towels and other items. She had to provide washing materials and fuel from her wages. The arrangements for the Queen were certainly similar, and it is clear that standards of personal hygiene were stringent for all at Court. The Eltham Ordinances, a detailed rulebook for courtiers of all levels, issued by Cardinal Wolsey in 1526, is full of prohibitions about the kind of behaviour that will not be tolerated, for example, specifying that the King's barber must ensure he is scrupulously clean, as he will, of course, be in close physical contact with the sovereign. In 1540, one of the reasons the King cited to Cromwell for his instant antipathy to Anne of Cleves was her 'displeasant airs' – evidently her personal hygiene was not up to his standards.

Among the other comforts Anne had as Queen was her own Privy Kitchen – this meant she could have meals whenever she wanted them, and without being dependent on the highly efficient, but industrial scale kitchens that serviced the rest of the court. At Hampton Court, these are still in existence, and it is possible to gain a sense of the scale of the operation, and of the level of expertise needed to feed over 1,000 people a day. For Anne, if she wished for an impromptu meal at any time of the day or night, then there would be no difficulty. The usual sequence of meals for the Queen as for others of high status, began with a breakfast of manchet bread – that is, the finest white wheaten bread – with a choice of butter and cold meat or fish depending on the season, accompanied by ale, first thing in the morning. The main meal of the day, dinner, was at ten or eleven, and this would offer a choice of ten or fifteen dishes, including delicately prepared stew and raised pies as well as joints and roast fowl, served in two courses. With this there would be wine and ale, with a dessert (known as a void) of sweet dishes to follow. There were some vegetable dishes and preserved fruits – raw fruit was regarded as indigestible. Supper, served at five or six, was a repetition of the same thing, but usually with fewer dishes. The Royal cooks were highly skilled, and ingredients from all over the known world were available – this included citrus and dried fruit, spices and preserved delicacies such as quince marmalade and gingerbread. On fast days and during Lent, the many meat dishes were replaced with fish, in profusion and in variety.

By 1533, this daily routine had been familiar to Anne ever since she had arrived at the English court more than a decade before. She had, of course, presided as Queen in all but name for perhaps two of those years. Now she had the official status too – and now she was six months pregnant with what she, the King and all their supporters were loud in predicting would turn out to be a male heir to the throne. As this was Anne's first pregnancy, she would, unknown to her, have been free of at least one potential difficulty. This was Henry's Kell's status. Among many theories about Henry Tudor's medical history, it has been suggested[2] that one of the reasons his six marriages produced only three children who lived past early childhood may have been that he was Kell's positive. This is a relatively rare condition – it does not affect an individual, but problems start if they have children with a partner who is Kell's negative. It does not affect a first pregnancy, but in the case of subsequent pregnancies, if the unborn baby has inherited the father's Kell's positive status, the immune system of the mother will attack the foetus, which will die in the womb or soon after birth, which usually takes place prematurely. This would certainly go some way to explain the pattern of Catherine of Aragon's repeated miscarriages and still births – her daughter Mary's survival is explained if she was, like her mother, Kell's negative. However, although the official line was given out that Anne was, in fact, in good health that summer, there is evidence that Anne was far from well. One commentator later claimed that the King was desperately anxious for her; certainly the usual Royal summer progress did not take place that year – instead, the King and Queen retired to Windsor. There was good hunting within reach, and Anne could rest as she waited for the birth.

The confinement was planned to take place at Greenwich, and in the case of a Tudor Queen, it was a confinement in a very literal sense. The protocol was that the pregnant Queen was expected to 'take her chamber' some weeks before she expected to give birth. There was a ceremony during which she took her leave of the outside world, her husband, officially at least, included, and withdrew into a specially modified suite of rooms, attended only by women. The room in which she was to give birth had walls lined with tapestries, with only one small section of window that could be opened to let in a little light. Her outer, or presence chamber, was divided by a curtain – the male officers of her household had to remain on the far side, all duties beyond being carried out by the Queen's ladies. In the event, Anne took her chamber just over a week before she went into labour. It may be that she had miscalculated her dates, or that the baby was a little premature, or indeed that the baby was full term but Anne was disinclined to advertise the fact that she had been pregnant on her wedding day. The labour appears to have been straightforward, and Anne's daughter was born at 3pm on Sunday, 7 September.

Famously, everyone, including Anne herself, had predicted a boy, the King had planned a joust and days of celebrations in his new son's honour, and hundreds of official letters announcing the birth of a prince had already been prepared. However, there has been much myth-making about the depth of Henry's disappointment at having another daughter instead of the much-longed-for son. The jousts were cancelled – the birth of a princess did not warrant them. However, free wine ran from the fountains of London, and we are told that bonfires were lit, although it is not clear by whom. The letters had to be hastily updated – there was so little space on them that the word 'princess' had to be spelled with only one 's'. Chapuys, delighted at the news, made the most of it, but Elizabeth was welcomed into the world with a proclamation by the King's herald, and the choristers of the Chapel Royal and at St Paul's sang a *Te Deum*. Henry appears to have been comforted – Anne had given birth without complication, his new daughter was perfect and took after him, and was simply the first of what he hoped would be many children with his new wife.

Elizabeth was called after Henry's own mother (and, indeed, Anne's), and was given a magnificent christening on 10 September. Henry took the opportunity to require a number of Catherine's friends to take part in the ceremony – the Marchioness of Exeter was a godmother, while her husband carried a wax taper in the procession. Mary's chamberlain, John, Lord Hussey, helped to carry the canopy over the baby. Alongside them, Anne's father, brother and Howard relatives took a prominent role. Thomas Cromwell may well have organised the event – certainly he was present at it, and equally certainly nothing was allowed to go wrong. As was usual, neither parent was present – the baby was presented to them at the end of proceedings. Only four days after the birth, Anne was still in bed, and would not go out until she had been 'churched' – a service of thanksgiving and purification after what was regarded as the taint of childbirth. Some writers have insisted that the King's absence was a sign of displeasure, but in fact his presence would have been a breach of protocol.

Londoners were happy to join in the celebration, and there is no record, even from Chapuys, of any kind of trouble. And when, a few weeks later, Elizabeth was taken to Hatfield, where she was to live in a household of her own, she was carried in procession through the streets of London on the way north – her first public appearance in London. Elizabeth had been declared heir to the throne and Mary was now officially illegitimate – a younger daughter preferred to an older. It would, of course, all have been much simpler if the arrival had been a boy. In that case few, even of the most loyal of Catherine's adherents, would have argued – no Tudor would have suggested that a son should not inherit, and it is likely that few would have continued to argue in the interest of Catherine or of Mary in the face of such an arrival. As it was, Anne still could not relax. She was a beloved wife, a crowned and anointed queen, and a mother, but she had not yet come up with the goods – it was regarded as every wife's duty to give birth to boys. Daughters just did not count, much as they might be loved. And everyone believed that if children failed to arrive, then the failure was that of the wife.

There is no agreement as to how good a prospect for fatherhood the King really was, even apart from his possible Kell's status. Some commentators argue that Catherine of Aragon's obstetrical misfortunes were no greater than many other women of her time, and point out the fact that Anne had become pregnant as soon as she began to have sex with the King. There was also no uncertainty about the paternity of Bessie Blount's son by him, and there is a strong possibility that he was the father of Mary Boleyn's daughter, Catherine, now known to have been her eldest child. But there are indications that the King was insecure about his virility – in April 1533 he had turned on Chapuys when he pointed out that a new wife in place of Catherine would not necessarily mean more children, asking 'Am I not a man like other men? Am I not? Am I not?'.[3] In 1536 one of the accusations made against Anne was that she had laughed with her brother about the King's inadequacies as a lover – this does not mean she had done so, or would have been justified in doing so, but it does suggest that rumours circulated on the subject. However, Anne evidently recovered quickly from the birth of Elizabeth, and conceived again only three or four months later. By April 1534 her condition was obvious, Henry had ordered a solid silver cradle with gold embroidered bedding, and all seemed well. Then, in July, late in the pregnancy, she miscarried, while the court was on summer progress. The secret was so well kept that Chapuys, not present on the progress, did not hear what had happened until September, and some writers have doubted that Anne was ever pregnant at this time. The likelihood is that both she and the King were desperate to keep the matter secret as, of course it was obvious that her enemies – and not only they – would be all too likely to start drawing comparisons between her and Catherine, and asking what, after all the trouble and trauma, the King had achieved by marrying her. Despite much speculation, it is unclear when the King started asking himself the same thing.

It is always a mistake to read history backwards, and it must be remembered that we are indebted to Chapuys for the early stories about the King's eye having wandered away from Anne. As early as August 1533, Chapuys was reporting hopefully that the King and Anne had been apart for weeks, and seeing this a good sign for Catherine. A month later he was claiming that the Royal couple had argued and not spoken for two or three days – but he himself dismissed this as a lovers' quarrel. At this time the gossip in the London merchant community, and in Europe, was that the King was besotted with his new wife, and delighted with his baby daughter, whom he visited once she had been given her own household (as all royal babies were). A year later, in September 1534, Chapuys was reporting that Henry had returned to a previous, unnamed flirt, that Anne had responded angrily, and that the King had retaliated by refusing to dismiss the girl, telling Anne 'that she had good reason to be content with what he had done with her, which he would not do again, if he were starting afresh, that she should remember where she had come from, and many other things.'[4] Chapuys' next instalment was a claim that Jane Boleyn, Anne's sister in law, had been dismissed from court for picking a quarrel with the girl, and that the girl was now sending encouraging messages to Mary. According to this narrative, the affair, if that is what it was, continued for the rest of the year, ending when Anne essentially procured her own cousin, Madge Shelton, brought her to the King's attention and the King obligingly began an affair with her instead.

This version of events is the one accepted by many writers, who take Chapuys' word for what is often read as being, if not a virtual breakdown of the marriage, then a growing distance between the couple, as early as summer 1534, with the King's passion for Anne having cooled some time before. This is distinctly questionable, not least because Chapuys fails even to give a name for the King's so-called new love. What does seem likely is that the King had lost little time in identifying a new partner in the game of courtly romance. This was an expected move: a gallant knight was expected to 'serve' an unattainable lady. Wives really didn't count, but Anne had played the part of the unattainable lady for too long to be prepared to give it up as, according to the rules of court etiquette, she should have done. Queens were not supposed to be players in the courtly game – they were supposed to preside, as indeed the Archduchess Margaret had done in the first court Anne had known. Certainly Henry VIII expected his new Queen to change roles – but did not expect to do so himself. It is likely, too, that he took it as a matter of course that he would find passing consolation elsewhere while his wife was pregnant. In this he was far from alone, not least as at this time it was regarded as both dangerous and inappropriate for a pregnant woman to have sex.

There is conflicting evidence about the tone Anne set for her household. As with so much else about her, different people remembered different things – and, in this instance, the disparate memories are not necessarily in conflict. Her personal piety and interest in religious matters are widely attested. The former was expected of any lady, both on her own behalf and on that of her household, for whose welfare and behaviour she had to be seen to take responsibility and, as Queen, Anne needed to set the tone for the rest of the Court. From the recollections of her silk woman, Rose Lok, and other eyewitnesses, Anne took care that she and her ladies should be seen to take religious matters seriously, as witnessed by the New Testament in her rooms, the prayer books carried by each, the sewing for the poor and the purse that Anne carried round with her containing ready money to give out at need. Once Anne and Henry had scribbled love-notes on the pages of a Book of Hours – now her cousin Madge Shelton was reprimanded when she was found to have scribbled 'idle poesies' on the pages of her prayer book.

As we have seen, Anne was interested in religious reform, partly because the arguments of some of its proponents put forward arguments that made her marriage a possibility. However, it is hard to doubt her genuine religious belief, or her desire to lead a Christian life. For her, a part of that life was learning – it would not have occurred to anyone at that time to make any distinction between the intellectual and religious part of that interest. It should be remembered that Anne would never have regarded herself as a Protestant (not, indeed, a term that was current in her lifetime) – she and her circle were interested in the reform of the Catholic church from within; in this she resembled Marguerite of Angouleme, the sister of the King of France, as well as his first wife, Claude, and her own sister. It was an interest that she shared with her brother, George – it was probably both an indicator and a cause of their undoubted closeness – and with many, if not most, of the court circle of which she formed the centre.

There were other parts of the picture. Margaret Roper, daughter of Thomas More, wrote to her father that 'there was nothing else in the court but sporting and dancing,' or so William Roper claimed in his biography of More. Admittedly, Margaret was highly unlikely to look at a court presided over by the woman who had, in her eyes, caused her father to lose his career, with anything other than hostility, but other observers reported large-scale partying in the Queen's rooms, including dancing in her bedchamber – which was essentially a reception room. Just after the coronation, Anne's chamberlain wrote to George Boleyn, away in France, that 'pastime in the Queen's chamber was never more. If any of you that be now departed have any ladies that favoured you, and some what would mourn at parting of their servants, I can no whit perceive the same by the dancing and pastime they do use here.'[5] Which was probably a piece of teasing aimed at either George himself or someone in his party. But Anne had gathered round herself a group of like-minded people – they were sophisticated, intelligent, and willing and able to take part in the music, dancing, discussion, hunting and gambling that formed an integral part of court life. As far as Anne was concerned, being deeply religious was absolutely no barrier to the enjoyment of earthly power, riches and taste and all that they brought, and all this social and cultural life took place within the context of the code of courtly love to which the King adhered.

Everyone concerned knew the rules of the game of playful, artificial flirtation by which the social life of the court operated.

It was, very evidently, a dangerous game when the language of artificial love proved, as it often did, an inadequate mask for all-too-real human passions. Anne, her brother, George, and a group of their friends appear to have formed an inner circle in the Queen's Side in Anne's time in power. Many if not most large groups have such an 'alpha' inner circle, its membership unofficial, shifting, but apparent, sharing aims, interests, jokes, secrets, probably, talent and, possibly, affection. It was a circle from which others felt excluded – and those who felt on the outside included their sister, Mary, George's wife, Jane, and, perhaps, the King. It was also a circle that those on its outer edge tried to get into – one of these was a musician named Mark Smeaton, a poor boy from the Low Countries who had been a chorister in the household of Thomas Wolsey and then talent spotted by the King. Mark was a skilled lute and keyboard player, and as such was valued and had access to much of the social life of the court. This allowed him to acquire money, fine clothes and privileges – and he may, for a while, have felt he was fully accepted. His musical ability allowed him to be on friendly terms with Anne and her brother, George, who gave him a book of music. He was still an outsider because he was not, and never would be, a gentleman.

Music was an immensely important part of life at court, and every report of Anne, including the most hostile, agrees that she was a skilled lutenist and dancer. A certain level of musical competence was expected in everyone in the Royal household, and greater skill invited greater favour. As we have seen, the King sang, danced, played several different instruments and composed music himself, and music was part of the education of high status children of both sexes; at the court of the Archduchess Margaret, the maids of honour were tutored in music by the organist Henri Bredemers, who was also involved in the writing and staging of many music and dance events. To be highly skilled as a performer was to be more employable as a courtier – especially if that courtier was knowledgeable about the latest fashions in musical pageantry. The fact that Anne was cast in Wolsey's high profile and very expensive

Assault on the Chateau Vert in 1522, almost as soon as she arrived at the English court, suggests that she was both highly talented and that she may well have had previous experience of this kind of event at both the Burgundian and the French courts. Anne's own songbook,[6] a collection of pieces evidently added to over a period, has been preserved and is now in the Royal College of Music. One of the manuscript pages bears the inscription 'Mistres A Bolleyn nowe thus' – proving both that the book is hers, and dating it to the period before her father became an earl, at which point Anne became Lady Anne Rochford. The motto 'now thus' is his – it may be that Anne shared it at this stage in her life. Once she became Queen, we may be sure that the 'pastime' in the Queen's Chamber' included both singing and rehearsing the latest dance steps. It is probably fair to imagine this kind of impromptu entertainment as being, along with card games and gossip, the most usual way of whiling away many winter afternoons when the weather was not fit for the tennis or archery riding that the courtiers also loved.

At this time, too, some of Europe's most accomplished painters were coming to England. One of the foremost was Hans Holbein, whose portraits of Tudor courtiers and Londoners form much of our view of them and their time. Holbein was in London in time to create some of the displays for Anne's coronation, together with designs for jewellery, tableware and furniture. His portraits of Henry VIII have formed our iconographic image of the King in his later years – the huge, wide-shouldered frame, with straddled legs and feet and unmissable codpiece from the painting created for the Presence Chamber at Whitehall, are imprinted in the mind of virtually anyone who has any concept of the word 'Tudor'. The series of drawings now in the Royal Collection, taken together, form a social commentary of life at court – the exquisite but almost brutally realistic representations, many with closed, anxious faces, tight mouths and hard eyes speak volumes about the stresses of life at Court. Holbein's first known regular employment by the King did not come until 1538, when we know that Anne was one the first of Holbein's patrons. Yet there is no portrait by him that can be proved to be of Anne. There are two drawings that are often claimed to be of her. One, still in the

Royal Collection, shows a woman in a high-necked smock, fur-trimmed robe and an undercap with the then-fashionable ear-irons, which leaves a few strands of fair hair showing. Her face is somewhat jowly, she looks into the middle distance and she looks tired. The caption on the picture says it is of Anne. The attributions on the Holbein drawings in the Royal Collection were based on identifications by John Cheke, tutor to Edward VI; several have been shown to be inaccurate; additionally, the coat of arms of the Wyatt family appears on the back of the drawing. In recent years some historians have again argued that Anne was the sitter,[7] suggesting that she was the only woman at court who would have taken the liberty of sitting for a portrait in such informal dress, and reasserting the idea, originally put about by a hostile commentator on her coronation, that she had a swollen, probably goitrous, neck and wore high collars to hide it. This is possible, but does not explain why a woman so concerned with her appearance, and a queen so concerned with her image, as Anne, would have chosen to sit for a portrait in such unbecoming clothes, including a head dress that emphasises the line of an already puffy jaw. If the image were of an informally but elegantly dressed woman, it would be much easier to believe the Anne Boleyn who spent huge sums of money on a black satin nightgown (meaning a loose over gown to wear in private but not in bed) might be the subject. It is also possible that this is a preparatory sketch for another portrait, now lost. There is, however, also the unanswered question of why the drawing has the Wyatt coat of arms on the back.

The second Holbein picture said to be of Anne, shows what, to modern eyes at least, is a more attractive woman. The lady shown is dark, with a vivid and pretty face – she is probably in her twenties, and has an open if thoughtful expression. She wears an English gable hood and the square-necked gown fashionable in the 1530s. This picture, too, has a caption, this time in a different hand, claiming it is of Anne Boleyn. This drawing is certainly by Holbein, and started off in the Royal Collection, but was sold sometime in the seventeenth century and is now in the British Museum. Its identification as a portrait of Anne appears to have begun in 1649. It is almost certainly not of the same sitter as the previous drawing, and this pretty lady bears little resemblance to any of the other pictures that may be of her. Additionally, this sitter is too young to be Anne, who was in her thirties by the time Holbein arrived for his second stay in England in 1532. The desire to identify a work by Holbein as being of Anne is understandable, but sadly it does seem all too likely that the elusive portrait did once exist but was destroyed, along with much else, immediately after her execution. It is possible to speculate that there was a painting, not just a drawing, and that it showed Anne in black gown, a pearl-trimmed French hood, much pearl jewellery and a pendant with her initials round her neck.

There are indeed several portraits of Anne Boleyn in just such clothes and jewels – one is now in the National Portrait Gallery, another at Hever Castle, a third at Ripon Cathedral. They are very alike, although not identical, and all date from the late sixteenth century. This is almost certainly because, once Anne's daughter, Elizabeth, became Queen, it was suddenly fashionable to possess a portrait of her mother, to display alongside a picture of Elizabeth herself and of her father. As so many of the extant portraits of this time are similar, it seems highly likely that they all relate to a lost original, but short of a near-miraculous new find, this cannot be proved. The two images we do have that may well tell us more about what Anne Boleyn actually looked like are frustratingly small. One is a portrait medal, produced in 1534, probably to commemorate the pregnancy that ended in miscarriage, and now in the British Museum. It is not only small but damaged too – however, it provides a memorable image of a very specific face. If this indeed an accurate image of Anne, the contemporaries who said she was no beauty were speaking the truth. This face, and its features, are long, and the woman shown is thin, lacking the delicately soft curves admired at this time. But there is something in the lift of her head that speaks of the intelligence and strength of will that we know Anne to have possessed. The second image that is likely to be authentic is even smaller in size. It is one of two tiny portraits in a ring, now in the collection at Chequers, and formerly a possession of Elizabeth I, who is said to have kept it by her bed. The face shown in the ring picture is very like that on the medal – a long face, long nose and an idiosyncratic lift to the head. As the other picture is of Elizabeth herself, this image clearly does not date from Anne's lifetime, but as there were a number of people in Elizabeth's household who remembered Anne, it seems very likely that this represents a recognisable likeness of the mother of whom she can have had no more than the haziest of memories.

Anne's style as Queen was very different from that of her predecessor. Her household had grown incrementally during the time when there had essentially been two Queens at court, as had her status as she progressed from maid to honour to earl's daughter and then to Marquess to Queen. It would have been very difficult, without a sudden, Henry V-like transformation, to have repudiated all her former friends once she was married. And, as Queen more than ever, she needed all the friends she had and more. From what evidence we have of conversation between her and her inner circle, she and they continued to talk and interact as they ever had, for all that she was now addressed as 'madam' or 'your grace' (the term 'your majesty' was reserved for the King alone). When Anne's relations with her uncle the Duke of Norfolk became strained, the Duke had no inhibitions about quarrelling with his niece, Queen though she might be. A certain amount of deference of speech was required, but much of the court was made up of people she had known for many years, some since her return to England in 1522. There was, however, a very distinct barrier between those of noble and gentle status, and those who were 'inferior persons'. In the informal atmosphere of the Queen's rooms, there is evidence this may not always have been maintained.

Like most people of her time, Anne placed a lot of reliance on the loyalty of her relatives – her household as Queen contained a number of uncles, aunts and cousins. Her mother was always there, but had the art of keeping very much in the background – whatever she thought of her daughter's career she kept to herself, and the two appear to have been close. On her arrest in 1536, one of Anne's first anxieties was for the effect on her ailing mother. Anne's relationship with her father was more difficult. Thomas Boleyn is sometimes portrayed as having owed his advancement to his daughters. This is unfair – as we have seen, he had climbed some way up the greasy pole of court advancement long before either Mary or Anne caught the Royal eye. Thomas was able and ambitious, but there is some evidence that he felt out of his depth when he found he was to be the father of the Queen. Most of these hints come from Chapuys and are uncorroborated from other sources, but it appears he may have made some attempt to dissuade the King from marrying Anne in 1532.

Mary was clearly the odd one out of the family. Until her husband William Carey died of sweating sickness in 1528, Mary appears to have stayed on good terms with her parents – but when she was widowed, and left with little money, the King had to intervene to persuade Thomas to help his daughter – although the King later assigned to Mary an annuity of £100 that had formerly been paid to her late husband. The relationship between the sisters can hardly have been easy by this time – the elder was a former lover of the King, the younger was trying to become his wife, and if it is true that one or both of Mary's children was by the King, then that must have complicated matters further. As we have seen, the King took a particular interest in Mary's daughter, Catherine, who it now appears was certainly the elder of the two, which does suggest that there was at least a possibility she was his child. But when William Carey died, Anne was given the wardship of his son, Henry, meaning that she had the right to make decisions concerning him. As Anne was by this time the Queen in waiting, it can be argued that this move was in the young boy's own interest, as it placed him under the protection of the most powerful member of the family. On a personal level, however, the evidence points to the following few years having been difficult ones for Mary. Although, thanks to the King, she now had an income of her own, it appears that Mary spent much of her time at Hever, where it is likely she shared the household with her daughter and grandmother. She is also on record as having visited court, for example taking a prominent part in the 1532 visit to Calais, where she was one of the six ladies in cloth of gold who joined Anne in dancing with the French King and lords before the assembled company. It is likely, too, that it was in Calais that she met William Stafford, who was to become her second husband. Mary was also in the procession at Anne's coronation, and was probably part of her entourage thereafter. Evidently, though, she was able to vanish for long periods without undue difficulty – when she appeared at Court, married to Stafford and pregnant, it seems that none of the Boleyn family had known where she was and what she was doing for several months previously.

In marrying Stafford at all, and in the way she handled the matter, Mary was to demonstrate how different in temperament she was to the rest of her family. To begin with, this was a mésalliance. Stafford, who was perhaps ten years younger than Mary, was a nobody in comparison with the Boleyns, despite the fact he was distantly related to the noble family of Stafford. At the time they met, William was either in the King's retinue for the Calais trip, or already serving in the garrison there, and Mary was to claim later that it was he who fell in love and pursued her. If so, he was taking a considerable risk, but it was one which evidently paid off in time. We do not know when or how they met again, but sometime early in 1534 they began an affair, then marrying once Mary was pregnant. When she appeared at court in September her condition was obvious – and all hell broke loose. This was hardly surprising, as at this time it was considered foolish for anyone of high status to marry solely for love, and outrageous for any member of the nobility, man or woman, to marry without family approval. For the Queen's sister to marry without approval, and on top of that to land the King with a family connection who was little better than a serving man, was outrageous.

The result was predictable. The Boleyns, headed by Anne and backed up by Thomas, George and the Duke of Norfolk, turned on Mary. They persuaded the King to banish her from court and cancel her annuity, and the additional allowance that her father had made her was discontinued, too. It was also predictable that the story provided Chapuys with a juicy piece of news to send to Charles V, writing with relish that Mary had been 'found guilty of misconduct' – the fact that she was pregnant when she married added the finishing touch. All this left Mary and her new husband in a very difficult position – it is likely that they took refuge with his parents, and they waited several months before Mary tried to plead for a reconciliation. Evidently she did not dare to approach any of her relatives directly, as her letter, which survives, was addressed to Thomas Cromwell. The first few sentences read:

'Master Secretary, After my poor recommendations, which is smally to be regarded of me, that am a poor banished creature, this shall be to desire you to be good to my poor husband and to me. I am sure it is not unknown to you the high displeasure that he and I have, both of the King's Highness and the Queen's Grace, by reason of our marriage without their knowledge, wherein we both do yield ourselves faulty, And acknowledge that we did not well to be so hasty nor so bold, without their knowledge. But one thing, good Master Secretary, consider: that he was young, and love overcame reason; and for my part, I saw so much honesty in him that I loved him as well as he did me; and was in bondage, and glad I was to be at liberty.'[8]

Despite her need to grovel for forgiveness and, just as importantly, the reinstatement of her income, Mary could not resist making it clear how unhappy she had been before her remarriage – the 'bondage' referring, presumably, to her position in the Boleyn family. This is reinforced later in the letter, when she states:

'So that, for my part, I saw all the world did set so little store by me, and he so much, that I thought I could take no better way than to take him and forsake all other ways and live a poor, honest life with him. And so I do put no doubt but we should, if we might once be so happy to recover the King's gracious favour and the Queen's.'

Having pleaded for Cromwell's intercession to get Stafford reinstated in his fairly lowly Court appointment, she makes it clear she knows it is Anne who is the most angry with her;

'And, good Master Secretary, sue for us to the King's Highness, and beseech his Highness, which ever was wont to take pity, to have pit on us; and that it would please his Grace, of his goodness, to speak to the Queen's Grace for us; for, so far as I can perceive, her Grace is so highly displeased with us both, that without the King be so good lord so us as to withdraw his rigour and sue for us, we are never likely to recover her Grace's favour, which is too heavy to bear.'

She goes on to ask Cromwell to intercede for her with her father, mother, brother and her uncle too, but Mary could not resist a barbed comment:

'But if I were at my liberty and might choose, I ensure you, good Master Secretary, for my little time, I have spied so much honesty to be in him that I would rather beg my bread with him that to be the greatest queen christened.'

Whatever the reader makes of the tone of the letter, it was written to little avail. Mary was never invited back to Court, although her husband was allowed to continue with his posting in Calais – it is likely that the Boleyns felt this embarrassing couple were best out of the way. Mary's actions at this time suggest that those historians who claim she was stupid, malleable or immoral are probably mistaken. Neither is the letter to Cromwell that of a nonentity – but it is that of a woman with a very different approach to life from that of her sister and brother.

Famously, and ultimately fatally, Anne and her brother, George, had become a close alliance against the rest of the world; although they can have seen little of each other in their teenage years, it is evident that Anne and George were very much alike. In his *Metrical Visions*, Wolsey's former servant Cavendish was to write after George's death:

'God gave me grace, Dame Nature did her part,
Endowed me with gifts of natural qualities
Dame Eloquence also taught me the art
In meter and verse to make pleasant ditties.'

As Cavendish was an enemy of the Boleyns, we may be sure that if he was prepared to allow any virtue or quality to his literary George Boleyn, it was probably there in real life. Even Thomas Wyatt, who was a friend of George's, was to accept that he was too proud. This quality he certainly shared with his sister, Anne. The two were drawn together, too, by their mutual musical and linguistic ability. As we have seen, they shared, too, an increasing interest in religious reform, and George was to help Anne to obtain some of the evangelical texts which were being produced in Europe, but which were illegal in both England and France. During his career George went on five diplomatic missions, and evidently used the opportunity to obtain and import some of the latest controversial works, including those by the scholar and humanist Jacques Lefevre d'Etaples, who was one of those who believed that the Bible must be made available in the vernacular. Accordingly, he published a New Testament in French, and also worked to promote the idea, shared with but not learned from Martin Luther, that humanity was to be saved by faith and not by good works. Lefevre, unlike Luther, always believed the Catholic Church could be reformed from the inside, but was passionate in his belief for the need for a living, scripture-based and active faith. It appears that Anne and George Boleyn shared these views, and George was to turn two of Lefevre's works, smuggled into England in the form of small, concealable volumes, into magnificent presentation works for his sister. Both were Biblical texts with accompanying commentaries, and both were exactly the kind of works that stimulated the kind of religious discussion in which the brother and sister delighted, and which they shared with others. George himself provided a translation into English of the commentaries, and included also a dedicatory preface in which he referred to himself as 'her most loving and friendly brother'.[9]

It has been suggested by some historians[10] that George was gay, and that he was the lover of, among others, Mark Smeaton. There are two pieces of evidence put forward in support of this – the fact that George once gave Mark a book, and an interpretation of a verse in Cavendish's *Metrical Visions*. The book concerned is a satirical poem attacking the institution of marriage, which some have seen as significant. As to the verse in Cavendish, it has George confessing to 'living bestial' and to having 'forced widows'. The former might indeed be interpreted as buggery; the latter has sometimes been taken to mean that George was a rapist. Those who support this theory also point to some of the reports of what

George said on the scaffold just before his execution, when he followed the accepted etiquette of the occasion by accepting that, as a sinner, he deserved death and that he had been better at taking an intellectual interest in the scriptures than in following their teachings. However, if there were anything in these claims, the rumours would surely have reached the ears of people other than the bitterly hostile Cavendish – and the confession he puts into George's mouth is anyway very unspecific. What does seem to have been the case was that George shared with Anne a capacity to antagonise and to exclude, and in some moments, even to enjoy doing so. It is beyond doubt that both were highly intelligent, and had been brought up by their father to be ruthlessly ambitious – it seems that, in these two children, he got more than he bargained for.

Anne and George Boleyn both used laughter as a weapon and as a defence. In one incident, Anne annoyed the French ambassador by laughing, as he thought, inappropriately, while they sat next to one another at dinner. He asked her why in some dudgeon, at which she explained that she had been watching the King, who had been distracted from where he was going by meeting a lady. Anne's way of dealing with this, as with other irritations, was to laugh wildly. As we have seen, she did this at the time of her hinting to Thomas Wyatt as to her pregnancy; and wild, hysterical laughter was to surface again at the time of her imprisonment. Sometimes, however, she would meet obstacles with fury, as, when she often did, she made hyperbolic statements in response to difficulties. As we have seen, one of those difficulties may well have been her own jealousy at seeing the King playing the courtly romance game with another, probably younger, woman. Another was certainly the ongoing problems relating to Catherine of Aragon and her daughter.

Catherine was staying firm, in what was either her resolve or her intransigence, depending on one's view of her, in insisting that she was still Queen. When her Chamberlain, Lord Mountjoy, briefed by Norfolk and the Council, spelled out to her that she was no longer to be addressed as Queen but as Princess Dowager of Wales, she had a moderately dignified tantrum. Reclining on a daybed, she restated her position, which was that she was the King's wife, his Queen and the mother of his only legitimate child and heir. She did not recognise Cranmer's court or its verdict, and if anyone in her household, or anyone else, were to address her as Princess, she would not answer – this was ultimately to result in her refusing to be in the same room with most of her household. The next day Mountjoy, as a courtesy, showed her the report of what had occurred that he was proposing to send to the King. In it, he referred to Catherine throughout as Princess Dowager. Her response was to take a pen and strike out the words[11] – Mountjoy, presumably to demonstrate what he was up against, sent the report to the King, complete with crossings-out. For the time being, both Catherine and her daughter, Mary, were left alone.

But when Anne's daughter, Elizabeth, was born, the King took the decision to tell his elder daughter that she no longer had the title of Princess, which would henceforward belong to Elizabeth alone (at this time, the term referred to an heir or heiress to the throne, not to any child of a sovereign). Additionally, Mary was to be ordered to leave New Hall in Essex and join Elizabeth's newly formed household at Hatfield – she would no longer have servants of her own as she had before. Elizabeth was paraded formally through London in December 1533 on the way to her new home at Hatfield, where she was to start her Royal life. The job of breaking this news to Mary went again to Norfolk, who visited her in person and escorted her to Hatfield. Chapuys, when he heard of this, was unhesitating in blaming Anne for the move, and thereafter began to refer to her in his reports as 'the whore' and the baby Elizabeth as 'the bastard'. Meanwhile, in Hertfordshire, the Duke of Norfolk, Mary and their servants arrived at Hatfield, and Norfolk asked whether Mary would like to go and pay her respects to the Princess. This, of course, gave Mary the opportunity of asserting she was the Princess, and Elizabeth was not. Perhaps as some form of olive branch, she said that, as she addressed the Duke of Richmond as 'brother' she would also be prepared to address Elizabeth as 'sister'. Norfolk, sensibly, did not stay to argue but asked if Mary wanted to send any message to the King – only to be told that she wanted him to say that 'his daughter, the Princess, asked for his blessing.' After that, Norfolk departed and Mary retired to weep in her room. We know that Catherine and her daughter had been corresponding, and that

Catherine had warned Mary to stand up for what they both regarded as her rights.

After this, a war of attrition began at Hatfield. Mary began to refuse to leave her own room, demanding to have her meals served in private as, if she went into the hall, she would not be served first. The household was told to stop taking food in to her, and to insist that Mary eat with everyone else in the hall – the point being that Mary's place in the hall was secondary to Elizabeth's, and this she was not prepared to tolerate. Chapuys, of course, blamed Anne for the whole thing, but may well have been mistaken in doing so, as the King appears to have been fully involved, and to have regarded this as being a question of a disobedient child – a serious matter. But Anne was certainly aware of what was going on, and sent a series of instructions to Lady Shelton, who was Lady Mistress of the household – and was also Anne's aunt. Anne wanted Lady Shelton to box Mary's ears if she tried to use the title of Princess, and to ensure without fail that the only food that was available, was to be served in the hall. Both Anne and Henry visited Hatfield often, and on several occasions Anne tried to be friendly with Mary, but the matter remained unresolved for the next year – and Mary responded to Anne's approaches with insults.

Meanwhile, Catherine was reducing herself to a state of near-hysteria. Chapuys claimed that Buckden, in Huntingdonshire, where she was lodged, was little short of a damp-infested prison. In fact, it was a large red brick mansion on the edge of the fens, where Catherine could have been tolerably comfortable had she wished. Her household had been reduced, but still comprised about 200 people, including 10 maids of honour. However, many of the 200 had been chosen by the King, and addressed her as Princess Dowager. So she would not allow any of these people near her, or allow them to prepare her food. Soon, she was camping out in her Privy Chamber, eating only such food as her own long-standing servants could prepare over the fire. Catherine apparently openly said she was afraid of being poisoned. Whether this was a genuine fear or not, she was to withdraw almost totally for the remaining two years of her life, living virtually as a recluse. The Pope had finally given a sentence in her favour in March 1534, stating that her marriage to Henry was valid and canonical, by coincidence on the same day that the Act of Succession was passed by Parliament in England, stating that the King was now married to Anne, that Catherine was now to be styled Princess Dowager, and that the succession was to go first to any male children of Henry and Anne or, if there were none, to Elizabeth. Mary was not mentioned at all. Catherine felt totally vindicated by the Papal sentence, and appears to have failed completely to come to terms with the brutal fact that no one, including the Pope, her nephew Charles V or any of the English nobles who offered sympathy, was going to lift a finger to help her in any practical way. More and Fisher might be preparing to die for their consciences, but that benefited her nothing. She had devoted friends, and many sympathisers, but without money and leadership none of them were in a position to help her. Chapuys, whom she addressed in her regular letters to him as 'her special friend', was completely in sympathy with her, but was himself fully aware that anything he said to the King in support of Catherine was serving only to annoy. Catherine was, of course, kept as far as possible from court. It might have comforted her had she known how much her uncompromising stance, and that of Mary, was infuriating and upsetting the Boleyns.

At the end of 1534, the Act of Treasons was passed. This stated unequivocally that it was treason either by action or by 'wish, will or desire, by words or in writing' to harm or disrespect Henry or Anne or their heirs in any way, or to call him heretic, tyrant or usurper. This, of course, strongly suggests what was feared. The scene was set for the first of a series of high-profile executions, the victims carefully selected to demonstrate what would happen to anyone who opposed the new order, and the deaths taking place in London. Those chosen were eighteen of the Carthusian monks who had refused to take the Oath of Supremacy, along with Bishop Fisher and Sir Thomas More. It has been convincingly said that the elimination of the monks was the most brutal act of the reign of Henry VIII. Nine of the monks were executed – they were dragged on hurdles through the city, still in their habits, and were then hung, drawn and quartered at Tyburn. The rest were simply left in prison to starve to death. One of those executed, Sebastian Newdigate, was a former courtier who had served in the Privy Chamber before he became a monk, and had been on friendly terms with the King. Newdigate was one of those imprisoned in Marshalsea Prison, in what is now Borough High Street. They are said to have been left chained to pillars for thirteen days, and then brought before the Privy Council. There is also a story (later current in recusant circles) that the King visited Newdigate in disguise, offering him riches and favour if he would take the oath. There is also a third story that, in the case of the monks left to starve, the King sent several messages wanting to know if they were dead yet, suspecting, probably correctly, that a sympathiser might be feeding them. More and Fisher came off better by comparison. Both were given the dignity of a trial, which the King supervised from Windsor, delaying the start of the 1535 summer progress in order to do so. Both of them were beheaded on Tower Hill, Fisher in June, and More in early July.

As was intended, these executions sent reverberations all around Europe. The position, to London, to England and to the whole world, could not have been made clearer – Henry VIII was Supreme Head of the Church. He was married to Anne Boleyn, and their children would succeed. Be prepared to swear that you agree to all that. Or prepare to die. According – as usual – to Chapuys, Anne was not only delighted by the deaths of people she had regarded as enemies, but was doing her best to persuade the King to have Catherine and Mary executed too.[12] There is no way of knowing how true this is – by this time the court had set off on the annual summer progress, and Chapuys was in London and dependent on his informers in the Royal party. What is certainly true is that the 1535 summer progress was a political road show. It was a tour of the West Country, taking in Bristol, second only to London in the number of religious reformers in the population, and including visits to a number of country houses where there lived courtiers and others sympathetic to reform. Among these were Sir William Baynton, Anne's Vice Chamberlain, Sir John and Lady Walsh, protectors of Tyndale, and Nicholas Poyntz of Iron Acton. Thomas Cromwell joined the progress for several weeks. The stopping places included Ewelme and Hook Norton, properties owned by the Duke of Suffolk but about to be surrendered to the King as part of the price of Suffolk's less-than enthusiastic support over the Great Matter. The presence of the King and Queen in these houses was a high profile – and very expensive – way of demonstrating Royal approval of these loyal, and reforming, friends. This was perhaps the most political progress of the reign, and the top item on the agenda was to show off the King in his new role as Head of the Church. It appears they had at least some success – Chapuys wrote that he had been told that 'many of the peasants' in places through which the progress had passed now believed the King had done right to repudiate both Catherine and the Pope.[13] This does not, of course, mean that the whole summer was devoted to politics. The chief entertainment, as in other years, was hunting.

Another piece of political drama took place during the progress. The process of dissolving the religious houses began – we could almost say launched – at Winchcombe Abbey. It was here that Cromwell briefed the visitors who were to travel round every monastery and nunnery in the country, with a brief to find fault. A set of injunctions was issued, to be handed over at each house, giving a list of reminders of the rules they were supposed to live by. The rules were not in contention – some of the interpretations were – and the visitors had orders to concentrate in their reports on any sexual failings of the monks and nuns, and any less-than authentic objects of veneration. Many religious houses owned relics of saints; often these had become places of pilgrimage and objects of veneration; some saints' altars were decked out with jewels, precious metals and fabrics worth a fortune, and brought in a very healthy income to the monastic orders that owned them. It was well known that, in come houses as least, there were criticisms to be made – the story of Mary Boleyn's would-be abbess sister in law and her two children by different priests was not unique, and there were notorious instances of sham relics deliberately set up to dupe the gullible faithful. All over England, Cromwell's men set out with a set of questions to ask and an agenda to fulfil – they knew what was expected of them.

This progress also included another famous stopping-off point – Wolf Hall, where the Royal party stayed for three nights. This was the home of the Seymours, the parents of Jane, Edward and Thomas. It is often claimed that it was during this visit that Henry met and fell in love with Jane – a good story, but as Jane, at about twenty-seven, was a seasoned courtier who had been a maid of honour to Catherine of Aragon before moving on to the household of Anne Boleyn, the King must have been acquainted with her for years. It is not even known for certain whether Jane was present during the visit, as not everyone who had a court appointment was required to go on the summer progress. However, as the visit was to her parents, it seems likely that she would have been there, even if she did not take part in the entire progress. If she was there, it is possible that she would have come more to the King's notice than ever before. But as the summer became autumn, and the day's outings generally took the form of hawking, the reports were that the King and Queen were both in good health, and 'merry together'. At around this time, Anne became pregnant once more. Later in October, the progress had reached the Vyne in Hampshire, home to Lord Sandys and a house the King had visited before.

The end of the month saw everyone back at Windsor – summer was officially over. As they settled back into the routine of the winter months, with the court dividing its time for the most part between Greenwich and Hampton Court, the King and Queen appeared on good terms. It is clear that they were not as happy together as they had once been – whatever the truth of the King's reported affairs, he was indulging in notable flirtations, if not more, with other women of the court. At this time the French ambassador wrote in a report that the King was less and less in love with Anne, and that he had other loves. Anne appears to have become far less tactful in her handling of him – she seems to have been bored of him, and to have made fun of him, certainly with her brother and perhaps with her ladies, too. Also, time had not been kind to the looks of either Henry or Anne. At forty-four he was now going bald, and so had had his previously long, wavy hair cut short. He had also grown a beard, which now became the fashion at court, and had begun to put on the excess weight that was an important factor in ruining his health over the next few years. Anne, always slender, was now referred to as being thin – from the descriptions she appears always to have been highly-strung and nervous, as is attested by her habit of going off into wild peals of laughter when life was complicated. Her temper, too, seems often to have been on a knife-edge, as is attested by her outbursts of irritation, and sometimes of fury, at the latest news of, for example, the intransigence of Catherine or of Mary. As for Henry, as well as his physical ageing, he was also showing signs of the paranoid suspicion that was to characterise him in his last years. He could still be affable, and was more than capable of dissembling, including being pleasant to people he was planning to destroy.

Henry and Anne had good reason to be pleased with their summer – but on returning to London, they were returning to political reality. While they were away, there had been a very public demonstration at Greenwich in favour of Mary.[14] The matter was very much hushed up, so we do not know the details. But evidently the wives of some leading London citizens took part, together with Anne's sister in law, Jane, Lady Rochford, and aunt Lady William Howard. The two were briefly imprisoned in the Tower, and banished from Court thereafter. According to some reports, Catherine of Aragon wrote to Charles V at this time, asking him directly to intervene. The story of the Royal summer progress was known; a new tax of 10 per cent on all clerical incomes was coming into force; Cromwell's agents were all over the country, inspecting the religious houses and making no secret of their contempt and disapproval of most of what they found; the London merchant community was rife with rumours of war with Charles V; the harvest had been one of the worst in Henry's reign; and it was a Plague year (bubonic plague was a regular summer visitor, not just in London but all over the country). Just before Christmas, the news of Catherine of Aragon's illness reached Greenwich – but at that stage it did not sound very serious. Most importantly, Anne was pregnant. It would be a merry Christmas after all.

Chapter 8

Fall: 1536

New Year 1535/6: at Court, this year, as usual, the royal household exchanged presents with the King and Queen. This was a cheerful Christmas season – although the days when Queen Anne had received a gold-hung room from her adoring husband may have seemed far away. Two years before, Anne had given Henry a silver gilt table fountain, designed by Hans Holbein, featuring naked nymphs that spurted rose water from their breasts. But this Christmas the Royal couple, after what may have been a sometimes rocky year, were observed at least to be 'merry together' as they had been during the summer progress. In London, John Husee, agent of Lord and Lady Lisle, wrote increasingly desperate letters to his bosses as suppliers refused to provide more goods until they were paid. He tried six times in five days to obtain the special livery kirtle the Queen had promised to Lady Lisle – still without success. In a luxuriously furnished but damp room in Cambridgeshire, Catherine of Aragon knew she was dying – her final letter to the king went unanswered. In her nursery in Hatfield, many miles from the infections of London, the Princess Elizabeth was taking pleasure in the many new clothes her mother sent her – among them a tawny silk petticoat and a variety of caps and coifs. Now over 2 years old, she was talking fluently and already had a strong will of her own. In Leicestershire, the Abbot of Garendon, his abbey already marked for closure, was prophesying the King's exile and death. At Greenwich, Anne Boleyn was entering the second trimester of a sickly, but much-wanted, pregnancy.

The new year (and, confusingly, most people called it new year even though the date did not officially change until 25 March) must have seemed to bring with it a number of reasons to be cheerful, not only for Anne Boleyn, but for anyone in support of the cause of religious reform.

The previous autumn's royal progress to the west country had underlined the high favour enjoyed by such families as the Poyntz and Walshes – and the itinerary had been expanded to allow Thomas Cromwell to organise early inspections of some of the local monasteries. Since then, his agents, armed with a list of standard questions, had been out working their way round the country, visiting all the smaller religious houses with a clearly understood agenda to find problems in each one. Some reformers, however, including the Queen, were of the view that there might be alternatives to closure, and it was by no means a foregone conclusion what should happen to the property and land of any monasteries that were closed.

Closest to home, and known only to the inner circle at Court, Anne was now sure she was pregnant again. There are some indications that this was another sickly pregnancy. Chapuys, who now seems to have had regular, and at least passably reliable, sources of information in the Queen's Side, mentions that he has been told that Anne was fearful of death[1] – he assumed she feared the King, but Anne may well have been afraid she might not survive childbirth, and her fears may have been exacerbated by her previous miscarriage. She was by now around 36, which in the sixteenth century was regarded as being an advanced age for a pregnant woman. But alongside the fears went hope that the longed-for son might at last be on his way.

True, in the wider country there was a mood of resentment against the King, but the simmering anger that was to boil over to become the Pilgrimage of Grace the following Autumn was scarcely yet discernible, especially from Court. In London it was, of course, Thomas Cromwell, at the centre of his network of informers, who was most aware of what was being said where and by whom. He was doing everything in his power not only to keep tabs on what was being said throughout the land, but to monitor who was building up what might be an undesirable amount of local influence. He was extremely aware of how controversial the monastery closures might turn out to be, and was in constant touch with his staff as to what appointment or payment should be offered to which person in order to damp down any fear of opposition. There is some possibility, too, that at this stage the intention was to keep some of the larger houses in operation.

168 Anne Boleyn in London

On the ground in London, the mood was as mixed as ever. The autumn's demonstration at Greenwich in support of Mary had been largely hushed up. It is not recorded when the ringleaders, including Anne's aunt by marriage, Lady William Howard, and sister in law, Jane, Lady Rochford, were released from the Tower. It seems likely that Jane was still unwelcome at Court, and that she was living at one of the Boleyn properties, perhaps Hever. As will appear, however, she was back in London by the spring. Regarding the unnamed wives of London citizens who were also involved, no action was taken. The fact that they had the time and the means to get to Greenwich suggests they were people of some status, and it may well be that the matter was dealt with by telling their husbands to keep them out of trouble in future, and that few people in London itself ever got to know of the incident, except on the uncontrollable gossip circuit that passed on everything it could find.

The death of Catherine of Aragon in Kimbolton on 6 January should not have come as a surprise. Catherine's health had been deteriorating for some time – she was suffering from what most historians agree was probably cancer of the stomach. By December 1535 she could not eat or sleep for more than an hour and a half at a time because of the pains in her stomach and abdomen. Chapuys was receiving regular updates from Catherine's personal physician, Dr de la Saa, and on 29 December de la Saa sent an urgent message warning that Catherine was dangerously ill. Chapuys went straight to Greenwich to obtain the King's permission to visit – he sent a detailed report of this meeting to Charles V. It was clear that the King was fully aware of what was happening in his former wife's household – it was he who told Chapuys that 'madame could not live long,' and was more interested in engaging the ambassador in conversation about the political implications of her likely death. He was, however, happy to give the necessary permission for Chapuys to visit, probably thinking that it would now make little difference. He still refused to allow Mary to visit her mother, however. The ambassador began his winter journey without delay, setting off on horseback for East Anglia.

Kimbolton Castle, today much altered but still standing, is on the edge of the fens, easily defensible and miles from anywhere. It was, and is, a low-lying and damp situation, but the mediaeval castle was well built, large and included a number of comfortable rooms, a chapel, kitchens and stables. Catherine of Aragon had been moved there, without her consent, in May 1534, from nearby Buckden. Despite her protests to the contrary, neither was exactly the depths of squalor – but Catherine hated the fenlands. At Kimbolton, as in all her other houses, she was allocated a household including a Steward, Chamberlain and all the other officers a royal lady had a right to expect. However, she was no longer allowed to choose the appointees for herself, and began to regard them as gaolers. At Kimbolton, she began to refuse to see anyone but her most trusted ladies, several of whom had been with her since her arrival in England, her confessor, her doctor and her apothecaries. This involved refusing also to move from her bedchamber for months at a time – she appears to have divided her days between praying and needlework. She was also terrified of being poisoned, and this meant that most of her food was prepared under her eye, in either her bedchamber or next door in the presence chamber. There was constant conflict, too, about how she was addressed, as she still insisted she was Queen, and would not accept, or even speak to, anyone who called her anything else – and all the household officers had been instructed that she was to be addressed as Princess Dowager of Wales. This all sounds petty, but was, of course a politically loaded subject. Catherine does not ever seem to have given up hoping the King would take her back, and she was certainly trying to defend the position of their daughter, Mary. There was, however, something of the martyr about her – at least some of the misery of her last months can be regarded as having been of her own making.

Chapuys arrived on 2 January and stayed for four days, visiting Catherine every afternoon, always in the presence of several witnesses so no one could accuse them of plotting against the King. During Chapuys' stay Catherine appears to have experienced a form of remission, as she regained some strength, began to eat and sleep again, and was able to sit up and tend to her own hair. When he left for London, Chapuys believed his old friend was on the mend – it is clear that her physical state had been improved by the comfort his visit brought her. However, on 6 January it became evident she was dying, which she herself accepted – she was conscious and coherent, receiving mass and extreme unction in the last hours of her life. Some historians say the last letter she is said to have dictated to the King from her deathbed, and which did not surface until later in the century, is a fabrication – it is short, but manages to combine forgiving Henry with accusing him. It addresses him as her husband, and ends 'in this life, mine eyes desire you alone.'[2] Even if Catherine did not write it, the letter probably represents how she felt in the last days of her life. And if the words are hers, she would have phrased them knowing that it was almost certain that her last letter to the King would become known. Her friends and supporters would in any case regard her as a martyr – the tone of the letter is either heroically forbearing or passive-aggressive depending on the degree of sympathy with which it is read.

Famously, the news of Catherine's death was welcomed at Greenwich. Henry is said to have exclaimed 'God be praised we are now free of all threat of war'.[3] This is perhaps not quite as heartless a response as it sounds, as it was, of course, absolutely true that, with Catherine dead, Charles V would no longer be under pressure to fight for her reinstatement – less cause of conflict, meaning fewer deaths (and less expense). What happened next appears in several different versions. Hall has the King appearing in purple, Anne in yellow 'for the mourning'. Chapuys describes the King in yellow from head to foot with a feather in his cap. Some writers say that yellow was the colour of Spanish royal mourning and that the colour was a mark of respect, although there is no supporting evidence of this. No one says the King and Queen were anything but happy that day and in those following. The Court was still at Greenwich for the Christmas season, and it appears that extra festivities, including a joust, were laid on. Chapuys also reports, with indignation, that Henry went to Anne's apartments after attending Mass, sent for the toddler Elizabeth, and, 'carrying her in his arms, he showed her first to one and then to another.' Chapuys records all of this in grief and outrage, but all it really tells us is that no one at Greenwich shared his sorrow – and he knew that anyway.

The King's next concerns were to ensure that Catherine's funeral was, in his terms, appropriate, and to get his hands on her remaining property. On the face of it, the two aims conflicted. If Catherine had never been his wife, then he had no right to her worldly goods. But then, Henry never allowed consistency to get in the way of what he wanted. The funeral, to take place at Peterborough Cathedral, honoured the dead woman as a princess of Spain and Dowager Princess of Wales, but great care was taken to stop short of the extra rites due to a queen. Thomas Cromwell's servant, Ralph Sadleir, placed in charge of some of the organisation, wrote to check a number of points, quoting the recent funeral of the King's sister, Mary, as a precedent, and was told very firmly that that was different, as Mary Tudor had been a queen of France. It was left to Richard Rich, Solicitor General, to find, or rather invent, a legal basis to allow the King to help himself to the property of a woman he was maintaining had never been anything other than his sister in law.

For most of the rest of January, the mood in Greenwich appears to have been exuberant, with more jousts and other entertainments added to the diary. The usually staid William Kingston, Lieutenant of the Tower, wrote to his friend Lord Lisle asking him to help him find a new horse so he could join in the fun. But on 24 January, the king had a mishap, falling from his horse during a joust – and it may be, too, that the horse fell on top of him. Chapuys says he 'fell so heavily that everyone thought it a miracle he was not killed.'[4] One source, Dr Pedro Ortiz, Charles V's ambassador in Rome, was to write on 6 March to the Empress claiming that 'the French king said that the king of England had fallen from his horse and been for two hours without speaking.'[5] It is clear that this claim is hearsay, and is not corroborated by anyone else writing at the time. The nature of the accident is important, as some historians take the view that the fall, and subsequent concussion, caused the King serious brain damage, and that this in turn led to a personality change, which explains much of his subsequent behaviour.[6] As the accident itself was evidently well known, but Dr Ortiz, writing several weeks later from many hundreds of miles away, is the only one to make the claim about the King's having been knocked unconscious, this does cast some doubt on the likelihood of his having suffered a brain injury, at least as a direct result of this particular accident although this fall may have contributed to a build up of damage acquired in accidents over a period of years. It may also be true, however, that, once recovered, the King wanted to make light of the accident, and that the claims that he had suffered nothing but bruising were part of the spin he wanted to put out to allay fears (or, possibly, hopes).

What is almost certainly true, too, is that hearing about the accident was a considerable shock to Anne Boleyn. She appears to have blamed it for causing the miscarriage she suffered four days later, on 29 January, the day of Catherine of Aragon's funeral. Ortiz, in his account, continues 'La Ana was so upset that she miscarried of a son.' Whatever the cause, most reports agree with Chapuys that the foetus 'seemed to be a male child which she had not borne three and a half months'. The rumour mill of the Court was, of course, hard at work to find causes for the mischance, and Anne's enemies were jubilant. It is worth saying, however, that none of them claimed that Anne had miscarried of a shapeless mass of flesh. That particular piece of *grande guignole* remained to be invented by Catholic commentators of fifty years after her time – and it is grotesque enough to have appealed to a certain kind of writer ever since. The king took the news badly, if Chapuys is to be believed: 'When she miscarried, (Henry) scarcely said anything to her, except that he saw clearly that God did not wish to give him male children.' Anne is said to have retorted that she had been upset by news of his accident and his infidelity.[7] On the same day that he reported this exchange, Chapuys also mentions Jane Seymour for the first time. But Anne was comforting her maids with the idea that the next baby would be conceived after the death of Catherine of Aragon, and would thus be of unassailable legitimacy. It is often said, in the famous but perhaps now somewhat over-used phrase, that Anne had 'miscarried of her saviour', and that her marriage was doomed from the moment she lost the baby. Certainly Chapuys in reporting the King as having scarcely spoke to Anne when he visited her, saying merely that he would speak to her when she had recovered, was as ever, construing this in the way most damaging to Anne, namely that the King was turning on her in anger over the failure of the pregnancy. Perhaps this was the case – but the reaction may well indicate grief and shock. Whatever the cause, as always with Henry VIII, his response was totally selfish. But it is clear, too, that the King had other worries – his other comment was that he saw God would not give him male children – not Anne's fault, but quite possibly a demonstration that the marriage had not been God's will. The writing was not quite on the wall, but an exit strategy had evidently entered the King's mind.

There is evidence to suggest that in the following weeks the King was considering his position with regard to his marriage to Anne. Naturally little of whatever was said, was said in public. In the preternaturally watchful world of the Court, all continued as usual. The Queen recovered in health, and went back to her usual routine. So did the King, but during the last weeks of that winter, the emotional and political landscape changed. The outcome was not definite – as others have said, Anne may have been tottering, but she had not fallen. And the end, at that stage, was most emphatically, uncertain. Greenwich, London and anywhere where the informed sat and talked or exchanged glances but said as little as possible, must have been very full of hedged bets in that late winter and early spring.

It is tempting to tell this, as other human stories, in terms of emotion and sex – and the events that follow have been the stuff of many novels. The King had a new interest – that had been known for some time. Jane Seymour may have seemed an unlikely choice. She was a member of the Queen's household, and had previously served Catherine of Aragon. So she had been a face about Court for the best part of a decade. She was, by now, in her late twenties (young, in twenty-first century terms, but, for a woman, verging on middle aged to the Tudors). She was quiet, discreet, appeared demure, and does not appear to have tickled Chapuys' fancy. His report on 'Mistress Semel' describes her as pale, self-effacing and of doubtful virtue (he suggests, rather spitefully, that any woman who had been at Court for any length of time was unlikely to be a virgin). She had evidently been on the diplomatic radar for some time – in an early reference to her, Chapuys describes her as 'the lady the king serves'. This was a very significant choice of words, as it makes it clear that Jane was the King's latest partner in the public games of courtly love that were a part of Court life. She was one of the ten children of Sir John Seymour of the now-famous Wolf Hall. Two of Jane's brothers, Edward and Thomas, were well-known faces at Court, and Edward, at least, had proved he had some military ability. He had been knighted on the field of battle at the age of eighteen. Not all of the ten siblings had survived to adulthood – and the oldest had settled for life as a country gentleman, but Edward and Thomas were, like their sister, already established at Court. In the cases of Edward and Jane at least, their personal style was very different from that of the Boleyns, but they were very similar in that they were every bit as personally ambitious.

Both at the time and later, many commentators have assumed that Jane Seymour's attraction for the King lay in her contrast to Anne Boleyn, and, in seeking to emphasise this, have assumed that she must have been as docile as the motto she was to choose as Queen – 'bound to obey and serve'. It should, however, be remembered that Jane's public image was, like Anne's, a matter of strategy. One theory is that she was taken up, and indeed taken over, by the Boleyns' enemies, perhaps especially Nicholas Carew, and coached as to what she should do and say. In particular she was to avoid being alone with the King, and was to be the epitome of virginal modesty. An incident on 1 April (perhaps an appropriate date) when the King sent her a purse of money and a letter, is, in this reading of her character, a triumph for her backers. According to the story offered by Chapuys, when the King's presents arrived, Jane kissed the letter but returned it, and the money, along with the message that she could accept such a present only when she had obtained 'some good marriage'. No points for subtlety, but many for laying her cards on the table. However, there is no reason to suppose that Jane was a mere puppet. The personal presentation was all respectability and docility, but it seems likely that her underlying character was as tough and resourceful as her brothers'. However, whether she played hard to get by inclination or as a result of a strategy not of her making, the game evidently had its desired effect. At some point during the early spring, Cromwell vacated his room at Greenwich – it is not clear whether by his own design or under orders

from the King – so that Jane Seymour and her family could take advantage
of the fact that it was joined by a passage to the King's private rooms.
Trysts could now take place in semi-respectability.

It is possible that Jane Seymour was quite capable of planning her
own strategy, too. As she had worked for Catherine of Aragon she may
well have felt a genuine loyalty, both for her and for Mary Tudor. If so,
once Catherine was dead, there was no disloyalty in accepting the king's
advances, especially if Jane could help restore Catherine's daughter,
Mary, to favour. Evidently, Jane felt no inhibitions about betraying her
new mistress, Anne Boleyn, oath of loyalty notwithstanding, and would
probably have argued that she was merely behaving in the same way that
Anne had done before her. From the limited evidence we have, it looks
as if Jane's relationship with the King started as a relatively casual fling,
beginning with a Court flirtation and going on from there. As we have
seen, it was a pattern with him, as with many other high status men of his
time, to stray while the current wife was pregnant and off limits sexually.
It seems that everyone concerned was expected to accept this and not to
take it seriously. George Wyatt was to suggest in his account of this time
that it was in part Anne's strong reaction to her husband's affair with Jane
that helped to provide the momentum to make it more serious.[8] Eric Ives
suggests that Anne had no choice other than to confront her husband over
his infidelity precisely because he and she had married for love.[9] There
may well be some truth in this, but it is hard not to suspect that at least
part of the reason lay also in Anne's nature – it was not in her to play
the part of a docile wife in the approved 'Patient Griselda' like model of
her time. Hostile observers during these months commented that she was
losing her looks, becoming 'old and thin'.

By the time of the encounter at the beginning of April, Jane had
evidently become potential wife material, confident enough in the
seriousness of the King's interest to send back his letter and present
without fear of repercussions. Not least among her charms for the King
may well have been her fecund family – there are indications that he was
less than deeply in love. Certainly, we are told that during the time she
was 'queen in waiting', Jane tried to intervene on Mary's behalf, only to

be told by the King that she was a fool to waste time on the matter – she should confine her attention to the children he and she would have together. If this story is true – and the tone of it sounds in tune with what we hear of the King from other sources – this is evidence both that Jane was being chosen as breeding stock, and that her influence was to be strictly limited. The conservative faction, however, were certainly hoping that Jane would soften the King's heart towards Mary. It is unclear how they, and Mary, felt about the likelihood of Jane's giving birth to a prince who would replace Mary as next heir to the throne.

Until a very late stage, it seems likely that Jane and her backers were working in the hope that the King would take the course of having his marriage to Anne annulled. There were two possibilities for finding grounds for this – Anne's likely pre-contract with Henry Percy, and the King's undoubted affair with Mary Boleyn. There appear to have been some exploratory talks with canon lawyers about the matter, and it may well be that at least some of Anne's own allies were expecting this to be a possibility. There might well have been those who would not have been altogether sorry, including some of her own relatives. By the spring of 1536 Anne had long fallen out with her uncle the Duke of Norfolk, and there are signs that relations between Anne and her father had become strained, as were those with various other relatives, including two of her aunts. However, not a word was written about her relationship with her mother, who may well have had the gift of keeping her own counsel about whatever she thought and felt about her children's careers – Elizabeth had been there in the background throughout the years overshadowed by the Great Matter, but there is no record of her making any public comment. It was Anne's brother, George Boleyn, who was perhaps her closest ally – and this alliance was shortly to cost him his life.

By this time Anne was increasingly under attack from within the Court, as she was certainly well aware – but her case was by no means hopeless. Although her relationship with the King had clearly deteriorated, it had not broken down. There is clear evidence, too, that they continued to co-operate politically. In the aftermath of Catherine of Aragon's death, the arena of foreign policy had changed dramatically, as there was now a possibility of a rapprochement with Charles V – and with this came increased possibilities for playing the Empire and France off against each other. The challenge for Anne was to continue to play a full part in negotiations, to distance herself from her previous identification with French interests, and to ensure that the position of her daughter as the King's heiress was maintained. It was this last requirement that was the greatest challenge, as keeping Elizabeth's status as first in line to the throne meant continuing to disbar Mary, and this was never going to be acceptable either to Charles V or to the conservative faction in England. As to the Boleyn marriage itself, Charles V was beginning to consider that it was to his advantage that at least Henry could not enter into a dynastic marriage with one of his enemies, so perhaps Anne was the least of a number of possible evils. At this stage Chapuys was still referring to her as the Concubine, and throughout the preceding years had allowed his genuine affection for Catherine of Aragon to colour his judgement about Anne. His colleague, Dr Ortiz, the Imperial Envoy in Rome, included news of England in his reports. His tone was less hostile but more gossipy; he referred to Anne as 'La Ana' – less pejorative, but still avoiding giving her any royal title.

But negotiations over Europe were by no means the only item on the political agenda in England. The Act of Parliament to suppress the minor religious houses had been passed by both houses of Parliament – now it required the king's signature, and, true to form, he was prevaricating about making up his mind. It was by no means a foregone conclusion that the dissolution would go ahead at all. Or, if it did, it was possible that so many exceptions would be made that in the event there would be few closures. The major point of contention was what would happen to proceeds. Even though these were the smaller monasteries and nunneries, up to the value of £300, their collective value was equivalent to billions of pounds today. This money was much needed for the King's increasingly cash-strapped exchequer, and it appears that Thomas Cromwell, in particular, was assuming that that was where the proceeds were destined. But this was new: when Wolsey, assisted by Cromwell, had presided over the dissolution of a number of religious houses in the 1520s, with the full blessing of the Pope, the proceeds had been used towards the setting up of Cardinal College, Oxford (later to be renamed Christchurch), and a second Cardinal College in Ipswich. Each of these occupied the site of a previous priory, and money raised from closing down several nearby religious houses was used to increase the endowment. This had been accepted practice, on a small scale, throughout the mediaeval period.

When Thomas Cromwell became Vicar General, he became responsible for the day-to-day running of all the country's religious houses. He had begun, with customary energy and efficiency, to set about the task of the destruction of at least some of them. It had taken only a few months for his visitors, who knew what they were looking for, to amass a dossier of evidence demonstrating the corrupt and run-down state of both the houses and their inhabitants. How much of that evidence was genuine is unlikely ever to be known for sure, but it had proved good enough for both houses of parliament. It was not yet quite good enough either for the King or for the Queen, and the fate of the profits, rather than the principle of closing down the houses, was very much under discussion. The bill for the dissolution went before the House of Lords at Shrovetide, and the King went to Whitehall to be on the spot, leaving Anne at Greenwich. Chapuys pounced on this as being further evidence of their estrangement,[10] claiming, too, that the King and Anne had spoken only ten times in three months. As Anne was almost certainly still recovering from her miscarriage, this is questionable. However, for two crucial weeks, the King and Anne were apart. It is certainly true that this was, if not unprecedented for the past seven years, then highly unusual.

It must have been during that couple of weeks that Anne and Thomas Cromwell fell out. It is open to question just how strong their alliance had ever been, but until this point their interests had lain in the same direction, and they appear to have co-operated without difficulty. The immediate cause of conflict was the use to which the monastery money was to be put. Anne evidently felt strongly that these profits should be used exclusively for religious and educational causes, and it was this that brought her and Cromwell into open conflict. Anne evidently considered that Cromwell and his supporters were preparing to help themselves to the assets of the monasteries, and was incensed by this. The Scottish reformer Alexander Ales, writing twenty years later, claimed that Cromwell and his allies by then 'hated the queen, because she had sharply rebuked them and threatened to inform the king, that under the guise of the gospel and religion they were advancing their own interests, that they had put everything up for sale and had received bribes to confer ecclesiastical benefices upon unworthy persons.'[11] Even allowing for the fact that Ales was writing to please Anne's daughter, this is probably close to the truth. Certainly Anne was to make her disillusionment with Cromwell very public just a few weeks later.

It is probably fair to suspect that there had never been anything warmer than grudging respect between Anne and Cromwell, and now the temperature had evidently dropped still further – Anne was certainly aware by now that Cromwell was on cosy terms with the Seymours, and would have known all about his giving up his room to them. By this time Cromwell was setting up an unlikely alliance with the rest of the conservative, anti-Anne faction – indeed, he appears to have been making bridges with Carew, at least, since the previous year – and now he made a point of meeting with Chapuys, and evidently had a series of ambiguous conversations with him. During these at one moment he talked openly about the possibility of the King taking another wife, then backtracked and said the King would 'live honourably and chastely, continuing in his marriage'. Chapuys, no fool, realised that Cromwell must now be signalling, however indirectly, that he was at loggerheads with the Queen – but he was concerned that Cromwell would come off worst from any encounter. Neither was Chapuys at all sure that Cromwell was in earnest or, if he was, that everything would not change again in a day or two.

But Anne had declared war on Cromwell, very publicly. On Passion Sunday, 2 April, the Queen's almoner, John Skip, preached a sermon on the theme of the Old Testament story of Queen Esther and her evil and avaricious enemy, Haman, who persecutes the Jews and tries to use their money to enrich the King. Haman's story ends with him facing death on the scaffold he had prepared for the Queen's protector – point sufficiently clear for anyone in the congregation to be in no doubt about who and what was meant. The sermon finished with a look at the final days of the life of King Solomon, whose last years featured giving in to his 'sensual and carnal appetites in the taking of many wives and concubines'. As the King had often been favourably compared to Solomon, this was two attacks for the price of one. It is not clear whether the King, or Cromwell, or both, were in the congregation. Some reports say that Skip was arrested and interrogated by the Council, but was released when it became clear that he had acted under the Queen's orders. Anne followed up this opening attack by persuading Cranmer to write to Cromwell on 22 April supporting her position on the appropriate use of monastery funds.

Alongside all this, the international negotiations continued, and during these Thomas Cromwell appears to have over-estimated his own influence. Cromwell's own inclination, like that of much of the City of London, was for an alliance with the Empire, which was considered better for trade of all kinds. And for the Reformers, good relations meant good communications with places such as Antwerp, from whence came ideas and books. Over the early weeks of April, the talks were going well, and Cromwell made arrangements for a visit to Court for Chapuys. In the detailed report the ambassador sent to Charles V, it is made very clear that Cromwell was trying to stage manage the whole day – he met Chapuys on the road, accompanied him, and gave him a lot of advice about what to say and do. Cromwell made it clear that part of the price of the alliance was that Chapuys should meet and acknowledge the Queen – as Chapuys had managed to avoid coming face to face with her in the three years since her marriage, this was a major issue. Chapuys was in no doubt that not only the court, but much of Europe would be agog to know about any encounter between the two.

Once at court, Chapuys was received by an obviously prepared George Boleyn, who escorted him to the chapel where the King and Queen would be attending Mass – there was no escape. At the end of the service, Anne descended from the Queen's closet where she had, as usual, been observing. She curtseyed to Chapuys, who bowed in return. That was the extent of the encounter, but the exchange of greetings was considered to signify Chapuys' acceptance of Anne as queen. After the service Chapuys hastily avoided an invitation to dine with the King and Queen, but was again scooped up by George Boleyn, who accompanied him to dinner in the presence chamber, where they evidently conversed very pleasantly. It was then time for Chapuys and Cromwell to have a private meeting with the King. This was only relatively private – there appears to have been perhaps thirty other people, including Audley and Edward Seymour, present. According to Chapuys' report, at first all went well, but, quite abruptly, the King's mood changed and he and Cromwell began to argue. Chapuys maintained that he had been out of earshot, but that he saw Cromwell, visibly upset, leave the group around the King, saying that he was thirsty. He then sat down out of sight of the King. At this stage the King called Chapuys back to him, and told him, very brusquely, that he needed to have the terms of the proposed alliance in writing so he could consider them – then going on to deliver what was little short of an angry tirade, going through the agreement that Chapuys and Cromwell had worked out, finding fault with its terms, and then going on to enumerate the various wrongs the Emperor had done him in the past. According to Chapuys, Cromwell, now back at the King's side, and Audley, were looking on aghast. The meeting ended with a stand off in the form of the King promising to look back over previous treaties and give a further opinion.

Chapuys and Cromwell then left Greenwich, travelling back to London together and commiserating over what had turned into a distinctly bad day for them both. Chapuys reported that Cromwell confided he had already spoken to the King about the matter (although he can have had little time in which to do so) and admitted to Chapuys that he had misread the king's intentions. He also claimed that he never said or did anything that was not a direct reflection of what the King wanted. Whether this was the exact truth is open to doubt. It does appear, however, that the day's events had been a shock to Cromwell. His relationship with the King had always been far more deferential than had been that between the King and Wolsey – one contemporary, George Paulet, was to claim that the king regularly abused Cromwell and hit him about the head[12] and that Cromwell had to laugh it off. While there is no other evidence of physical violence not only the king, but many others at Court regarded Cromwell with contempt because of his low birth. If Chapuys is to be believed the events of 21 April were a frightening demonstration to Cromwell not only of how easily his own influence could vanish, but of how much Anne still possessed, and how she could well come back into full favour. If it was indeed Cromwell who brought about Anne's fall – and Chapuys was convinced that it was[13] – then it was at this point that the decision was made. We know that at this point Cromwell retired from Court for a week, pleading illness. He appears to have spent the time in London, and may well have been building a case against the Queen. It is, of course, entirely possible that Cromwell was doing so with the King's knowledge, or even on his instruction.

It was probably in the next couple of days that a crucial incident took place – although it is impossible to tell how closely the officially hinted-at version of events followed the truth. Elizabeth Somerset, née Browne, Countess of Worcester, was a senior member of Anne Boleyn's household. Elizabeth had been close to Anne for years – the two were of an age, and Elizabeth had been one of the ladies chosen to attend Anne at her coronation dinner. Anne had arranged for a payment for a midwife for her in 1530, suggesting that the two had been friends for some years. The fact that she appears to have been unable to pay the midwife herself suggests Elizabeth may have been in financial difficulty – and in early April 1536, she was to borrow the very large sum of £100 from the Queen. At this time, Elizabeth was pregnant once more. It appears that, sometime in the third week of the month, she quarrelled with her brother, Sir Anthony Browne, who was a member of the conservative faction ar Court. We are not told the exact cause of the quarrel, but it seems to have centred around Elizabeth's conduct at court; he was to claim that during the disagreement she said, in effect, that whatever she had been doing. her behaviour was cast in the shade by that of her mistress, who had been conducting affairs with several people, including Mark Smeaton, one of her musicians. Browne appears then to have reported what his sister had said to the King's Council, or possibly to the King himself.

This possible sequence of events is pieced together from several sources, including letters from the LIsles' agent, John Hussee, and a report in the form of a poem written by Lancelet de Carles, a member of the French ambassador's staff, both of whom were writing within weeks of what happened – but after Anne's death. Both were well connected and on the spot in London in 1536, but neither was either at court or a member of the Royal household. We are told the Council went into emergency session – possibly recalling Cromwell from London to take part – and that an immediate, and highly secret, investigation ensued. There is no evidence that either the Countess of Worcester or any other of the Queen's ladies was interviewed.

Cromwell may well have been busy during his week at home in London. During his absence, on 24 April, the Chancellor, Audley, appointed two commissions of oyer and terminer, covering Middlesex and Kent. This was a legal mechanism for hearing and judging evidence for possible full-scale court cases – a form of grand jury. Although the procedure had been known for at least 200 years, it was rarely used, was reserved for the most serious cases and involved setting up special hearings in the county in which an alleged crime had taken place. If, as most historians agree, these commissions were put in place as the first stage in the legal process against Anne, Cromwell had worked quickly enough to have established where her alleged crimes were supposed to have taken place. The next day, 25 April, Parliament was recalled, only a few weeks after it was prorogued.

So it is certain that, whatever had precipitated the legal action against Anne, it was in place before 24 April. Some historians[14] take the view that the fall of Anne Boleyn was precipitated almost entirely by a catastrophically unlucky build-up of circumstantial evidence, the first, and most crucial, piece of which was Lady Worcester's quarrel with her brother, during which she must, to support this view, have lied in the heat of the moment and then failed to retract her accusation about Mark Smeaton and the Queen. This is possible, but seems unlikely, as she must have been questioned further, if not by the full Council then certainly by some members of it. Another possible explanation is that she was bullied or blackmailed into implicating Anne, and that she was vulnerable because it was she who was having the affair. Or the row between the brother and sister may have started off at a less poisonous level – he accused her of being too flirtatious, and she replied by saying everyone in the Queen's household behaved like that – going on, perhaps, to give examples. Or she, may, of course, have said exactly what is reported, and had been telling the exact truth.

It has been suggested that Lady Worcester was having an affair with Cromwell, and that the child she was carrying was his. The only evidence to support this idea is a letter, written by Lady Worcester in 1538, thanking Cromwell for his kindness in keeping the matter of the £100 loan a secret and asking him to continue to do so, for fear of what her husband would say if he found out. This seems more like evidence that Cromwell had been threatening to tell her husband about the loan than any indication of closeness – Cromwell was certainly not above blackmail, and it seems possible that this was the threat used to induce Lady Worcester to speak against Anne. What is known is that her baby, a daughter, was born safely despite the difficult pregnancy. Poignantly, she was named Anne – and appears to have been accepted without question by her legal father. Less poignantly, Elizabeth Worcester went on to be one of Jane Seymour's ladies in waiting – but all this tells us is that she, like several of her colleagues, was a pragmatist. She was not the only one of Anne Boleyn's ladies who went on to serve Jane Seymour – so did Anne Gainsford, Lady Zouche and Margery Horsman.

Life at Court continued, superficially normally, until the end of April. It is clear that Anne knew by the 26th that she was under serious threat, as on that day she spoke to her chaplain, Matthew Parker, and entrusted him with the spiritual welfare of her daughter, Elizabeth, if anything should happen to her. On the 28th, two different commentators, Chapuys and Thomas Warley, a correspondent of Lord Lisle's, both noted that the King's Council was meeting in closed session for the whole day. By this time Cromwell appears to have been back at Greenwich, and, according to Chapuys, had extra meetings of his own, with an eminent canon lawyer, Dr Richard Sampson. Meanwhile, Chapuys was reporting to Charles V that the Bishop of London had told him that the King had asked for his opinion as to whether he might legally leave Anne, but that the Bishop was warily refusing to commit himself in case the King changed his mind and

Anne came back into favour. It is likely, then, that at this stage the King was indeed taking advice about whether it might be possible to annul his marriage to Anne without making too many waves – but he had not made up his mind.

Two seemingly minor events took place on 29 April that may have tipped the balance. Each was brief, superficially trivial and involved Anne. Both have become famous – and we know Anne's own version of what happened.

In the first, Anne encountered Mark Smeaton standing on his own in a window in her presence chamber, seemingly lost in thought. She asked him why he was so sad, and he replied that it 'was no matter'. This abrupt reply fell far short of the deferential way that a man of his status was expected to use in speaking to the Queen, so her response is unsurprising: 'You may not look to have me speak to you as I would to a nobleman, because you be an inferior person' – to which Smeaton replied 'No, no madam, a look sufficeth me, and thus fare you well.' It appears he then left the room without waiting for her permission to do so – another breach of royal etiquette. This brief exchange has been endlessly unpacked for possible meaning. Certainly it points to a very high emotional temperature in the room. One possible explanation, as others have speculated, is that Mark Smeaton, trying hard to make his way at Court and climb the slippery ladder of success, had fallen obsessively in love with the Queen. If this was the case, and Anne was aware of it, that would explain the snub she delivered – an unkind, but in sixteenth-century terms, justified, reminder that Mark was not even a gentleman, let alone a nobleman, and so not a fit player of the courtly love game by which so much of his world operated. It is, of course, also possible that Anne had had a brief affair with Mark and was choosing this distinctly ruthless way of letting him know he was now out of favour.

In the second encounter, it was Anne herself who broke the rules of the game. It may have been later that same day when Anne quarrelled with Henry Norris. The cause of the trouble was Norris' prevarication about when he might marry again, four years after his wife's death. Anne's favoured candidate was her cousin and lady in waiting, Madge Shelton – and on this occasion, when Anne pressured Norris to commit himself and he still would not, she appears to have lost her temper and her judgement. Anne herself admitted that she said to Norris 'you look for dead men's shoes, for if aught came to the king but good, you would look to have me.' Norris, evidently appalled by the direct accusation, retorted that 'if he should have any such thought, he would his head were off.' Anne, realising what she had said, sent him off to her chaplain to swear that the conversation was innocent and she was a good woman. This conversation was almost certainly, in some respects, in the tradition of so many others – it was, of course, the common currency of the Court for its gentlemen to declare their undying devotion to the unattainable high status lady of their choice – the Queen being the most popular object for this. A conversation on the basis that Norris was not marrying anyone else because he could not have the Queen would not have raised even the most censorious eyebrow in that time and place. It is her accusation that appears to put the exchange into a different category. Again, the encounter has been analysed hundreds of times, with a variety of supposed results – everything from a conclusion that Anne and Norris were indeed in the throes of an affair to maintaining that there was nothing unusual about the conversation until, in the tense atmosphere of those days, others began adding two and two and making five. What does not usually get discussed is the possibility that, at this time, Anne may have been already on the verge of hysteria. It is fully documented that, three days later, on her arrival in the Tower, she collapsed in alternating tears and wild laughter, followed, once she was in her lodging, by what sounds like ill-considered talk. All of which is only too understandable given the danger in which she found herself. But if we are to assume that, in the last days before her arrest, Anne suspected her enemies were about to move against her but did not know what form the attack would take, then she must have been under considerable nervous strain. Given what we know of her character, this kind of mock-aggressive semi-jocularity seems a likely way for stress to have taken her. And she seems always to have been one for hyperbole. It may well be that this conversation, although ill considered, meant very little until the tattle-mongers got busy – and, when she realised her error, she compounded it with the matter of the oath.

The next day, Sunday, 30 April, Mark Smeaton had a flattering invitation to dinner. He had been invited to Thomas Cromwell's house in Stepney, and he appears to have walked unsuspectingly into the trap. We do not know whether Cromwell either fed him or made any attempt at polite conversation before he accused Mark of having had sex with the queen. In the highly coloured version of events provided by the Spanish Chronicle, Cromwell was accompanied by heavies who tried to torture a confession out of Mark by tying a piece of rope round his head and twisting it. It may be true – he appears to have been in Cromwell's house for several hours, and may have made a confession while he was there, but later that same day he was formally arrested and taken to the Tower of London, where he was probably shown the rack. It appears that, while still in Cromwell's house, he confessed to having had sex with the Queen on three occasions. It is likely that, in return, he was promised either a royal pardon, or at least the quick and more homourable death of beheading rather than the horrors of hanging, drawing and quartering, possibly preceded by torture. Certainly he kept to his side of the bargain, never retracting his confession of adultery – and in return he was allowed to die 'above his station'. And there is always the possibility that he was telling the truth.

On the same day, Alexander Alesius witnessed a memorable scene.[15] Writing to Anne's daughter, Elizabeth, in the 1550s, he described seeing the king looking out of a window. Outside, Anne was standing with Elizabeth in her arms, pleading with her husband, who was visibly angry. Alesius was too far away to hear what was being said, but was in no doubt that he was witnessing a major altercation: 'Never shall I forget the sorrow which I felt when I saw the most serene queen, your most religious mother, carrying you, still a little baby in her arms and entreating the most serene king, your father.... I did not perfectly understand what had been going on, but the faces and the gestures of the speakers plainly showed that the king was angry.' If he saw what was happening, it is likely others did. It is fair to suppose that the story of Anne's encounter with Norris the day before was now all over the court. Anne's attempt at damage limitation in sending Norris to her chaplain to swear that she was a good woman would certainly only have served to add an extra fillip to the story. Ales went on to mention that the King's Council met that day and went on sitting until late at night. Later that evening the planned visit by the King and Queen to Calais, due to start two days later, was postponed, with a view to travelling a week later.[16]

The next day, Mayday, was one of the traditional holidays. At Greenwich, the usual joust went ahead, and both the King and Queen attended as planned. George Boleyn led one team of participants, Henry Norris the other. We are told the King appeared to be in a pleasant mood, offering Norris a replacement horse when his own started playing up. At some point during the day, the King received a letter from Cromwell. And at the end of the tournament, he left, suddenly and without explanation, for London, not as usual by boat, but on horseback, taking only six attendants with him. Among these was Norris. We are told that on the journey the King interrogated Norris, pressing him to admit to an affair with Anne, and promising him a pardon if he would confess. By most accounts Norris protested his innocence, and there the matter was left overnight.

At dawn on Tuesday, 2 May, Norris was arrested at Whitehall and taken to the Tower. Later that morning, Anne was also arrested while watching a game of tennis at Greenwich. She was questioned by some members of the council, including her uncle the Duke of Norfolk, and was told that she was accused of adultery, and would be taken to the Tower. Anne evidently maintained her composure during a wait of several hours at Greenwich for the tide, and during the journey by water. But when she arrived at the Tower, she was in a state of near hysteria. When she was greeted by William Kingston, she asked if she was to be put in a dungeon, and upon being reassured she would be lodged in the royal apartment she had occupied before her coronation, she collapsed in tears followed by frantic laughter.

Once in the royal apartments of the Tower, the ladies who awaited Anne cannot have been a welcome sight. There were only five – a paltry number for a queen, and none of them were her friends. There was her aunt by marriage, Elizabeth Wood, Lady Boleyn (wife of Sir James Boleyn of Blickling), who had previously been close to Catherine of Aragon.

There was Mrs Margaret Coffin, the wife of Anne's Master of Horse – a professional courtier, and not known to have been particularly close to Anne. There was Mary Scrope, Lady Kingston, wife of Sir William, obviously placed there as a spy. There was Mrs Elizabeth Stoner, Mistress of the Maids at Court. The fifth was Lady Shelton, her father's sister, mother of the Madge Shelton who was one of Anne's household and previously governess to Mary Tudor. In fact all of them were instructed to spy on Anne and report everything she said or did to Kingston, who was to report to Thomas Cromwell. The two chamberers – the women who did the more menial work for the Queen – were a kinder choice. One was Anne's old nurse from Hever days, Mrs Mary Orchard, the other, Mrs Margaret Stonor, was the wife of the King's sergeant at arms. There were also two men servants and a boy.

That the small household proved to be an efficient spy network is demonstrated by the fact that Sir William Kingston was able to send extensive detailed reports to Cromwell describing Anne's words, actions and moods. The original letters survive in part, although they were damaged in a fire in the eighteenth century – but before that happened, they had been transcribed by John Strype. It may seem curious that two women closely related to Anne should have been chosen to spy on her. There have been many speculations about why this might have been.[17] A strong element in the motivation of both of them may well have been a straightforward desire to survive. It had been true of Wolsey before her, and it was true of Anne now that once it became clear her fall was inevitable, friends, family, household and clients fell over one another to distance themselves from her. Ladies Boleyn and Shelton may have reasoned that there was nothing they could do to help Anne, so they might as well co-operate and demonstrate their loyalty to the King. However, Anne was to say that she considered it 'great unkindness in the king' to place around her 'such as she had never loved'.

It was also arranged that Anne and her ladies would take their meals with Sir William Kingston – this was usual in the case of prisoners of high rank. So Kingston was able to send some of his reports at first hand. One of Anne's first requests was that she should have the Sacrament reserved in the closet next to her bedchamber. This was arranged, and she took Holy Communion late that evening. Anne took the opportunity of declaring in front of Kingston 'My God, bear witness there is no truth in these charges, for I am as clear from the company of man as from sin, as I am clear from you' – knowing that Kingston would report her words back. She was to maintain her innocence throughout. At this stage Anne knew that Mark Smeaton and Sir Henry Norris had also been arrested, but was asking for news of her father and brother. At this stage she became tearful – 'Oh, my mother, thou shalt die for sorrow.' Two weeks before this Lady Wiltshire had been described in a letter to Lady Lisle as 'sore diseased of the cough', and her daughter was evidently distressed at the thought of the effect the news was likely to have. Anne's next anxiety was for the Countess of Worcester – she evidently had no idea the Countess was implicated in her arrest – worrying that her unborn baby had not quickened. Lady Kingston asked Anne why she thought this might be, and the reply was 'for the sorrow she took for me'. This might refer back to Anne's miscarriage in January, or to more recent days. It is also possible that Anne knew of Elizabeth's scene with her brother and that Elizabeth had expressed anxiety about the consequences.

Anne then asked 'Master Kingston, shall I die without justice?' The Constable, mindful of his report, replied 'The poorest subject of the king hath justice,' provoking frantic laughter from Anne. Considering that she would have been fully aware that few prisoners accused of high treason were ever acquitted, this was unsurprising. Neither were the accused allowed access to a lawyer or any legal advice, or the opportunity to cross examine witnesses in Court. Although she was to go through many changes of mood in the remaining seventeen days of her life, Anne surely already knew that she would die.

At around the same time, the King was crying over his son, Henry Fitzroy, Duke of Richmond, who had come to say goodnight and ask for a blessing. 'The King began to weep, saying that he and his sister were greatly bound to God for having escaped the hands of that accursed whore, who had determined to poison them.' By that evening everyone at Court must have known of Anne's arrest. Sir Francis Bryan was to write a few weeks later that the consensus among the gentlemen of the Privy Chamber was that they 'rejoiced the king had escaped this great peril and danger' – which suggests that they had also been told that the Queen had been plotting the King's death. At around this time, too, Chapuys was writing a gloating letter to Charles V – they had been expecting that the King would repudiate his marriage to Anne, and her arrest on charges of adultery came as a delightful extra. At this stage Chapuys knew about the charge of adultery with Smeaton, but thought that Norris was under arrest for having covered up the affair. Chapuys was at home in Austin Friars, and was clearly not completely up to date with the news. This suggests that some news had leaked out from Court and the Tower, but even the Imperial Ambassador was not fully informed.

Many Londoners would certainly have seen Anne and her entourage arriving at the Tower by boat. By that token alone, the news of her arrest would have gone immediately around the city. A London lawyer, Roland Buckley, wrote in haste to his brother, Sir Richard Buckley, a friend and ally of Henry Norris, to come to London immediately to try to intercede with the King. It is a measure of how effective Cromwell's spy system was that the courier with the letter was intercepted and imprisoned, and the letter sent to Cromwell. Buckley's letter has some details incorrect, but he knew that Norris was accused of having 'had ado with the Queen'. If Cromwell's agents were thorough enough to track one letter from a not-very-important lawyer to his brother, it is certain that there were informers in place throughout the city, not only listening for any sign that anyone might be attempting to help Anne or her remaining allies, but planting their own version of, and spin on, events. Aless, who appears to have been staying in London, wrote his memories of that day to Elizabeth I:

'Those who were present well know how deep was the grief of all the godly, how loud the joy of the hypocrites, the enemies of the Gospel, when the report spread in the morning that the Queen had been thrown in the Tower. They will remember the tears and lamentations of the faithful, who were lamenting over the snare laid for the Queen, and the boastful triumph of the foes of the true doctrine. I remained a sorrowful man at home, waiting for the result, for it was easy to perceive that, in the event of the Queen's death, a change of religion was inevitable.'

Aless' perception of the events of the time in terms of a halt in the progress of religious reform does not mask the fact that he believed that the news of Anne's arrest had divided London along religious lines. Those who opposed reform – in the view of Aless, 'enemies of the Gospel', were jubilant, and 'the faithful' – the reformers – were horrified. Aless does not say whether they believed in Anne's guilt, only that they immediately recognised their cause was likely to be set back. It is clear, too, just how quickly the news spread 'in the morning' – the day after Anne's arrival in the Tower.

It is possible to have a good idea of the story that was being put out by Cromwell's agents – the one that Cromwell himself was writing to the King's envoys abroad. He was to write, before Anne's trial, to Gardiner and Wallop, the King's ambassadors in France, apprising them of the government's spin on the situation. He wrote that he had to 'inform them of a most detestable scheme, happily discovered and notoriously known to all men'. Cromwell explained that the Queen and her brother had still to be tried, and there was no doubt as to the outcome. As to the evidence, 'I write no particularities, the things be so abominable, and therefore I doubt not but this shall be sufficient instruction to declare the truth if you have occasion to do so.' Naturally, the arrest and trials were the talk not only of London but of all Europe. Cromwell never appears to have added to what he circulated among English ambassadors in foreign courts, but he did give a fuller version to the French ambassador, one of whose staff, Lancelot de Carles, wrote up the story in verse.

The coup appears to have taken almost everyone completely by surprise. But, as soon as the news was out, no one was in any doubt as to the outcome. This appears to have applied to everyone from Charles V, who was writing to Chapuys about possible new brides for the King as soon as he heard of Anne's arrest, to the London reformers referred to by

Aless in his memoir. The only person who made any attempt to intercede for Anne was Cranmer, who wrote the King a letter redolent of anxiety and doubt. He appears to have tried to see the King, only to be intercepted and taken to a meeting of the Star Chamber court (make up of members of the main Council). Whether they managed to convince him of Anne's guilt, or merely of the hopelessness of her case, he added a postscript to his letter to the King, saying he had heard enough. Wildly garbled versions of events started circulating, and continue to this day. All over Europe, correspondents exchanged details, of varying accuracy, of who had been arrested, accused of what. Versified and fictionalised accounts sold well. The one provided by de Carles survives in several different versions, and is probably closest to the government's official line on the matter. It cites one of the Queen's ladies as being the source of the story of her misdemeanours, and claims that the unnamed lady's brother, to whom she had spoken, had then taken the story to the council. De Carles mentions affairs with Smeaton and Norris, and incest with Rochford, with Anne as the seducer in all three cases. But this did not stop even more lurid stories from getting rapidly into circulation.

The King was chief among the fantasists. As we have seen, on the evening of Anne's arrest he was accusing her of plotting to poison both Fitzroy and Mary. During the period between the arrest and the start of the trials, we are told he was seeing very few people (and Cromwell seems to have been controlling who got to see him). He had left Greenwich for Whitehall, and was making trips by river to visit Jane Seymour, now living in semi-royal splendour in Sir Thomas More's old house in Chelsea. Jane was being looked after by Sir William Paulet, comptroller of the royal household. Her parents appear to have come to join her, and she was 'served very splendidly by the servants, cooks and certain of the king's officers in very rich liveries' – all very respectable. The Seymours were evidently on good terms with Chapuys and Mary's other supporters, all confidently expecting that, once Anne was disposed of and the King married to Jane, Mary would be restored to her former status as princess and heir to the throne. It appears that Jane was not the only lady to party with the King during these few days. Chapuys was also told about suppers with Court ladies (probably including some who had been in Anne's household) with music and more river trips. He was also, if Chapuys is to be believed, carrying about with him the manuscript of a play telling the story of his version of Anne's betrayal, which he was offering about for his guests to read.

It would have been more usual for Tudor treason trials to go ahead immediately after the arrests of the accused. The delay was almost certainly because Cromwell was making use of the reports of what Anne was saying during her captivity. The first instructions to Kingston had been that no one in attendance on the Queen should encourage her to talk. But, in the first days of her captivity, Anne appears to have veered between frantic despair and frantic hope, talking constantly to those around her about why she was imprisoned and what possible evidence might be found against her. She gave her own versions of the crucial conversations with Smeaton and Norris. And she spoke about an earlier incident during which Sir Francis Weston, another member of the King's household, had spoken of his 'service' to her, which he claimed was a stronger tie that that to his wife or to Madge Shelton, with whom he was conducting a flirtation. This appears to have been a bonus to Cromwell, who duly had Weston arrested and added to the list of Anne's supposed lovers. Cromwell had also had Thomas Wyatt and Richard Page arrested – it seems likely that he was holding both in reserve in case more victims were needed, rather than any genuine enquiry being made as to their likely guilt. So it was not until Tuesday, 9 May that the sheriffs of London were instructed to assemble a grand jury to decide whether there was evidence enough to proceed to full trial. They were able to do this at twenty-four hours' notice – it is likely that they had been forewarned to have their appointees at the ready, headed by Sir Thomas More's son-in-law, Sir Giles Heron. Given charges of that seriousness, the jury had little option other than to send the case for trial.

The trial of the commoners Norris, Weston, Brereton and Smeaton, was set to take place in Westminster Hall on Friday, 12 May. Cromwell had again been careful about the jury, which was headed by one Edward Willoughby, who we are told owed Brereton money,[18] and included an assortment of Cromwell clients, relatives of Sir Thomas More and Boleyn enemies. However, given the nature of Tudor treason trials – no access to lawyers for the accused, no defence counsel and no cross-examination of witnesses – the men had little chance anyway. It would have taken a brave and foolhardy juryman to go against the wishes of the King and his minister. The four accused must have known from the start that their case was hopeless.

All four were accused of 'violating' the Queen and of having conspired the King's death with her. Smeaton pleaded guilty to adultery but not guilty to conspiracy, the others, not guilty on all counts. The official records of the trial are incomplete. We have the justices' instructions to the Sheriff of London[19] in which Smeaton's name is erased, suggesting that, as he had confessed, he was not questioned in court. The other three were, and as Chapuys, who was ill and did not attend the trial, says that no witnesses were called to testify against Brereton, who was 'condemned upon a presumption and circumstances, not by proof or valid confession, and without any witnesses.'[20] This may mean that there were witnesses called to support the cases against the other three; Norris was said to have made some kind of confession, but retracted it in court, saying he had been tricked by Fitzwilliam into making an unconsidered statement. We do not know what was in the statement, whether it was read out in court or if anyone corroborated it. Neither do we know how long the trial lasted – probably not long. The verdict was inevitable: all four were found guilty on all counts, and condemned to be hung, drawn and quartered.

Evidently the news was soon out. The Lisles' agent John Hussee wrote 'This day Mr Norris, Weston, Brereton and Mark hath been arraigned, and are judged to be drawn, hanged and quartered. I pray God have mercy on them. They shall die tomorrow, or Monday at the furthest.'[21] Hussee goes on to speculate about when the Queen might come to trial, although in fact the date had already been set for Monday, 15 May, four days before. The order of the trials was, of course, completely deliberate. Not only did it further the expectation that she would be found guilty, but, as convicted felons, the four could not give evidence at her trial. They were now returned to the Tower to wait for death. It was the expectation of the time that the condemned men should now cease to concern themselves with earthly things except to attempt to right any wrongs they had done. However, those around them had no such inhibitions – as soon as news of the verdicts was out, Cromwell was making lists of their assets, was evidently receiving approaches from people hopeful of a cut of the spoils, and was promising the ambassadors serving in Paris a share. The latter promises were made in same letter that gave news of the Queen's fall. Hussee was busy finding out who was getting what, reporting by letter to Lord Lisle, and reminding him to 'remember Mr Secretary with wine and letters' to ensure some of the spoils came his way. The day after the men's trial, on Saturday. 13 May, the King ordered that the Queen's household be broken up, and her servants released from their allegiance. This was, of course, a strong indication that Anne's trial was simply a formality, especially in the light of the trials of the men. Fitzwilliam, the royal treasurer, and Paulet, the comptroller, were sent to Greenwich to do this. Evidently the people of the Queen's side had been left at Greenwich kicking their heels since Anne's arrest. Many of Anne's ladies, including Margery Horsman and Elizabeth, Countess of Worcester, would soon transfer to the household of Jane Seymour.

At the Tower, seating was being put into the great hall, which had been redecorated for Anne's coronation – there was space for 2,000 people, and the structure was still in place in 1778. Evidently it was felt that this show trial should be held as publicly as possible and with a high degree of ceremonial. On the dais at one end of the hall there was a canopy and chair of estate, provided for the Duke of Norfolk who, as Lord High Steward, would be representing the King. A wonderful chance, of course, for the duke to demonstrate his complete loyalty to the King, and lack of involvement with his niece. The trial appears to have been conducted with great formality. It started with Norfolk taking his place, staff of office in hand and with his 19-year-old son seated at his feet. Audley, the Lord Chancellor, sat at his right, ready to offer legal advice, and the Duke of Suffolk was at his left side. Then there was a row of twenty-seven peers, seated in order of precedence. This represented around a third of all the peers of the realm, who had been 'chosen' – Wriothesley's word – to try the Queen and her brother. It is extremely likely Cromwell had done the choosing, handpicking the lords who would be sure to convict without any fuss. Those present included the Earl of Sussex, a confidant of the king, the Earl of Worcester, husband of Elizabeth who may have provided evidence against Anne, and Lords Exeter and Montagu, great supporters of Mary Tudor. Lord Morley, Rochford's father-in-law, was also present, as was Lord Clinton, husband of Bessie Blount, the King's former mistress and mother of the Duke of Richmond. Richmond himself was not there – perhaps because he was not yet seventeen.

The original list preserved in the *Baga de Secretis* – the top secret file – is perished, and not all the judges' names are legible. It is often stated that Lord Wiltshire was not among his daughter and son's judges, but this appears to be supposition, and several contemporary sources contradict this. It is certainly true that, having served on the jury for the trial of the 'lovers', Wiltshire had already helped to make the executions of his children inevitable. While it is almost certainly true that there was nothing he could have done to help them, it is hard to find his pragmatism anything other than brutal. There are indications that he had been on less than good terms with Anne for some time – this may have been in part because he disagreed with her reformist views – and it is probably significant that, during her imprisonment she was reported as having expressed concern for her mother and brother, but appears only to have asked Kingston, shortly after her arrest, where her father was. If, indeed, he was one of the judges, there is no record of Anne's having reacted in any visible way to his presence.

In addition to the peers, there were judges chosen from City livery companies and the law – in total there were over ninety. One of them was Sir John Spelman, a justice of the King's Bench, who was to leave an account of the trial. In addition, members of the public were admitted to observe; we are told, too, that there were large crowds outside the hall. There were to be no accusations that justice was not seen to be done. The ceremonial and the spectators were all in place – the content of the case was more questionable.

There is some debate as to what evidence was presented against Anne. Some historians believe that no witnesses were called on the day, and only prepared statements were read out. She was accused of having taken the active role in seducing all five of her lovers, and of having given money and presents as an inducement. In each case, dates and specifics were given – and it is notable, that, even after nearly 500 years, it can be demonstrated that, in most cases, either she was somewhere else, or her so-called lover was, or, in one instance, she was recovering from childbirth. Cromwell was to tell Chapuys that he had gone to a lot of trouble over the details of the trial, but he had certainly not bothered to get the detail right on this. He would, of course, have been aware that there would be no one who was in a position to challenge him. With no defence counsel and no opportunity for the defendant to review the evidence, he was on very safe ground.

The accusation of incest should have been, in public relations terms, a winner. It was intended to be so shocking that the hearer might stop thinking critically, and might assume that this woman was so depraved that no accusation was unbelievable. But where did the idea come from? At least one novelist has recently provided scenes not only of incestuous sex but also of Anne's giving birth to the formless mass of flesh that makes its first monstrous appearance in Sander's account of her life, written during the reign of her daughter. But whatever else Sander invented, he did not invent the incest charge. Despite a recent biography that attempts to rehabilitate her, Rochford's wife, Jane Parker, remains the most likely source for the accusation – this is confirmed by a number of contemporary sources. And there is, of course, the possibility that either it was true or that Jane believed it was true. Or she may have been misquoted or misunderstood. Or she may have said something indiscreet that was exaggerated and distorted. There is evidence that the marriage between Jane and George was unhappy. It appears that they had no children – the George Boleyn who was Dean of Lichfield later in the century is likely to have been an illegitimate son of the earlier George, or another relative entirely. Jane's career at Court, including at least two periods of banishment for trouble-making, suggest that she was at odds with Anne by 1534. We know, too, that Jane's father, Lord Morley, was a friend of Mary Tudor – not a position that was likely to endear him to George. We know, too, that George Boleyn was an unswerving ally of his sister, Anne. It is very possible that Jane felt excluded from their closeness, and the accusation of incest was her revenge.

The Crown's case also included the accusation that Anne had not loved the King, and that she and Rochford had laughed together about his clothes and his poetry. Presumably this was intended to help form a picture of Anne as heartless and disloyal to her husband, but as evidence of crime it leaves something to be desired. It also included hearsay evidence from an alleged deathbed confession of a woman who had been a friend of Anne's from former days. Spelman wrote about this, 'Note that this matter was disclosed by a woman called the Lady Wingfield, who had been a servant of the Queen and shared the same tendencies; and suddenly the said Wingfield became ill, and a little time before her death she showed the letter to one of those – etc.'[22] It was claimed that her dying words had been repeated to Cromwell by an un-named third party. This, it appears, was admitted as evidence.

It is notable that even those such as Charles Wriothesley, who were inclined to favour the conservative faction, were impressed by Anne's performance in court: 'She made so wise and discreet answers to all things laid against her, excusing herself with her words so clearly as though she had never been faulty to the same'.[23] Sir John Spelman recorded that all the evidence against the Queen 'was of bawdery and lechery, so that there was never such a whore in the realm'. Cromwell was relying on shock to carry his case – he had included, not only a lover who was perhaps the nearest to a friend the King had, two extras to play off against him, plus Mark Smeaton who was of such low status that most people would be shocked by the idea that a Queen would regard him as a potential sexual partner, and then, salacious treat, the accusation she had seduced her own brother. But Spelman was not the only one to be sceptical. Even the hostile Chapuys, still laid up with a fever, commented on the lack of substantive evidence. Writing at the end of the century, George Wyatt commented 'For the evidence, as I never could hear of any, small I believe it was. The accusers must have doubted whether their proofs would not prove their reproofs.' In common with legal practice in Tudor trials, Anne could not call her own witnesses, cross-question any of the Crown's witnesses or speak on her own behalf. As she was being tried for treason, she was not allowed any legal representation.

But the peers present, who were the ones who actually got to vote on the verdict, were in no doubt about what was expected of them. They consulted together, and then each, beginning with the youngest, pronounced her guilty. Some observers said that the watching crowd was expecting her to be acquitted, and in the confusion the wrong information was passed on those waiting outside for news. Wyatt makes a slightly confusing claim that some of the peers were saying semi-publicly that she 'had cleared herself with a most wise and noble speech' – presumably meaning her answers to the accusations. We are told that a hush then descended as Norfolk pronounced the sentence of death on his niece – the tears that poured down his face may well have been largely for himself and his own loss of prestige. The sentence, that she should be burned or beheaded at the King's pleasure, offended some of the lawyers present, Spelman among them, because it was imprecise. Chapuys reported he had been told that 'when the sentence was read she preserved her composure, saying that she had held herself always ready to greet death, but was extremely sorry to hear that others, who were innocent and the King's loyal subjects, should share her fate and die through her. She asked only for a short space for the disposing of her conscience.' Other sources, Aless included, give similar but slightly expanded versions of the same thing – all agree that she remained calm, curtseying to the peers before withdrawing from the court, accompanied by Kingston, Lady Kingston and Lady Boleyn. After her departure, the Lord Mayor of London is said to have spoken out against both the way the case had been handled and the verdict: 'I could not observe anything in the proceedings against her, but that they were resolved to make an occasion to get rid of her at any price.'[24]

The trail of Rochford followed later in the day. He was, inevitably, under the same restrictions as Anne with regard to the legal process, and it appears that, again, the Crown's case consisted of prepared statements and hearsay evidence. Wriothesley's opinion was that he 'made answer so prudently and wisely to all articles laid against him, that marvel it was to hear, but never would confess to anything, but made himself as clear as though he had never offended'. The centrepiece of the case against him, the charge of incest, certainly once again figured largely. According to de Carles, Rochford commented on this 'On the evidence of only one woman you are willing to believe this great evil of me, and on the basis of her allegations you are deciding my judgement' – most contemporary commentators appear to have been in no doubt that the source of the accusation was his wife, Jane. Opinion was divided as to whether she was telling the truth or motivated by malice. During the trial Rochford was passed a piece of paper on which the story about his laughing with Anne about the King's sexual inadequacies was written. He was warned not to read the charge aloud, but promptly did so, to the fury of the Crown lawyers. Chapuys relayed that his informant had told him that observers were betting ten to one in favour of an acquittal for George – but, in his case too, the peers brought in a unanimous verdict of guilty on all counts. Norfolk also condemned another of his sister's children to death – we are not told whether to the accompaniment of tears this time. Rochford made a speech accepting that he was to die, but appears to have been very much concerned to try to ensure his various creditors were paid.

So the Crown case had prevailed, and in some quarters the adages about mud sticking and no smoke without a fire seem also to have prevailed. The day after, a scandalised Hussee was writing to Lady Lisle:

'Madam, I think verily, if all the books and chronicles were totally revolved, and to the uttermost persecuted and tried, which against women hath been penned, contrived and written since Adam and Eve, those same were, I think, verily nothing in comparison of that which hath been done and committed by Anne the Queen; which though I presume be not all thing as it is now rumoured, yet that which hath been by her confessed, and others, offenders with her, by her own alluring, procurement and instigation, is so abhominable and destestable that I am ashamed that any good woman should give ear thereunto. I pray God give her grace to repent while she now liveth. I think not the contrary that she and all they shall suffer.'[25]

So, even allowing a certain percentage for exaggeration, Hussee was sure that Anne was guilty of a great deal – and, a full century before the appearance of the first newspaper gossip columns, here is a foretaste of their tone. Cromwell would have been satisfied if he had been shown this letter, and it is likely to have been typical of other letters and conversations being written and held in London that week.

Anne's remaining allies were understandably keeping very quiet and hoping that they would not fall under suspicion. Page and Wyatt were still in the Tower, and still very far from certain that they were going to escape with their lives. As we have seen, Anne's household had been broken up before her trial – we do not know how many, if any, had remained at Greenwich. But given the number, not only of Anne's ladies but the male officers too, who reappeared within weeks in the service of Jane Seymour, it is reasonable to suppose that many of them had not gone far. In London, if Aless's account is to be believed, the reformers who had regarded Anne as their greatest ally were horrified. Whatever they believed about her guilt or otherwise, her fall was a disaster to their cause. We know that the story of the King's pursuit of Jane Seymour had been current for some time –and the King had written to warn his new love of 'a ballad made lately of great derision against us, which if it go abroad and is seen by you, I pray you to pay no manner of regard to it. I am not at present informed who is the setter forth of this malignant writing; but if he is found, he shall be straitly punished for it.'[26] Whatever the truth of the many claims of Anne's previous virtually universal unpopularity, it seems that at least some Londoners were unimpressed by the King's behaviour at this time. Chapuys was scandalised by tales of river parties and of a gathering at the house of the Bishop of Carlisle, who visited Chapuys to describe the jollifications,[27] but was still insisting that 'everybody' was rejoicing at Anne's downfall.

There was still one legal preliminary to fulfil before Anne was to be allowed to die – her marriage was to be annulled and Elizabeth bastardised. The Queen had wanted to make her confession, and on 16 May Cranmer visited her. Some historians have suggested that Cranmer discussed the annulment with Anne in the course of that visit, and may even have suggested she might be allowed to live in return for providing evidence as to the invalidity of her marriage. The case papers relating to the annulment have disappeared, so we do not know what reasons were finally used. It is known that Cranmer had been in touch before Anne's trial with the Earl of Northumberland about the possible pre-contract with him, which he firmly denied, even when visited and pressurised by one of Cromwell's household. It appears likely that Cranmer had to use the fact that the King had had a sexual relationship with Anne's sister, Mary, as the grounds, which had placed him within the forbidden degrees of affinity with Anne. If these grounds were indeed used, Cranmer conveniently ignored the fact that the Pope had granted a general dispensation for the King to remarry within the forbidden degrees, in 1528. This would all have been somewhat embarrassing if discussed in public, and if these grounds were indeed used, it would explain why the papers were made to vanish so completely. If Cranmer persuaded Anne to confess that she had known of this bar to her marriage to Henry, it might explain why she talked to Kingston at dinner of being allowed to retire to a nunnery. It may be that Cranmer had suggested she might be granted her life in return for her co-operation. Certainly Kingston was soon reporting what she had said in his next letter to Cromwell.

Meanwhile, Weston's wealthy family were trying to save him, offering 100,000 marks – the equivalent of several million pounds – in return for his life. It is not clear whether the King was ever told about this, or whether it was Cromwell who resisted the offer of this much gold. Chapuys was told that the French ambassadors had tried to plead for him. However, Kingston visited the King the day after the final trials, and it was on his return that he told all the men that they were to die the next day, not at Tyburn or within the Tower, but on Tower Hill. It is therefore likely that the decision was made personally by the King. This then left Kingston with all the arrangements to make in a hurry, as he wrote to Cromwell:

'The time is short, for the King supposeth the gentlemen to die tomorrow, and my lord of Rochford with the residue of gentlemen.'

They had not yet been visited by the priest who was to hear their final confessions, and the King had not yet confirmed he would commute the hanging, drawing and quartering to which they had been condemned to the quicker death of beheading. Both Weston and Rochford appear to have spent much of their last day on Earth in dealing with practical matters. Weston wrote out a list of his debts – he owed money to several of his own family, to the King, to various friends and to a number of tailors and embroiderers for some very elaborate clothes, including a cloth of gold doublet – and a last letter to his parents, asking them to pay the debts and forgive him for anything he might have done to offend them. Brereton sent his wife a gold bracelet, which she was one day to leave to their son, Thomas. Rochford was also worrying about money, and about a monk of Tower Hill whom he had helped to obtain promotion as an Abbot, and who would soon now be losing his job when his abbey was dissolved – Kingston felt enough sympathy for him to write to Cromwell to enlist his help in the matter: 'You must help my lord of Rochford's conscience for the monk.' We do not know what Norris or Smeaton did or said that day. Neither do we know which of the five men carved a falcon – now without a crown – in the stone wall of the Beauchamp Tower, where it remains to this day.

By this time the arrangements were also under way for Anne's execution. Indeed, they had been for some time. Famously, she was beheaded not with an axe but in the French fashion with a sword, wielded by an expert executioner from Calais. At that time, it took a fast horseman two days to ride to Dover and in the best weather another day to cross by boat to Calais – a round trip of a minimum of six days. As there were to be only four days between Anne's trial and her execution, it is clear that someone had decided not only that Anne would be condemned to death, but was making detailed plans as to exactly how she was to die, at least two days before her trial. Kingston, told of the arrangement when writing to Cromwell that he was 'very glad of the executioner of Calais, for he can handle the matter.'

The five men were all beheaded on the morning of Wednesday, 17 May, on a specially built high scaffold on Tower Hill. It is recorded that large crowds were present, including a number of observers from Court. As the time must have been finalised only hours in advance, it is a matter for speculation how those present knew when to arrive. The building of the scaffold must, of course, have indicated what was going to happen, and there may have been messages sent to at least some prominent citizens to let them know when. Chapuys wrote that Anne saw the executions from the Tower 'to aggravate her grief', but this is unlikely as Tower Hill was not visible from the Royal apartments on the other side of the Tower – unless she was deliberately moved to the Bell Tower and made to watch. Kingston would certainly not have done this without direct orders from the King or Cromwell, and there is no record of anything of the kind. It was Thomas Wyatt who witnessed the executions – according to the highly debatable *Spanish Chronicle*, he had already been told he was to go free, but as he does not appear to have been released for several weeks after this, he may well still have been in fear of his life. Certainly rumours were flying around that more of the Queen's lovers were to be arrested and tried. He was to write a poem about that time –beginning 'These bloody days have broken my heart.'

> 'The Bell Tower showed me such a sight
> That in my head sticks day and night:
> There did I lean out of a grate,
> For all favour, glory or might
> That yet circa Regna tonat.'

All observers, including John Husee, agreed that the men died 'charitably'. This means that each of them followed the accepted conventions of the day in the way they met their deaths. It was the custom that each one would have the opportunity of making a short speech of farewell, and it was expected that the condemned man would try to demonstrate that he had forgiven his enemies and was ready to leave this world at peace with God, accepting the need for divine forgiveness and asking for the prayers of those present. All five of them followed these conventions. One of the observers, George Constantine, who was within earshot of each of them, reported to Cromwell that they all confessed that, in general terms, they deserved to die for having lived sinful lives. Rochford, as being of the highest rank, was to die first, and made a long and pious speech, of which there are several versions, which do differ, but agree that he regretted that he 'did read the Gospel of Christ but did not follow it.' Some historians have taken this to mean that Rochford was making a specific, if coded, confession to the crimes of which he had been accused – but there is really no evidence of this. Norris, Weston and Brereton in turn made what appear to have been rather shorter speeches, each confessing to having led sinful lives, but making no specific admissions. Each asked the onlookers to pray for him. Smeaton, as being of the lowest rank, died last. He too asked for prayers: 'Masters, I pray you all to pray for me, for I have deserved the death.' This has been taken to mean he was renewing his confession to adultery with the Queen, but as he was a native Dutch speaker and had just watched four men being killed in the way he was about to suffer, it is just as likely that his command of English was less than perfect in the last moments of his life. However, those present at the executions did not agree among themselves – Constantine wrote to Cromwell that, having heard the five last speeches, he had come reluctantly to believe that they were all guilty as charged. It is impossible to know whether he was genuine in what he wrote, or whether he was writing what he knew Cromwell would want to read. Crispin de Milherve, in contrast, concluded that all five 'suffered a death which they had no way deserved'. The heads and bodies of all five were taken away in a cart and buried at the chapel of St Peter ad Vincula within the Tower – Rochford, as a nobleman, before the high altar, the others in the churchyard. There seems to be no record as to whether a funeral service was held for them.

Anne appears to have assumed that she was to die the next day too, and prepared herself accordingly. In fact, across the river at Lambeth,

Cranmer and a roomful of ecclesiastical lawyers were trying to come up with a form of words for the annulment of her marriage that would be acceptable to the King. No one seems to have pointed out that if she had never been married, she could hardly be considered guilty of treasonable adultery. She did not retire to bed on that Wednesday night, spending the hours with her almoner, and by two o'clock on the Thursday morning was ready to take the sacrament for the last time. She asked Kingston to hear mass with her and, before and after doing so, took a solemn oath that she had never been unfaithful to the King. It must be emphasised that, to any believing Christian at this time – and almost everyone, including Anne, belonged in that category – to lie when swearing an oath on the sacrament would have been blasphemy. To do so in the hours before death would have cut the liar off from any possibility of God's mercy. It is, of course, possible to argue that Anne was prepared to lie on oath to protect her posthumous reputation, and to point out that Smeaton, at least, had never withdrawn his confession. One recent writer, G. W. Bernard, has argued that if, as he is inclined to believe, Anne had committed adultery, then 'what she faced in the world to come was already dire: she might thus risk another untruth.'[28] However, this argument does not acknowledge the teaching of the Church that a sinner who died repentant, after confessing and, preferably, receiving the sacrament, would be likely to receive mercy, while someone who died with unconfessed sins on their conscience would not.

The morning was spent waiting – she made arrangements to distribute the £20 the King had sent her to give as alms. Then there was nothing left to do. Around mid-morning she sent for Kingston, having been told she was not to die until noon, and said she had been sorry to hear that news, as she had expected to be dead and past her pain by then. Kingston had no definite news for her, and did not tell her that he had just received a letter from Cromwell instructing him to clear the Tower of foreigners. Kingston tried to reassure her that there would be no pain, as the blow was 'so subtle', to which she replied 'I heard say the executioner was very good, and I have a little neck' – and she put her hands round her neck and laughed. Kingston commented on this exchange: 'I have seen many men, and also women, executed, and all they have been in great sorrow, but to my knowledge, this lady has much joy and pleasure in death. Sir, her almoner is continually with her, and hath been since two of the clock after midnight.' In fact, Anne's 'wild laugher in the throat of death' may seem less bewildering to us than it did to Kingston – her world had fallen apart, her preparations for death were made and she just wanted to go. The near-hysterical laughter was part of the way she operated.

It was not stated why foreigners were to be excluded from seeing Anne's execution – perhaps Cromwell, or the King, or both, were afraid that ambassadors and others might send home reports sympathetic to Anne and critical of the King. It is unlikely that they had expected trouble – Kingston was to report to Cromwell that there were only about thirty foreigners to exclude. It may also be, however, that the King and Cromwell were afraid of demonstrations by Londoners in Anne's favour, and were vacillating between this and the desire to make sure there was a reasonable number of observers so that justice could be seen to be done. Whatever the reasoning, the execution was now delayed until the following day – and when this news was taken to Anne, she pleaded to die immediately, as she was in a state of preparedness. She said it was 'not that she feared death, but she had thought herself prepared to die, and feared that the delay might weaken her resolve.' But there was nothing Kingston could do – she had to endure through that day and another night, spending most of the time in prayer or in conversation with her attendants. Meanwhile, that evening, the King was rowed to Chelsea to visit Jane Seymour, who was evidently behaving as if she were a queen already – but in relative privacy.

There is a tradition that Anne wrote a poem during these last hours. It survives in a manuscript in the British Library,[29] and was set to music a few years later by Robert Jordan, one of her former chaplains. It is impossible to know whether it was indeed written by her, but it may well represent something of her state of mind:

> 'Oh, Death, rock me asleep,
> Bring on my quiet rest,
> Let pass my very guiltless ghost

Out of my careful breast.
Toll on thou passing bell,
Ring out my doleful knell,
Let thy sound my death tell,
Death doth draw nigh,
There is no remedy.'

It seems that either the word was deliberately put round in London or that the news leaked out. Certainly over a thousand people made their way to the Tower to witness the first-ever execution of a Queen of England. Alexander Aless was to write that he had a nightmare early that morning, dreaming he saw Anne's mutilated body after her execution – and he knew nothing of the plans, having been ill in bed for a week. His response on waking was to visit Cranmer at Lambeth, finding him walking in his garden at four in the morning. Aless wrote that he told Cranmer of his dream, and in response Cranmer told him: 'She who has been Queen of England upon Earth will today become a queen in Heaven' – after which he burst into tears. If this story is true, it is highly significant that Cranmer, having just heard Anne's final confession, was evidently now sure of her innocence of the charges made against her.

At seven that morning, Anne heard mass and received the sacrament once more. At eight, Kingston appeared to tell her she should make ready. She chose to wear a black robe with a cape furred with ermine – this to emphasise her Royal status – with an English, gable hood. Some observers said she wore a crimson kirtle under the robe: red for martyrdom. Both garments had low necklines so she had no need to remove them for the execution. She told Kingston 'Acquit yourself of your charge, for I have long been prepared.' Several eyewitness accounts say that Anne was attended by four young ladies as well as two older ones, Ladies Kingston and Boleyn. The identities of the young ladies have been much speculated over, but may have included Margaret Wyatt, sister of Thomas. The likelihood, however, is that they were four of the maids of honour from her household.

The procession that made its way from the Royal apartments to the scaffold was as formal and as theatrical as any other regal occasion – and more dignified than many. Two hundred Yeomen of the Guard went first, followed by Anne, accompanied by Kingston and her ladies, and possibly her almoner, walking through the Cole Harbour Gate, past the White Tower and to the scaffold. She must have seen many familiar faces among those present – Cromwell, there to see the fruits of his labours, the Duke of Suffolk, her stepson the Duke of Richmond and her uncle the Duke of Norfolk, along with a sprinkling of senior Liverymen. Aless was to record that he could not bear to be present, although his landlord, who was a servant of Cromwell, attended and, when he returned home, told Aless what he had seen. De Carles, who was not present, was to claim in his poem that she had frequently looked behind her at her ladies as she walked, which has led some writers to speculate she was hoping for a last-minute reprieve: this seems unlikely. The scaffold was a platform of 4 or 5 feet high; the Constable helped Anne up the steps, and she walked forward to address the crowd. All the eye-witness accounts except one say that she appeared composed and even smiling (the exception states that she looked 'feeble and stupefied' – as well she might after two sleepless nights). She asked Kingston for permission to speak, which he gave.

There are, again, several contemporary versions of what she said. As ever, Chapuys provides one. Others are given by Hall and Wriothesley in their Chronicles, and another by de Carles and a further one by Milherve. Although the details vary, they agree that she started by saying that she was there to die, and as she had been judged by the law, she was accusing no one. In Hall's version, she continued that if ever she had offended the King, she was about to atone for it in her death:

> 'I submit to death with good will, asking pardon of all the world. If any person will meddle with my cause, I require them to judge the best. Thus I take my leave of the world, and of you, and I heartily desire you all to pray for me.'

Hall's version became the source for a number of other later accounts, including that of George Wyatt. All agree that Anne then exchanged her gable hood for a linen cap, embraced her ladies in farewell and, as was the custom, forgave the executioner. She then knelt upright, saying a final prayer. Several observers say that most of those present also knelt in respect for her passing. Spelman, who was also present, said that the executioner 'did his office very well, before you could say a Paternoster'. Her head fell to the ground with her eyes and lips still moving. Her ladies then covered her head and body, and carried her remains away for burial. Spelman says no proper coffin had been provided, and that Anne was buried in an old elm bow-chest, which had been found at the last minute. The only people who attended her burial were her four ladies and, as it was now afternoon, there could not be a full Mass, so one of her chaplains, Father Thirlwall, simply pronounced a blessing over the chest before it was interred in the chancel of St Peter ad Vincula. As the execution had taken place at around nine in the morning, the delay was probably so a grave could be dug. Writing that same day, another of her chaplains, Matthew Parker, was in no doubt that her soul 'was in blessed felicity with God'.

At a pre-arranged signal, a gun was fired within the Tower to announce Anne Boleyn's death to the world. An assortment of apocryphal stories place the King in a variety of hideaways waiting to hear the gunfire – the reality seems to have been that he was at Whitehall. As soon as the signal came, he set off by boat to the house where Jane Seymour was waiting for him. In the wider world, opinion was, as ever, divided. But for the rest of his life, no one dared bring up the subject of Anne Boleyn in the King's presence. In all the Royal residences, work was already in hand removing the HA monograms from walls, windows and ceilings. A few escaped the attentions of the destroyers and remain to this day, joined by the thousands of reconstructions that have been added as her posthumous fame has grown.

Chapter 9

Ever After

From the day of her arrest, Anne Boleyn became a non-person – a subject best avoided. At Court her memory was not so much obliterated as covered over. Anne's household was disbanded before her trial took place[1] and her servants released from their oaths of allegiance, but the rooms were not empty for long. Jane Seymour married the King less than a fortnight after her predecessor's death, and there was no rebuilding and remodelling for her as there had been for Anne – she lived in the same spaces, with the same furniture, cared for by the same servants and living by the same routines. A number of Anne Boleyn's ladies returned to serve the new Queen – these included Anne Gainsford, Margery Horsman, Margaret Coffin and Elizabeth Stoner. When Jane dined for the first time as Queen in her Presence Chamber at Greenwich, she sat in the chair occupied by Anne Boleyn five weeks before. It is likely, too, that much of her jewellery and household plate had belonged to Anne.

At the Tower of London, the new graves at St Peter and Vincula were scarcely filled in before the river walls of the Tower were decorated with streamers in preparation for a river procession[2] on 7 June to welcome the new Queen into London. There was a 400-gun salute from the Tower, music from musicians onboard a variety of boats, and a welcome from Eustace Chapuys, resplendent in purple satin, as the Emperor's ambassador. The King and Queen passed by in their barge (probably the one that had belonged to both Catherine of Aragon and Anne Boleyn), accompanied by a number of what Wriothesly simply describes as 'lords', in their own barges – but the flotilla did not stop, passing straight on to York Place. Everyone was advised to write and congratulate the King on his new marriage – Sir John Russell suggested Lord Lisle should say "you do rejoice that he is so well matched with so gracious a woman as she is

... wherein you shall content his Grace."[3] Others also hastened to write carefully phrased letters.

In houses throughout London, people of reforming sympathies were devastated. Cromwell and his informers had done their job well, putting out the agreed line on Anne's conduct. For many people, such as the Lisles' agent John Hussee, she had been found guilty by innuendo – if so much was being said against her, surely some of it must be true. It is impossible to know how many of her sympathisers believed she was guilty and, if so, of what. She had been convicted of everything from plotting murder, to incest, to laughing at the King's poetry. But given the extreme nature of some of the crimes for which she had been condemned, it was, for the time being, virtually impossible to speak publicly in her favour – or to mention her in public at all. Like Cranmer, they had to hope that it was not true that Anne had 'professed His Gospel in her mouth and not in heart and deed'[4] Some of those who had supported Catherine of Aragon were not surprised to hear of anything 'the concubine' might have done. But as time went on, and news of the King's nocturnal river parties had spread, so the tide of the sympathy of many Londoners turned in Anne's favour. Cromwell had been afraid of public demonstrations in her favour at the time of her execution – he knew the ways of London crowds, who were always liable to support someone they thought was being treated unjustly.

As the weeks after Anne's death went by, there were other things to think of – those Londoners who sympathised with the Lady Mary, and had been expecting her restoration as Princess, were disappointed when this did not happen. The King was adamant that he would not see his elder daughter again until she had sworn that she agreed that her parents' marriage had been unlawful – thus swearing that she considered herself illegitimate. It look the combined efforts of Cromwell and the Council, alternately bribing and bullying, to persuade her to submit. Finally, in July, she gave in. The King, Queen Jane and much of the Court visited Mary in Hackney, where father and daughter were formally reconciled. Soon Mary was being showered with presents, from a good horse from Cromwell, to money from the King, to a supply of court dresses from the Queen, who arranged for her to have rooms at Hampton Court. But Mary does not appear ever to have forgiven herself, or her father, for what had happened, and for the rest of her life she was to suffer from headaches, toothache and hysterical palpitations. Mary's relationship with Anne's daughter, Elizabeth, was always to veer between a rather queasy-seeming affection and a resentment that began to border on hatred. A few weeks after Mary's submission, her half brother, Henry Fitzroy, died of tuberculosis after a short illness – leaving the King the father only of two daughters, both of whom he regarded as illegitimate. Already he had begun to fret that his new wife had not conceived.

Throughout 1536, no longer hampered by Anne Boleyn, the dissolution of the smaller monasteries and nunneries went ahead, with no question of the proceeds going either to other religious purposes or to educational causes – it all went to the Crown. The King's income was doubled, and for the next few years he was able to finance a number of pet building schemes, including the wildly luxurious Nonsuch Palace, as well as the high cost of his bellicose foreign policy. Magnificent jewels from the dismantled shrines of saints were also welcome – the ruby given in 1179 by the King of France to adorn the shrine of Thomas A Becket at Canterbury made a fine thumb ring for Henry, who was certainly aware of the irony of a king wearing the spoils of the shrine of this particular saint, murdered at the behest of Henry II. Conscious of the need to keep significant people onside, the King and Cromwell set up a Court of Augmentations to oversee the distribution of roughly one fifth of England's land. Some was given away to the influential, some sold cheap and some at the full price.

But this did not make everyone happy – through the northern counties of England, the unrest that had been building up in the previous few years over the imposition of the new religious order boiled over into an uprising in Lincolnshire in early October. At first this consisted of burning books and angry meetings, but it soon escalated into lynchings of unpopular officials. The Lincolnshire rising was put down, but unrest spread to Yorkshire, escalated and finally involved around 40,000 people. The Duke of Norfolk, sent north with only 12,000 men, negotiated with the rebels, whose leaders naively believed his promises of concessions and a Parliament to be held in York. Some of them were invited to Court for Christmas, where they met the King at his most charming. London was to see nothing of what happened except, a few months later, the executions of some of the leading rebels. But when the King interfered with the mayoral election that year, dictating that his candidate, the reformist Ralph Warren, be elected, the Aldermen did as they were told with scarcely a murmur.

An initial 'J' instead of an 'A' had appeared, at Hampton Court and at other Royal palaces, entwined with the King's 'H', in the places where the decorative schemes were most visible. Anne's falcon needed little alteration to become Jane's phoenix (itself hastily adopted instead of her family's peacock, which would hardly have been on message in view of peacocks' connections with pride as well as eternal life). Jane's motto, 'bound to obey and serve', replaced Anne's 'the most happy'. But in the year that passed between the wedding and Jane's becoming pregnant, it was apparent to all just how little influence she had over the King, who took care to keep her away from any significant discussions. When she cast herself at her husband's feet, begging him to restore the monasteries, he pushed her away, reminding her he had often warned her 'not to meddle with his affairs', and of the fate of her predecessor[5]. As the reporter observed – 'enough to frighten a woman who is not very secure'. Evidently the title of Queen of England was no longer one that was necessarily a permanency.

Queen Jane was also surrounded by many of the same ladies who had served her predecessor – they were once her colleagues, now her attendants. Several of them, including Margery Horsman and Mrs Stoner, Mother of the Maids, had started their Court careers in Catherine of Aragon's time, going on to serve Anne Boleyn alongside Jane and now swearing allegiance to a third Queen. Bess Holland, the lover of The Duke of Norfolk and friend of Anne Boleyn, was soon added to the number, as was Jane, Lady Rochford, Anne Boleyn's sister in law. If these ladies are regarded as career civil servants, rather than as the personal friends or allies of either Anne or Jane, their continuing presence seems less odd, but given the close proximity in which they all lived, the adjustments involved may have been something of a challenge to those concerned. This must have been the case given that the long-serving ladies must have seen for themselves the exact circumstances of how Jane Seymour replaced Anne Boleyn as Queen.

As Queen, Jane, in contrast to her meek motto, gained a reputation for being imperious and demanding. In keeping with the image of modesty she had decided upon, the racy, hair-revealing French hood was banned in her household, and her ladies were required to revert to the modest, and highly unbecoming, English gable hoods. However, Jane insisted on grandeur – when Lady Lisle's daughter, Anne Bassett, became a Maid of Honour, she was given a very expensive shopping list, told to provide a servant and bedding at her own expense, and instructed to replace all her fashionable French-style clothes with English gowns with long trains. The combination of conservatism in dress, modesty and formality were perhaps part of a public relations message to help underline the difference between Jane and her predecessor. She may also have had a desire to ensure her ladies were less likely to catch the King's eye. Once she became pregnant, which took some months, Jane seems to have relaxed a little, and she acquired a craving for quails that had much of the court expending considerable time and energy in sourcing enough birds so that she could have them for both dinner and supper. The new Queen was, of course, fully aware of what was expected of her – in May 1537 most of official London attended a 'Te Deum' (a thanksgiving service) at St Paul's. The thankfulness was for the quickening of her unborn child, who was indeed born safely in October, albeit after a gruelling thirty-six-hour labour. Once she had given birth to the longed-for prince, Henry would probably have ensured Jane could eat quails every day forever – however, she died of child-bed fever only ten days after the birth, leaving her widower inconsolable. He remained so for all of three months.

Jane, Lady Rochford, had been left briefly destitute after the execution of her husband, George, since, as a convicted traitor, all his property was forfeit to the Crown. Sensibly, she asked Thomas Cromwell to intervene for her, with the result that her reluctant father in law was induced to provide for her out of his own, now somewhat reduced, income. By

1537 she, too, rejoined the ranks of court ladies, going on to take part in Jane Seymour's funeral procession and in the short-lived household of Anne of Cleves. In 1539, after the death of Thomas Boleyn, two Acts of Parliament gave Jane many of the Boleyn lands, including Blickling – this was possibly Cromwell paying for services rendered. A year later Thomas Cromwell was dead, and two years after that Jane, too, came to grief, and was executed, without the dignity of a trial, for her involvement in the fall of Henry's fifth Queen, Catherine Howard, who conducted an extra-marital affair with the help of Jane. Few have had a good word for Jane Rochford, and she is generally assumed to have been both mad and bad. A recent biography[6] has made some attempt to depict her as a victim of circumstance – but the evidence of spite and mental instability is strong. So is that of the King's spite against her: after the arrest of Catherine Howard, Jane Rochford was kept under comfortable house arrest, attended by one of the Royal physicians. That is until a special Act of Parliament was passed to legalise the execution for treason of the insane.

The 1536 executions had unleashed a Court feeding frenzy among those who hoped for grants from the property of the dead. Anne's brother, Rochford, had relatively little, as the Boleyn family lands were still held by his father; but Brereton and Norris had each held at least £1,000 a year's worth of Court appointments. Unsurprisingly, Cromwell presided over the division of the spoils. The victorious Seymour faction claimed a share, along with appointments and grants for Jane's brothers – both Edward and Thomas were preferred, with Edward becoming Earl of Hertford. Both were to remain in favour even after their sister's death. Plans were begun for a coronation for Jane in the first year of her marriage, but the King called them off on the excuse that there was plague about. It is likely that, had she lived, a coronation would have been her reward for producing a healthy son. Some of the documentation for the original plans survive, and make clear that it would have been deliberately more splendid than that of Anne Boleyn.

Thomas Boleyn set about making good his losses. He retained his seat in the King's Council, but lost the office of Lord Privy Seal to Cromwell in June 1536. Keen to demonstrate his loyalty, he served the King during the Pilgrimage of Grace later that year, paid his taxes on time and turned up to the annual Garter ceremonies, lending a chain to Thomas Cromwell on one occasion. Elizabeth Boleyn, already ill at the time of her daughter's arrest, died in April 1538 and received a fitting funeral. There is some indication of a rift between Thomas and Elizabeth – she was staying with a friend at the time of her death, and her funeral and burial took place under the auspices of her own family, the Howards. Elizabeth had only been dead a few weeks when the court gossip mill started predicting a second marriage for Thomas, perhaps to the King's niece, Margaret Douglas. But the next year Thomas also died, at Hever – his memorial brass is still in the church there. Some of the Boleyn lands were inherited by Thomas' brother, James, who was not allowed to claim the earldom of Wiltshire – and Cromwell had ensured that Jane Rochford received a major share. James Boleyn sold Hever to the King, who soon afterwards, possibly with a sense of irony, leased it to Anne of Cleves as part of her divorce settlement. James lived on into his eighties, and saw his great niece, Elizabeth, become Queen of England. When he died in 1561, the Boleyn male line died with him. That is if we discount the George Boleyn who became Dean of Lichfield, lived until 1609 and may have been the bastard son of George Rochford – there is nothing on record about who his mother may have been.

Mary Boleyn was the only one of Anne's close relatives to live on in what appears to have been contentment – at least for a few years. It is likely that Mary was in Calais with her young husband, William Stafford, at the time of Anne and George's deaths, and so probably escaped much of the horror of those few months. Her second marriage seems to have turned out well, although there is no record of the birth of the baby whose conception had precipitated the marriage, or of any more children. But after Anne's death, Mary was finally granted the wardship of her son, Henry Carey – her daughter, Catherine, married at about this time. Mary and her husband were also awarded the tenancy of Rochford Hall in Essex, where they settled until Mary's death in 1543, after which William married again. A convinced Protestant, he went into exile during the reign of Mary Tudor. Both the Carey children lived long lives, had children and grandchildren of their own, and were much favoured once their cousin, Elizabeth, became Queen. The stories of Mary's daughter, Catherine, and granddaughter, Lettice Knollys, were intimately connected to that of Elizabeth I – and the relationship between Elizabeth and Lettice was to be as complicated, and probably as unhappy, as that between Anne and Mary Boleyn.

Thomas Cromwell continued to spend most of his time at his homes in Austin Friars and Stepney, directing much of the business of the kingdom. Among the rewards that came his way in the months and years following the executions were not only the appointment of Lord Privy Seal, but both a knighthood and a barony. Alongside the official recognition were numerous stewardships and keeperships which generated little work but substantial sums in income. That was in addition to the bribes and presents from people he had helped. In early June 1536, he had a long meeting with Chapuys, during which, almost as an aside, he said he had gone to a lot of trouble to bring about the fall of Anne Boleyn, and that he respected 'the sense, wit and courage of the said concubine and of her brother'. Cromwell's own luck was to last another four years and when it ran out, it was partly because he had never learned to operate as successfully at Court as he had always done in London.

For the rest of Henry VIII's reign, no one spoke of Anne Boleyn in the King's presence, and it is likely that most of her portraits and many of her possessions were destroyed. Henry appears to have kept a few items, whether by mistake or as souvenirs is hard to tell – but the apparent randomness of the selection that appears among the 17,810 items that belonged to Henry VIII at the time of his death in 1547 suggests that the gilt bottles, embroidered cushions and candlesticks, all bearing Anne's cipher, may simply have been overlooked. Anne's daughter, Elizabeth, now officially a bastard but acknowledged as the King's daughter, after some time in an official limbo during which her household began to run out of clothes for her, began to make occasional appearances at Court. At the age of three she was carried as she took part in the christening of her baby brother, Edward, in October 1537. A few years later Henry

VIII's sixth wife, Catherine Parr, took trouble to bring the ill–assorted half siblings and their father together, and tried even to set up some kind of family life for them all. It appears to have worked, up to a point. From 1542 all three of the King's children spent more time at Court, and the next year both Mary and Elizabeth were restored to the succession.

As Elizabeth grew, so too did her resemblance to both parents – she had inherited her father's red gold hair and her mother's pale, pointed features and dark eyes. Elizabeth was under 3 years old at the time of her mother's execution, and may have had no conscious memory of her. However, as the little girl had been visiting her parents in Greenwich in April 1536, it is equally possible that she may have had some recollection of what happened. We do not know what she was told had taken place, either at the time or as she grew up. Among Elizabeth's inheritances from Anne was the charm that was to win her popularity with the London crowds who saw her when she took part in public events. When, after narrowly escaping execution during her half sister Mary's reign, Elizabeth came to the throne, it was to great acclaim in London. And one of her coronation pageants, at Gracechurch Street, featured figures representing her ancestry. So there, for the first time since 1536, stood Anne Boleyn next to her husband. There is no record of Elizabeth's having commented on this – but, after she had stayed in the Tower of London in time-honoured fashion as part of the Coronation festivities, she avoided the place for the rest of her life. In fact, Elizabeth I very rarely spoke in public of her mother, and certainly never made any attempt to provide her with a memorial. She could hardly have done so without appearing to be disloyal to her father's memory. However, she always kept with her a ring holding two miniature portraits, one of herself and one of Anne. As there is a strong resemblance between the picture in the ring and the medal that is the only definitely attested image of Anne made in her lifetime, there is a distinct possibility that the painting is a copy of a lost contemporary original.

When she became Queen, Elizabeth gave Court appointments to many of her mother's family and friends. Two of her four Ladies of the Bedchamber (the most senior women in the Queen's household) were relatives and her cousin, Henry Carey, Baron Hunsdon, was always welcome. So, too, were Catherine Carey, her husband Sir Francis Knollys, and, in the course of time, their many children. But one of them, Lettice, was to hurt Elizabeth immeasurably when she married Robert Dudley, the man the Queen loved but could not marry. In time Robert was forgiven, but not Lettice, who was barred from Court for the rest of her life. Matthew Parker, a former Chaplain of Anne Boleyn, was Elizabeth's first Archbishop of Canterbury, and it is on record that, although she disapproved of married clergy, she would dine with him and his wife.

In London, Anne's name could be spoken again, and she became something of a Protestant icon – Foxe and others wrote of her as having been learned and serious, a proponent of reform and a seeker after truth. Elizabeth I appears to have been happy to receive recollections of her mother, as the theologian Alexander Alesius (or Ales), who was in London in 1536 and had witnessed some of what took place, wrote a detailed letter to her about his memories. We do not know if she replied. During Elizabeth's reign, too, John Foxe included Anne Boleyn among his martyrs – a hugely influential book that had a number of editions from the 1560s onwards. Foxe was, of course, seeking to present those whom he regarded as Protestant martyrs in a positive light, but he was certainly able to speak to people who had known Anne, and the anecdotes he uses, such as her keeping a purse of money with her so as to be able to give alms as the need arose, ring true. It is likely he spoke to Rose Lok, who told him about the decorum that she had seen maintained among Anne's ladies during her visits as a silk woman.

By the time Elizabeth came to the throne, much of the London where her mother had made her home in 1522 was changed forever. In the years immediately following Anne's death, as the city's monastic houses were dissolved, immense and long-lasting consequences overtook almost every aspect of life in London. In terms of the look of the city, much of the land and many of the buildings went to the nobility and prosperous merchants who could afford them; some of the monastic churches, such as St Bartholomew the Great, were reduced in size and used as parish churches, while others, for example that of the Blackfriars, vanished altogether. Many monks and nuns received some sort of redundancy or pension payment but were then left adrift with no home or occupation, and were threatened with dire consequences if they kept wearing their religious habits. And, with brutal suddenness, London lost its entire hospital service. It was to be nearly ten years before the King and the City fathers came to an arrangement about payment for the premises of the various hospitals and, in the meantime, the sick poor starved. In the sixteenth century it was usual to find the corpses of the dispossessed in city gutters; after the dissolution, foreign visitors commented on the numbers of the starved dead to be found in London streets. At much the same time, one of Anne Boleyn's aims came to fruition – a Bible in English was placed in every parish church in England. But, panicking over the subversive nature of some of what the laiety would find there, the King and Parliament passed legislation limiting who could read it. 'Women, artificers, apprentices, journeymen, serving men of the rank of yeoman and under, husbandmen and labourers' had to wait to have suitable passages read to them. Noblewomen and gentlewomen could read for themselves in private, but not in church[7]. But it was too late – the need to pass such an Act indicates how widespread reading had become.

In recusant circles, the many propagandists who sought to tarnish Elizabeth's reputation, fell to myth-making about her mother. The second half of the sixteenth century saw the emergence of most of the stories that hang about her still. Anne had been called a whore, adulteress and witch in her lifetime; her daughter was to be targeted with what was essentially a curse by the Pope of the day. This came about when Elizabeth was excommunicated in 1570 in a statement that referred to her as 'the pretended Queen of England and servant of crime'. Once this was published, Roman Catholic writers could and did give their misogyny full rein. Foremost among these was Nicholas Sander, who, in his Rise and Growth of the Anglican Schism, published in 1585, endowed Anne with a jaundiced complexion, a projecting tooth, six fingers and a large wen under her chin. It is also to him that we owe the story of Anne's having given birth to 'a shapeless mass of flesh' in 1536, and the claim that Henry VIII was in fact her father. This was before Sander had even embarked on his vision of Anne's moral ugliness. As he was born in 1530, Sander was, of course, too young to have had any involvement in the events he was writing about, but may well have spoken to older people in recusant circles, and would certainly have had stories passed on to him. Sander had a personal hatred for Elizabeth I because he felt he had to go into exile on her accession, and he was supportive of the various attempts to overthrow Elizabeth in obedience to her excommunication by the Pope. After this, any good Catholic would have received only Papal praise for murdering her. Sander's book presents the English Reformation as a cynical and political act by a corrupt monarch.

It was to be the publication of a French edition of Sander's book that persuaded the seventeenth-century divine, and shrewd and intelligent courtier, Dr Gilbert Burnet, to write his History of the Reformation of the English Church. This long, detailed and insightful account of the reign of Henry VIII draws on many sources, some of them now lost. Burnet states in his book that he had taken a lot of trouble to draw together the evidence for what brought about Anne Boleyn's fall, as it was such a significant event and takes the view that it was a combination of the work of her enemies, the possibility of the King's making a new, dynastic marriage, the King's increasing distaste for her combined with his increasing paranoia and suspicion, and also her own personality. Burnet describes her as having been 'of a very cheerful temper, which was not always limited within the bounds of exact decency and discretion'[8], but did not believe Anne was guilty of any of the charges against her.

In the mid-nineteenth century, Agnes Strickland and her contemporaries began the process of rediscovering the history of women. Strickland's account of Anne Boleyn, one of her Lives of the Queens of England, is in many respects a sympathetic one; it clearly seeks to be a balanced one. Certainly it takes Anne's political role seriously, and is clear that there was no evidence of her guilt of any of the charges made against her at her trial. However, Strickland takes the view that Anne was largely responsible for the King's refusal to allow Catherine of Aragon and her daughter to meet for so long, and makes much of the remorse that Anne 'must' have felt at the end of her life when she was facing the fact that her own daughter would now be brought up by a stepmother; Strickland treats as fact a story to the effect that, the day before her execution, Anne wanted to beg for Mary's forgiveness. The summary Strickland gives of Anne's personality and reputation are interesting:

'There is no name in the annals of female royalty over which the enchantments of poetry and romance have cast such bewildering spells as that of Anne Boleyn. Her wit, her beauty, and the striking vicissitudes of her fate, combined with the peculiar mobility of her character, have invested her with an interest not commonly excited by a woman in whom vanity and ambition were the leading traits.'[9]

Strickland adds that, like Poppea, Anne regarded love as being part of the art of diplomacy – she was evidently in no doubt of Anne's overwhelming desire for power. Some male historians of the time continued to take a different line – for example: 'It must be admitted that (Anne) behaved in a very improper manner, as a wife and a queen, and if we acquit her of the crime laid to her charge, we must find the witnesses guilty of perjury and the peers of injustice.'[10]. (As we have seen, there were no witnesses). And some of them commented condescendingly about what they termed a ladies' view of history, presumably in an attempt to belittle both the influence over events any woman might have had, as well as giving their take on the level of seriousness to allow to any woman historian. Sadly, this dinosaur breed is not yet extinct. To Charles Dickens, while Henry VIII was 'a blot of blood and grease upon the history of England', Anne, in exchanging letters with him before the divorce, was, in Dickens' view, showing herself 'very worthy of the fate which afterwards befell her'. At this time, most writers were firmly in either the Catherine of Aragon or the Anne Boleyn camp, and, curiously, this continued even after the publication of the various Calendars of State papers made much primary source material easily available for the first time. Writing in 1884, Paul Friedmann, although he admitted grudgingly that there was not enough evidence to convict Anne, announced himself to be 'by no means convinced' that she was not guilty of something just as bad. He summarises his view of her:

'Her place in English history is due solely to the circumstance that she appealed to the less refined side of Henry's nature; she was pre-eminent neither in beauty nor in intellect, and her virtue was not of a character to command or deserve the respect of her own or subsequent ages.'[11]

Meanwhile, the heritage industry was growing up. For hundreds of years visitors to London had visited the Tower, but its greatest attractions for many were the wild animals that were kept there and the chance to see the Royal Mint. Until the mid-nineteenth century, the Tower of London still had a real military role to play, but in 1850 the architect Anthony Salvin, famous for his work in the Gothic style, was commissioned to make the Tower look more mediaeval, partly to please the increasing numbers of Victorian tourists. First to be refaced and re-presented was the Beauchamp Tower so prisoners' graffiti could go on show. Over the next decade the whole site was transformed, including removing some genuinely mediaeval parts and putting in new ones that were considered more in keeping. The first ticket office had already been in use by 1838, and by the end of the nineteenth century over half a million people were visiting each year. At least one of those Victorian visitors has added a layer to the story: since the late nineteenth century, every year on 19 May a bouquet of red roses is delivered to the Tower in Anne's memory, and is placed on her grave. They are ordered by a firm of London solicitors on behalf of a long-ago client.

At Hampton Court there was a similar story. Once the Hanoverians had grown tired of living there, the palace was used for nearly a hundred years as grace-and-favour apartments for retired courtiers and others. Some of the flats were of up to forty rooms, others as few as four; all were magnificent, draughty and virtually impossible to heat. It had always been possible to have a rapid guided tour of a few of the 1,300-odd rooms in the palace on production of a suitable fee to the housekeeper, but in 1838 the young Queen Victoria decided that Hampton Court should henceforward be open and accessible to all. As this was the time of the Chartist movement, some of those around the Queen disapproved, thinking extremists might come and pull down tapestries, but in the event all went well. As at the Tower of London, it was decided to make the building look more historical – so the great hall, gatehouse and west front were 're-Tudorised'. It was at this time the 'Anne Boleyn Gateway' acquired its 'HA' motifs – although the restorers did find a falcon from the design of her day, which is on display in the Great Hall. The Crown spent about £7,000 a year on the place for the next decade and, in time, many Georgian sash windows vanished, making way for casements. Partitions that had been added by some of the tenants to create rooms of a more manageable size were removed, and the privy garden was cleared and tended. Much of what we see now is the early Victorian idea of Tudor magnificence.

Windsor Castle, although it retains much of its mediaeval structure, is also much changed since Anne Boleyn's time, as it was considerably altered by George IV, who enlarged it, made it more comfortable, and at the same time, and to his way of thinking, more historical – it is to him and his architect, Jeffry Wyattville, that we owe most of the crenellations, turrets and towers we see today. The desire for comfort is understandable, as in Tudor times the place must have been as unheatable as it was magnificent – most of the references to the Court spending time there relate to the summer months. Windsor was on the tourist trail at least as early as 1785, when Charles Knight published The Windsor Guide – in this Henry VIII figures as a monstrous tyrant, with Anne as the 'unfortunate' wife who died 'to gratify the capricious passions of her husband'[12]. By the early nineteenth century, there were plenty of guidebooks available, both for London and for the whole country. Interestingly, many of them concentrate on 'things to do' in the capital. One, an annually updated late Georgian precursor of a 'Rough Guide', devotes a whole chapter to the Tower of London, of which two pages list the animals kept in the Tower, their species, origins and names, while Anne merits just two references, including one mentioning that the exhibits in the Tower including an axe said to have been the means of her execution.[13]

Of the other London houses associated with Anne Boleyn, most have vanished. The Bridewell Palace, by then a women's prison, was largely destroyed in the Great Fire of London, but rebuilt as a school. Today Unilever House occupies much of the site. Durham House has long gone. After the fall of the Boleyns it reverted to the ownership of the Bishop of Durham, who exchanged it with the King for some other London properties. The Duke of Northumberland, Protector to the young Edward VI, then lived there in the 1540s, and it was there that Northumberland's son was married to Lady Jane Grey. Later in the century, Elizabeth I lent the house to Sir Walter Raleigh, who invited many of his less mainstream associates to dine there – these included the Queen's astrologer, Dr John Dee. By the early years of the seventeenth century Durham House was in a bad way, and its decline was exacerbated when it was used as a barrack in the civil wars. It was largely demolished in the 1660s and its site used as building plots, leaving only the gate house standing for another century. Whitehall Palace went on being a Royal residence until it was destroyed by fire in 1698 – all but the Banqueting House, but that was not built until the time of James I.

Later Victorian tourist bosses were very much aware of Anne Boleyn. Finally, in 1876, St Peter ad Vincula was restored, having been in an extremely poor state. It was necessary to stabilise the floor, and as a result the graves inside the chapel had to be disturbed. The remains were supposedly identified, examined and reburied, and a booklet, The Remarkable Persons Buried in this Chapel, went on sale, including a lovingly detailed account of the state of the bones found. Those supposed to be of Anne Boleyn were described as being the remains of a woman in her late twenties, of around 5ft 3ins and with small, tapering hands and feet; the bones had been disturbed at some time, probably when a later burial was made in 1750, but were all present and undamaged. Doyne Bell, the civil servant in charge of the operation, had prepared a plan of where, according to the Tudor record, the graves should be located. Nothing was found of either George Rochford, who may have been buried in an area undisturbed by the restoration, or of Catherine Howard. It has been suggested that this may have been because she was only in her teens when she died, and young bones decay more quickly. Some writers have questioned whether the identifications are correct but the likelihood seems to be that it is Anne Boleyn's bones that lie under the tile that bears her name. Already in 1866 Queen Victoria had personally asked for a memorial plaque to be placed on what was then believed was the site of Anne's execution. Then, as now, the Yeoman Warders showed visitors round, with much emphasis on blood, bones and ghosts.

At Hampton Court, as the numbers of tourists increased until by the 1850s there were hundreds of thousands a year (as the Queen had forbidden making any charge for entry, nobody quite knew how many), those in charge produced several different kinds of guidebook. One was for those interested in the natural history of the gardens, one offered an itinerary for those travelling from London, and one offering a short history of the place, including the stories of Cardinal Wolsey and Anne Boleyn. It appears that, in the early years at least, Hampton Court attracted a rather different kind of visitor, with a preponderance of families wanting a day out and a walk rather than the seriously historically inclined. We are told there was a guidebook in 1817; another, dating from 1840, is entitled A Stranger's Guide to Hampton Court Palace Gardens. This was partly because so many of the rooms in the palace were, at that time, divided up and furnished for people to live in; by the early nineteenth century there was a community of several hundred living there; most were not pleased when the state rooms were opened to the public, and some residents continued to fight a rearguard action against public access. But, evidently, the numbers were increasing. For example, in 1878 one resident, Lady Grey, wrote to the Lord Chamberlain complaining about the number of tourists and finding the 'din of their voices and penny trumpets and whistles and similar toys is so distracting'. The age of mass tourism was reaching Hampton Court.

Of the London locations known to Anne Boleyn, Westminster Abbey is one of the few that would look familiar to her. The western towers, designed by Sir Christopher Wren, are the only external feature added since her time and, allowing for some internal re-ordering, Anne would certainly recognise the scene of her coronation. She certainly sat in the coronation chair of Edward the Confessor as she was anointed and crowned. She would also know Westminster Hall, where she presided over her coronation banquet, and which was furnished with tables and hung with tapestries for the occasion. Around the corner, the Jewel Tower is the only other section left of the Palace of Westminster of Anne's day – by her time it no longer held many of the King's jewels, but was packed with every imaginable luxury in the way of clothing and household furnishings, from precious hangings to silver walking sticks.

Anne has been the subject of innumerable novels, films, plays and at least one opera, Donizetti's Anna Bolena, which was staged in London in 1830. When it opened at the King's Theatre, it was to great acclaim; London audiences evidently delighting in the opulently imaginative retelling of the story. Tom Taylor wrote a play about Anne, which was staged in London and also met with success – again, it presents the world with a wronged and passive victim who pleads with Henry VIII to leave her and return to Catherine. This view of her also produced a number of paintings of Anne (and some of Lady Jane Grey) as she endured imprisonment in the Tower. The first film about her was made in 1922, since when hardly a year has passed without a new addition. And she has made it onto the popular stage, with the song Stanley Holloway made famous:

> 'With her head tucked underneath her arm
> She walks the Bloody Tower,
> With her head tucked underneath her arm
> At the midnight hour....'

It is unexpected that this song became famous as recently as 1934, as it clearly displays its ancestry to the Victorian music hall – it is darkly humorous and offers a picture of outrageous ghostly goings-on at the Tower: 'She comes to haunt King Henry. She means giving him what for. Gadzooks, she's going to tell him off. She's feeling very sore....' And it is still a song of which many visitors to the Tower appear to know at least two lines.

In recent years, the old accusation of witchcraft has resurfaced. Norah Lofts, researching her 1979 biography, was trying to discover if there was truth to the story that Anne's heart is buried in Salle Church in Norfolk, when, on talking to the sexton there, she was told the story of a hare that appeared in the church every 19 May. Excitedly, Lofts told him that this was one of the shapes that could be taken by a witch. It is unclear how seriously the sexton had been intending his story to be taken. In 1989 Retha Warnicke's biography re-examined this possibility, taking care not to dismiss it out of hand, and accompanied it with a number of the more extreme accusations made by Sander and others. This, in turn, inspired Philippa Gregory's novel The Other Boleyn Girl, which offers the reader an Anne guilty of every last aspersion cast at her, including witchcraft, incest and the monstrous birth of 1536 thrown in for good measure (the author confirms in a note that she considers that this version of events is likely to be the true one). In return we are offered a long-suffering and kindly Mary Boleyn in the role of wronged, and ultimately vindicated, heroine. And, in the corridors of J.K. Rowling's Hogwarts, Anne's portrait hangs among those of the witches of history, presiding over the education of Harry Potter.

There is also at least one book on the subject of Anne Boleyn's ghost[14], as well as many websites. Among them there are stories from all over England – some, not all, feature a white figure carrying its head under its arm. The most violent emanate from Blickling and include not only a headless ghost of Anne, but a carriage drawn by headless horses, driven by a headless and accursed coachman – the ghost of Thomas Boleyn – and followed later on the night of each 19 May by a spectral George Boleyn wandering the gardens seeking justice. At the Tower of London there have been claimed sightings in at least six different locations. In 1864 a sentry accused of having fallen asleep at his post excused himself on the grounds that he had charged at a faceless woman in Tudor dress who had approached him, and he had then collapsed. A colleague claimed he had seen her too, from inside the Bloody Tower, and the charge was dropped. The most spectacular of the tales is located in St Peter ad Vincula and features an entire torchlight procession of Tudor notables, headed by a figure resembling the portraits of Anne Boleyn who walks with her face turned away. Any visit to the Tower today may be accompanied by a ghost story from a Yeoman Warder. Sometimes they say they are recounting the experience of a colleague, and almost all tell you that Anne Boleyn had six fingers on one of her hands. Some visitors to Hampton Court claim to have seen her, too, but here the most prevalent story is, perhaps understandably, that of Queen Catherine Howard, who was arrested there and, by some accounts, dragged screaming back to her rooms when she tried to escape her captors in an attempt to get to the King and plead for mercy. The same applies to Windsor Castle, where the ghosts of both Anne and of Henry VIII are said to visit; however, the most prevalent ghost story there is of Anne's daughter, Elizabeth I, who is said to appear in the Royal Library, dressed in black, and preceded by the sound of her high-heeled shoes on the stone floor. Rather pleasingly, we are told that she has appeared to a number of successor monarchs, including the present Queen, especially in time of war.

There have been at least three major television series featuring Henry VIII and his wives in the past three decades, two intending to represent an interpretation of history and one, The Tudors, complete fantasy, but with superb if totally anachronistic costumes. In contemporary theatre, Hilary Mantel's Wolf Hall has been dramatised, with successful runs in London and on Broadway – despite Mantel's efforts to avoid making Anne into the heroine of the piece, inevitably the character is a notable one. There have been several site specific plays about Anne performed at the Tower of London and at other places associated with her, ranging from romantic fantasies to dramatisations of letters and music of Anne's own time. Most years see an Anne Boleyn-related conference or meeting, often at Blickling or Hever, often with her biographers, and those who have written novels featuring her, as speakers. Itineraries have included Tudor themed parties, with participants being encouraged to bring suitable costumes.

In the current age of social media, there are multiple websites and Facebook groups devoted to Tudor history in general, and the story of Anne Boleyn in particular. A variety of history related blogs are devoted to the observations of women who feel they have a particular connection with Anne Boleyn. There are several highly successful, and professionally run, websites devoted to Anne and anything related to her, with attendant Facebook pages, research updates, discussions and opportunities to buy anything from the latest biography, to sets of Christmas tree ornaments in the shapes of Henry VIII and his wives. The shop at Hever Castle offers Anne Boleyn hot water bottles – the stopper is the head of the figure. At the last count there were over seventy Twitter accounts using some version of her name, a number adorned either with her portrait or with the photograph of a modern woman in Tudor costume. Several offer a day-by-day account of Anne's last days; one or two are publicising books; one appears to be a front for the English Defence League. Catherine of Aragon, Jane Seymour and Elizabeth I have their adherents, too.

In London there are walks, seminars and conferences devoted to Anne. As elsewhere there are events where the participants are invited to attend in costume, and days are spent finding and tracing the places where Anne Boleyn and her contemporaries lived and walked. A recent book gives descriptions, map references and opening times for many of the places associated with Anne, sometimes tracking down locations. Also, dotted round the London area there are a number of Anne Boleyn and Boleyn roads, walks, and a well. The well, at Carshalton, is ancient and long dry and must have been in existence long before the sixteenth century. The story of its naming can be traced back to 1827, when a local historian wrote that 'Legend has Anne Boleyn and Henry VIII riding from Nonsuch Palace to see Sir Nicholas Carew"[15] – and, her horse happening to stumble, a spring appeared where she had passed. Historically, the problem with this is that the foundations of Nonsuch Palace were not dug until after Anne Boleyn's death. The likelihood appears to be that the well was once known as that of 'Our Lady of Boulogne' – there is a local tradition that until the mid-nineteenth century there was an ancient cottage in the corner of the nearby churchyard that could well have been a minor pilgrim site. Unless more evidence comes to light, there is no knowing at what point between the Reformation and 1827 this legend grew, complete with its overtones of Olwen and Arthurian damsels. It meshes beautifully, of course, with the view of Anne as a wronged, and innocent, heroine. Possibly, more recently, a verse has come into circulation:

'There is a well at Carshalton, a neater one was never seen,
And there's not a maid in Carshalton but had heard of the
Well of Boleyn. It stands by the rustic churchyard, not far
From the village green; and the villagers show with rustic
Pride, the quaint old well of Boleyn.'

The verse crops up on a variety of local history websites, but without
attribution.

If the reader was to walk into any primary school in England, at the
time of writing, and ask to spend ten minutes with a group of 9 year olds,
they would most likely have an enlightening conversation about Henry
VIII and Anne Boleyn. Given even the smallest encouragement, the
children would show the huge, intimidating and square shape of the King,
tell the escalating and murderous story of his marriages, remember that
Anne was beheaded, and perhaps recollect that Anne was the mother of a
great Queen. Perhaps those same 9 year olds will be taken on a trip to the
Tower of London, Hever Castle or Hampton Court, where they will have
the opportunity to buy souvenirs such as sets of Christmas decorations
in the shape of Henry VIII and his six wives with, in appropriate cases,
removable heads. It may be both a blessing and a curse that the British
remember their collective past, but insist on turning it into a joke. In the
case of Anne, as she was a catalyst, if not in part an agent, of such an
immense series of national changes that, whatever changes there may be
in future in the National Curriculum, it seems likely that she will keep
her fame.

Anne Boleyn is not the only historical personality to have been accorded
celebrity status. Limiting the discussion to women and to Londoners, it
is a distinction she shares with her daughter Elizabeth and with Queen
Victoria. They are joined by Nell Gwynn and perhaps by Florence
Nightingale – the only one without Royal connections. All are tourist
draws. To qualify, the women concerned must be instantly recognisable,
certainly by name and probably by face, to most Londoners coming
through, for example, Euston Station – perhaps someone will organise a
survey. Not only are there thousands of women, all over the world, who

want to be Anne, and a few who think they are – but there are now some who are writing about that phenomenon and others[16]. Anne Boleyn seems unlikely to lose her power to fascinate and to provoke, and likely to retain her ability to elude analysis. It is impossible to know what she thought; as to what those who knew her thought and felt about her, one of the most evocative indications is the hastily-carved falcon etched into the wall of the Beauchamp Tower by one of the men also destroyed by her fall. The carved bird perches on a tree stump, as does the one on Anne's crest as Queen – but now it is uncrowned. As for Anne Boleyn's physical world, in a London which would be largely unrecognisable to her, perhaps the closest we can get to her is in a boat on the Thames, travelling the choppy water she knew so well.

Appendix

Tudor Money and Prices

In the earlier years of the sixteenth century some of the currency is familiar to that of the early twenty-first century. There were pounds and pence, but it is much more complicated. As anyone who remembers as far back as the 1970s will be aware, twelve pence made a shilling, and twenty shillings made a pound. The pound is expressed as £, the shilling as, for example, two shillings as 2s or 2/-, and the penny as, for example, two pence as 2d. There is more, however: the crown was worth five shillings, and half a crown was therefore 2s 6d, and a groat was worth 4d.

In Henrician England some people worked in marks, which were worth two thirds of a pound, or 13s 4d, or angels, which were one third of a pound, or 6s 8d.

As to values, some historians attempt to be prescriptive about this – there are a number of websites that give what purport to be precise equivalents between Tudor and present-day prices, and some writers give Tudor prices followed by an exact su that they offer as an equivalent at the time of the writing. This cannot be anything other than problematic, for many reasons. It may, however, be useful for the reader of this book to give some examples of prices and incomes relating to the 1520s and 30s.

It is very difficult to give precise modern equivalents, as some things were comparatively much more expensive than others. For example, housing was comparatively cheaper than it is today. In 1531 the King bought Anne Boleyn a large farm in Greenwich – the freehold price was £86 13s 4d. At this time a modestly paid schoolmaster might earn £20 a year – so the farm, complete with house, land and stock, cost less than five times his annual income

Food was a major item of expenditure and then, as now, the poorer a person was, the higher the proportion of their income was likely to go towards eating and drinking. Food prices varied considerably from year to year. But some typical London 'shopping basket' items might include a loaf of good bread for 2d, a chicken for 1d and oysters – plentiful and cheap in London – at 4s a bushel (100-150 oysters depending on the size). At the luxury end of the market, a quail might sell for 1s 2d, and spices were astronomically expensive – cloves went for 11s a pound, and cinnamon might be even more.

Clothes, too, were highly priced and highly prized. A decent pair of gloves could be had for 10d, while good, made-to-measure boots might set you back £4. Wool fabric was anything from 6d a yard depending on quality; crimson satin, for those who were allowed to wear silk fabric, was around 3s a yard, while Anne Boleyn's bill for furs in 1531 was £40 15s 8d – the King paid this, and all her other expenses that year. Tailors were highly skilled people: the King paid £1 1s 8d to one of his tailors for twenty days' work.

As regards to income for anyone on a salary at court, the official payment was often far less than the appointment was worth. Everyone expected officials to receive extra payments, in cash or in kind. Courtiers in particular would receive presents from everyone from the King, to anyone hoping for their custom. Another complication was that it was commonplace for courtiers to receive regular payments for representing the interests of a person or organisation at court – the Tudor equivalent of the lobby system. So, the comparatively modest £10 or £20 a year that a court appointment might appear to pay, might well be the least part of the benefits it brought to the appointee.

Wages for everyone else varied from the 8d a day, paid to labourers for digging and clearing fish ponds at Ampthill, to £10 a year for a falconer or £20 a year for the King's head gardener at Greenwich. £20 a year was reckoned a decent income for a parish priest as well as for the schoolmaster mentioned earlier.

For those on a relatively low wage, tips could be very important – for example, the servant of the Lord Mayor who brought Anne Boleyn a supply of cherries in 1532 was given 6s 8d as a thank you. John, the King's own bargeman did even better – on one occasion he received a present of £1 3s 4d for transporting a boat load of books to York Place (this was on top of his usual wage).

In the early years of the century Thomas Boleyn had felt poor on an annuity of £50 – but he had not only a family, but at least one country house to maintain, and servants to pay. And he almost certainly had expensive tastes.

Notes

Chapter 1

1. Discussed in Vanessa Harding et. al: *People in Place – Families, Households and Housing in Early Modern London* (London, 2008).
2. Wilfrid Hooper: *The Tudor Sumptuary Laws* (English Historical Review, 1915 ccc(cxix) 443–449).
3. LP xii ii 802.
4. John Fitzherbert: *The Boke of Husbandry* (London, 1533).
5. Discussed in John B. Gleason: *John Colet* (Los Angeles, 1989).
6. This estimate is discussed in Arthur Kinney: *An Encyclopaedia of Tudor England* (London, 2000).
7. John Stow: *A Survey of London* (reprinted from the text of 1603, Oxford, 1908).
8. Discussed in Alison Sim: *Food and Feast in Tudor England* (Stroud, 1997).
9. John Stow: *A Survey* … op. cit. p. 97.

Chapter 2

1. Calendar of the Patent Rolls, 1446-1509, pp. 294, 349. First reference for Chapter 2.
2. Alison Weir: *Mary Boleyn, the Great and Infamous Whore* (London, 2011).
3. Hugh Paget: 'The Youth of Anne Boleyn', in the *Bulletin of the Institute of Historical Research* no. 54, 1981.
4. Paget, op. cit.
5. Eric Ives, *The Life and Death of Anne Boleyn*, p. 20.
6. Paget, op. cit.
7. LP x.
8. Alison Weir: *Mary Boleyn*, pp. 112–3.

Chapter 3

1. LP xii (2) 952.
2. LP.
3. Philip Mowatt: *History and Antiquities of the County of Essex* (1768) vol, p. 154.
4. George Wyatt, in *Wolsey*, ed. Singer, p. 424.
5. Eric Ives, *The Life and Death of Anne Boleyn* p. 65.
6. David Starkey: *Six Wives: The Queens of Henry VIII* pp. 276–7.
7. Susan Brigden: *Thomas Wyatt – The Heart's Forest*.
8. BL, additional MS 62135 folio 52v/Brigden, op. cit.
9. This story, which was told by George Wyatt, is discussed in Susan Brigden and Jonathan Woolfson's article in *Renaissance Quarterly* vo. 58, no. 2, 2005.

10. Ives, op. cit. p. 90.
11. LP iv 33325.
12. Hall: *Chronicle* p. 754.
13. Hall: Op. cit. p. 755.
14. Calendar of State Papers Spanish, 1527-9, pp. 845–6.
15. G.W. Bernard: 'Anne Boleyn: Fatal Attractions' pp. 31–2.
16. Eric Ives, op. cit.pp. 105–107.
17. LP iv 5936.
18. Eric Ives, op. cit. pp. 123–5.
19. LP iv 6011.
20. Cavendish: *Wolsey* p. 137.
21. LP iv 6114.
22. LP v 238.
23. LP v 216.
24. LP v 1139.
25. Described in David Starkey, *Six Wives: The Queens of Henry VIII* pp. 465–6.
26. Nicholas Harpsfield: *Treatise on the Pretended Divorce between Henry VIII and Catherine of Aragon.*
27. Ives, op. cit. p. 162.
28. This anecdote forms one of Chapuys' reports, and this was found by Paul Friedmann, who retold the story in *Anne Boleyn* (1884) vol. 1 pp. 189–90. The original does not name Wyatt, but describes him.
29. LP vi 351.

Chapter 4

1. LP vi 351.
2. Hall: *Chronicle* p. 794.
3. LP vi 160.
4. LP v 1139.
5. LP vi 983.
6. Ellis: *Original Letters* – 1st series II p. 38.
7. Ellis: *Original Letters* – 1st series II p. 39.
8. Hall: *Chronicle* pp. 804–5.
9. NOTE MISSING.
10. LP vi 585 – the original of this paper has been lost, and it is impossible to be sure who wrote it.
11. LP vii 1257 and 1259.
12. Ascoli: *l'Opinion* pp. 111–27.

Chapter 5

1. Steve Rappaport: *Worlds within Worlds: Structures of life in Sixteenth Century London* (Cambridge, 2002),
2. Thesis by N. Adamson, cited by S. Rappaport, op. cit.
3. LP 1 357,
4. BL Ms Add 43827A f.6,

5. LP xii /2 91,
6. *Acts of Court of the Mercers' Company 1453–1527* ed L. Lyell and F.D. Watney p. 443.
7. CLRO Repertory 3, folio 194.
8. Ibid. Repertory 3, folio 164.
9. *London and the Reformation* by Susan Brigden, p. 136.
10. Hall: *Chronicle*, p. 728.
11. Goldsmiths' Company, Court Book D, folios 237r–238r.
12. LP iv/2 4539.
13. Edward Hall: *Chronicle* p. 754.
14. LP x 909.
15. Tom Standage: *How Luther Went Viral* (The Economist, 17 December 2011).
16. Hall: *Chronicle* p. 754.
17. *Calendar of State Papers relating to English Affairs in the Archives of Venice* vol. 4, 1527-33, no. 694.
18. *Two London Chronicles*, p. 8.
19. CSP Ven. Iv. 878.
20. M.L. Robertson: Thomas Cromwell's Servants (PhD thesis, University of California, 1975), cit. in Tracy Borman: *Thomas Cromwell* (2014).
21. Stow: *A Survey of London* pp. 191–2.
22. LP iv 1732.
23. LP iii 2214.
24. Cit. Terry Trainor: *Bedlam: St Mary of Bethlehem* (London, 2010).
25. LP x 699.

Chapter 6

1. From Historic Royal Palaces First reference for Chapter 6 – the Court.
2. This was a claim by Henry's seventeenth–century biographer, Lord Herbert, who may had had access to sources now lost.
3. David Starkey: *Henry*, p. 230, cites Bernard Andre on this – Starkey does not believe Henry was ever allowed to take part in the full sport of jousting in his father's lifetime.
4. 'Correspondencia de Fuensalida, 519–20, cited in David Starkey: *Henry: The Prince who would Turn Tyrant*.
5. LP ii no. 227.
6. R.W. Hoyle: *The Pilgrimage of Grace and the Politics of the 1530s* p. 99.
7. Calendar of State Papers, Spanish supplement, p. 25.
8. Quoted by Kelly Hart in *The Mistresses of Henry VIII* p. 104.
9. Calendar of State Papers Spanish Supp to vols 1 and 2, pp39-41
10. Calendar of State Papers Spanish 1531-33 no. 967
11. Cit. Alison Weir, *The Six Wives of Henry VIII*, p. 123.
12. Described in www.stagingthehenriciancourt.brooke.ac.uk.

Chapter 7

1. LP xi 613.
2. *A New Explanation for the Reproductive Woes and Midlife Decline of Henry VIII* by Catrina Banks Whitley and Kyra Kramer (*Historical Journal* vol. 53, December 2010).
3. LP vi 351.
4. LP vii 1193.
5. LP vi 613.
6. RCM Ms 1070.
7. John Rowlands and David Starkey: An Old Tradition Reasserted: Holbein's Portrait of Anne Boleyn (*Burlington Magazine* vol. 125, no. 959, Feb 1983, pp. 88–92).
8. LP vii 1655.
9. J.P. Carley: Her moost loving and fryndely brother sendeth gretyng in *Illuminating the Book Makers and Interpreters: Essays in Honour of Janet Backhouse* pp. 261–72.
10. Firstly by Retha M. Warnicke in *The Rise and Fall of Anne Boleyn* pp. 216–220.
11. LP vi, 760, 765.
12. LP viii 1105.
13. LP ix 58.
14. LP vi 1164.

Chapter 8

1. LP ix 199.
2. Quoted, and discussed in full in Giles Tremlett: *Catherine of Aragon: Henry VIII's Spanish Queen.*
3. LP X 141.
4. LP X 200.
5. LP X 427.
6. Eg Suzannah Lipscombe in *1536*, p. 58.
7. LP X 351.
8. *Wolsey*, p. 444.
9. Ives in *The Life and Death of Anne Boleyn* p. 303.
10. LP x 282.
11. Calendar of State Papers Foreign Series vol. 1, 1303.
12. State Papers of the Reign of Henry VIII vol 2 p. 551.
13. Calenders of Letters, Despatches and State Papers, Spain, vol 5, pt 2, p. 137.
14. Eg Suzannah Lipscomb in *1536*, pp. 76–7.
15. Ales – Letter – in Calendar of State Papers, Foreign, 1558–59, 1303.
16. LP x 789.
17. Eg Alison Weir: *The Lady in the Tower* pp. 174–6.
18. Ives, op. cit. p. 339.
19. From the 'Baga de Secretis', quoted in Wriotheseley's *Chronicle.*
20. LP x 908.
21. From the Lisle Letters.

22. Spelman: *The Reports of Sir John Spelman*.
23. Wriothesley: *Chronicle* i. 37–8.
24. Cited in Alison Weir: *The Lady in the Tower*, p. 280.
25. LP x 866/*The Lisle Letters*.
26. Strickland: *Queens of England*, ii, 274, Ives, op. cit.
27. LP x 908.
28. G.W. Bernard: *Anne Boleyn: Fatal Attractions* p. 172.
29. BL Additional MS XV, f117.

Chapter 9
1. Wriothesley: 'Chronicle', 37.
2. Wriothesely: 'Chronicle' vol. 1 p. 44.
3. LP x 1047.
4. LP x 792.
5. LP xi 860.
6. Julia Fox: *Jane Boleyn: The Infamous Lady Rochford* (London, 2008).
7. 'Act for the Advancement of True Religion' passed in 1543.
8. Gilbert Burnet: *The History of the Reformation of the English Church* book iii, p. 197 (London, 1679).
9. Agnes Strickland: *Lives of the Queens of England* vol 4, pp. 156–7 (London, 1842).
10. Major F. Sadleir Stoney: *The Life and Times of the Right Honourable Sir Ralph Sadleir*, p. 29 (London, 1877).
11. Paul Friedmann: *Anne Boleyn: A Chapter of English History* (London, 1884).
12. Charles Knight: *The Windsor Guide* (London, 1785).
13. John Feltham: *The Picture of London for 1802* (London, 1802, and updated annually until 1817).
14. Liam Archer: *Anne Boleyn's Ghost*.
15. G.B. Brighting: *The History and Antiquities of Carshalton* (London, 1827).
16. For example, Susan Bordo: *The Creation of Anne Boleyn – A New Look at England's Most Notorious Queen* (Kentucky, 2012).

Index